# *The* PRACTICE *of*
# DREAM HEALING

# The PRACTICE of DREAM HEALING

*Bringing Ancient Greek Mysteries
into Modern Medicine*

EDWARD TICK, PH.D.

## Quest Books

Theosophical Publishing House

Wheaton, Illinois ♦ Chennai (Madras), India

The Theosophical Society wishes to acknowledge
the generous support of the Kern Foundation
in the publication of this book.

Quest Books
Theosophical Publishing House
PO Box 270
Wheaton, IL 60187-0270
www.questbooks.net

Chapter 1 appeared as "In the Healing God's Sanctuary," in *Pilgrimage:
Reflections on the Human Journey*, vol. 27 (2001/2). Parts of chapters
2 and 3 first appeared in somewhat different and shorter versions as
"Asklepios: Myth and Meaning of the Healer Archetype," in *Voices:
The Art and Science of Psychotherapy*, vol. 32, no. 1 (Spring 1996):
65–73. Parts of chapter 12 appeared under the title "Before the Medical
Model: Hippocrates and the Origins of Western Medicine," in *Journal of
Family Life*, vol. 5, no. 3 (Winter 1999): 39–40, and in *Progressive Health*,
vol. 4, no. 3 (December 2000). Much of chapter 19 first appeared as "A
Journey into the Ancient Greek Origins of Experiential Psychotherapy,"
in *Voices: The Art and Science of Psychotherapy*, vol. 37, no. 1
(Spring 2001).

**Library of Congress Cataloging-in-Publication Data**
Tick, Edward.
The practice of dream healing: bringing ancient Greek mysteries
into modern medicine / Edward Tick.—1st Quest ed.
    p.   cm.
Includes bibliographical references.
ISBN 978-0-8356-0806-0 (cloth)    ISBN 978-0-8356-0799-5 (pbk.)
1. Dreams—Therapeutic use. 2. Psychotherapy. 3. Medicine—magic,
mystic, and spagiric. 4. Mythology, Greek. I. Title.
RC489.D74 T53 2001
616.89'14—dc21                     2001019791

Και συ μεν ουτω χαιρε, αναξ. Λιτομαι δε σ' αοιδη.

# HOMERIC HYMN TO ASKLEPIOS

*Doctor of our ailing, Asklepios, I begin your praise,*
*Son of Apollo, awakened through Mother Koronis*
*Of the Dotian Plains, daughter of King Flegion,*
*Great to humanity, soother of cruel suffering.*
*And thus are you welcomed, Master. By this song I beseech you.*

—Translated by Edward Tick

For my parents
Maurice and Sharon Tick
your devotion and sacrifice
gave me the freedom to dream

# Contents

PART IV: ASKLEPIAN HEALING TODAY

PART V: BENEDICTION

# FOREWORD

STEPHEN LARSEN

The manuscript for *The Practice of Dream Healing* arrived at my home as an early Christmas gift. I had promised to read it and write something about it, and here was the holiday. Would it be another task or an unexpected gift?

I found more in the package than I had hoped for: A mythic history of Asklepios, the gentle pan-Hellenic god of healing (a favorite subject of mine for more than twenty years); a history of the Asklepian roots of modern medicine, interesting for any modern physician or therapist in search of the roots of his/her profession; narratives of travels through Greece so evocative you could smell and taste them; and, above all, a journal of spiritual discovery and healing so compelling that you can't put it down.

My mind went back to my first meeting with Ed Tick, about ten years ago. Our daughter Gwyneth was part of an alternative school on our farm in the rural Hudson Valley. One year she initiated a social studies project involving Vietnam vets that changed us all. The year was 1990, and the awful aftermath of the Vietnam War was sinking in. Statistics said that the numbers of veterans dead from suicide or self-destructive behaviors had eclipsed the numbers of war casualties. The most unpopular war in American history had left a legacy of psychically wounded men and women.

The children in Gwyneth's school, at the threshold of adulthood, wanted to peer into the face of war. It was a self-imposed "rite of passage," as we had talked about in the school. They also had specific questions: Out of all the wars of history, why was it that these returned warriors fared so badly? And why wasn't anyone doing anything about the problem?

ix

I had read Ed Tick's book *Sacred Mountain,* an encounter with what Tick called "The Beast," the inner daemon that overtakes people who go to war and kill and see others killed. It is a walk into personal and collective hells written by a psychotherapist who had not fought in the war and, in fact, actively protested it, as did many people of conscience at that time. But when he saw those who returned broken from it, neither would his conscience let him look away.

A psychotherapist myself, I had first encountered Ed Tick's writing in *Voices,* a journal for professional psychotherapists. Now I picked up *Sacred Mountain* again. The book seemed a mythic journey for the therapist as well as the wounded warriors he endeavored to heal, for he did the only thing that really seemed to work—he let them tell their stories in his own way. Inevitably, deeply poignant tales emerged of the soul's journey into darkness.

Since Dr. Tick practiced in nearby Albany, he was our choice for the school. The visit took place on a spring afternoon. Tick brought with him several of his veteran patients. It was an unforgettable scene: Wounded warriors sitting calmly on the deck in the sunshine among the elfin children of artists, therapists, and ecologists. It was evident how mindful Tick was of the needs of both the children and the vets. Enough was said to honor the children's wish to know about war and its horrors and yet respect was given to what they could handle.

Out of all the events of that year, this presentation was the one that most moved the children. Everyone seemed to grow from the occasion. The warriors who had been working with Dr. Tick healed a little more as they spoke their truth and received the beautiful attention and empathy of the youngsters. From his writing I felt I had already glimpsed Ed Tick the therapist. At our little school, I experienced Ed Tick the skilled teacher. He showed more than told us how to walk into hell with an open heart.

Joseph Campbell used to speak of the *Odyssey* as the psychological journey of a warrior returning from war. The hero had to encounter the dreamlike wonders and terrors that are the subject of the *Odyssey*: storms and winds of fury, whirlpools and clashing rocks, sorceresses and temptresses, cyclopes and sirens, a dip into the underworld. "This is what it takes," Campbell would say, "to bring home a battle-hardened warrior with blood on his hands," now to become again an adequate husband to his wife and father for his almost-grown son.

On the threshold of World War II, Campbell had been asked by the Bollingen Foundation to do a mythic and psychological commentary on *Where the Two Came to Their Father: A Navajo War Ceremonial.*[1] For a scholarly exercise, it was amazingly timely. The ceremonial was meant to prepare Native American young men to make the transition from daily life into the alien and terrible zone of war, comport themselves with integrity, and finally return home and be reintegrated into the tribe.

Young men were being drafted off the reservations for the war even as Campbell wrote his essay. Again and again he pointed out how mythologies contain an age-old wisdom that we moderns seem to have forgotten. And it was very obvious to those of us who studied with him in the sixties and seventies that Campbell felt this wisdom to be lacking in our own culture.

It was into this vacuum that Ed Tick and other maverick therapists and social workers stepped. In effect, they set out to redress an imbalance in a culture that itself was wounded by its lack of healing myths. For Tick, the vastness of the wounds of war initiated a deep search for the generic roots of healing, in particular for soul healing.

Tick began to embark upon vision quests and healings for himself as well as his clients. He did Native American sweat lodges and vision quests under the tutelage of indigenous shamans, finally being initiated as Elder Pipe Carrier in the Earth Tribe by William Taegel, in the lineage of the Creek shaman Bearheart.

Even before completing his Ph.D. in 1981 at Rensselaer Polytechnic Institute, Tick began to work with post-traumatic stress disorder (PTSD) in its various forms, in fact before the diagnostic category was formally recognized or discussed in psychiatric circles. From 1987–91 he directed a Vietnam Veterans Treatment program in the Catskill Mountains, treating literally hundreds of vets and their families. But Tick also worked with survivors of all kinds of severe trauma and violence, including victims of childhood sexual and physical abuse; veterans from all wars, including World War II, Korea, and the Gulf War; Holocaust survivors; Eastern European refugees; and boat people. He edited *The Frontiers of Psychotherapy* (Ablex Publishing) book series from 1988–94. In this series as well as his role as editor of *Voices*, the publication of the American Academy of Psychotherapists, and his writings in *Spring*, a journal of archetypal psychology edited by James Hillman, he introduced depth psychological work with trauma victims to large sectors of the profession and brought to therapists a new awareness of the special problems of returning veterans.

Recognizing that deep wounds required equally deep remedies, Ed turned to spiritual traditions to find the roots of healing. He became ordained as a pastoral psychotherapist and broadened his work to assisting the dying and the bereaved. As an adult, Ed renewed his relationship to his Jewish roots and found them to be full of wisdom. But he and his family also participate in services in a variety of churches, or even pagan temples, as you will see in this book. As an initiated pipe carrier, Tick often uses rituals such as the vision quest, sweat lodge, and pipe ceremony for healing his clients.

But Ed Tick has always been on the track of a Greater Healing. For a wound almost as big as the world itself, something grand was needed, and this quest leads us into the subject of this book.

In the 1980s, Ed began to lead sacred journeys. The landscape and the mythology that called to him most strongly were those of Greece. Many of the insights and haunting tales of this book take place on these journeys, a revival, perhaps, of the medieval practice of sacred pilgrimage. As Tick writes:

We may identify with a mythic tradition to such a degree that we undertake a journey that replicates the mythic hero's journey as recorded in ancient sources . . . We go beyond association into a living identification. We do not forget who we are as modern people with a modern consciousness. But we accept and believe that the ancients had access to transpersonal dimensions that we have lost and that by following their teachings we may regain and achieve success as well.

The mythic tradition Tick was pursuing on these journeys was vast and influential. By the fifth century BCE, a healing religion had spread throughout the pan-Hellenic world. Its central figure was Asklepios, a gentle healer and teacher. Like Christ, he was the off-spring of a divine father and a human mother, the sun god Apollo and the mortal woman Koronis. Like Christianity, the new religion stepped down an unapproachable burning godhead to a son who was both god and man, who walked the earth barefoot and per-formed miracle healings.

Some estimates place the number of healing sanctuaries be-longing to the god at more than three hundred, stretching from Asia Minor to Rome, many in operation for over a thousand years. The largest was the great complex at Epidauros on the Greek Peloponnese, with its ancient theater, beautifully described in the first chapter of this book. But there were also centers in archaic Korinthos; next to the Akropolis in Athens; on the island of Kos, where Hippokrates studied; and a peculiar and haunting one, in the form of an island shaped like a great ship in the middle of the Tiber River of Rome. Tick takes us to these as well in the course of this book.

The mysterious process behind the whole tradition was called "temple sleep" or "incubation." Those in need of healing, from the highest to the humblest levels of society, cast off the garments of their roles in the outer world, bathed ceremonially and donned white robes, and presented themselves to the *therapeutes,* the first "thera-pists," the healing priests of the temple of Asklepios. Stone stelae describing the healings may be seen at many of the major Asklepian sites. The god was believed to visit the supplicant through a dream, or in his *theriomorphic* (animal-shaped) form, as a snake or a dog. Through the theophany itself (the apparition of the god) or through one of the first "prescriptions"—for instance, "after fasting for three days, the supplicant should immerse himself in the pool of Parthenius, though it be winter, and pray to Artemis"—the healing would come.

The cult of the healing god endured until about the fifth century CE. But the zealots of a new religion, Christianity, decided there wasn't room in the world for two divine physicians. Where the statues and sites of the healing god were not defaced or destroyed outright, the image of Asklepios was appropriated and reidentified as the figure of Christ.

In the early twentieth century, Asklepios caught the attention of the depth psychologists. Sigmund Freud mentions Asklepios only once in his writings, citing the existence of the cult as an early vindication of the fact that dreams had psychological meaning. But the Swiss psychiatrist Carl Jung made a greater conceptual leap. He took seriously the belief system of the ancient supplicants who visited the temples: that they were visiting a god. That god, Jung thought, was a symbol of the Self, the god image in the soul, that spoke in numinous portents.

Drawing on shamanic lore of the Naskapi Indians of the Labrador Peninsula, Jung developed a theory of "big dreams" and "little dreams." Little dreams often recapitulated events or frustrations of the day or of ordinary life, full of Freud's "day residues." But "big" dreams were messages from *Mistap'eo*, the million-year-old man who speaks to each human being, especially in moments of crisis or important decision. These dreams would not only be folly to ignore, but could offer positive suggestions for directions in life.

Others took up the issue: Austrian analyst Herbert Silberer, a brilliant early student of the imaginal, called these suggestions the *anagogic* or guiding function of dreams. Roberto Assagioli, the founder of *Psychosynthesis*, postulated that a higher spiritual or transpersonal self dwelled in the human psyche and could be accessed through guiding dreams.

Jung's colleague and associate C. A. Meier took the study of Asklepios to new depths with his *Ancient Incubation and Modern Psychotherapy*, claiming that the contemporary psychotherapist could learn much from this elder tradition.[2] When you record your dreams and present them to a therapist in a private place, a sanctuary of sorts, and work on them, you are incubating the ancient wisdom function in the psyche. Meier said modern psychotherapy was a place where, accompanied by an attitude of respect, modern incubation *could* occur. The god could speak.

Another colleague of Jung's, Hungarian scholar and professor of classics, Karl Kerényi, a "philologist," as he defined himself, rather than a psychologist, said that the myths should not be reduced to *anything*, including psychology: They stand in their own right. In his book, *Asklepios: Archetypal Image of the Physician's Existence*, Kerényi posited that in order truly to understand the healing cult, we need to put ourselves into the mind-set of the original supplicants.[3] We may not reduce the religion of Asklepios to anything but itself, if we truly wish to connect with this ancient spirit.[4]

Mircea Eliade and Joseph Campbell followed suit in the realm of comparative mythology. Instead of turning myth into something recognizable in our world, and thus explaining it, they said we must enter phenomenologically into the world of the myth creator and the mythic experience. This quest for firsthand experience, following on Campbell, characterizes the spiritual journey of the latter part of the twentieth century.

Ed Tick's approach to Asklepios exemplifies the very best of this experiential attitude. He has not only immersed himself in ancient Greek culture and religion, he has gone to the sites themselves, inviting the *genius loci,* the spirit of the place, to speak to him. Using the reverence and focus he learned from Native American ways, he has reevoked a spiritual and healing practice that languished for fifteen centuries, remembering for all of us that it was a *living* tradition.

As I was reading this manuscript, I reflected on the unique nature of creative genius in our time. In a world that has more information in it than any modern Renaissance man or woman could hope to encompass, the modern seeker after truth and knowledge may become a specialist—and run the risk of narrow isolation—or a generalist—and run the risk of dissipating in superficiality. Similarly, the contemporary spiritual seeker, who has options broader than at any time in history, may drown among an embarrassment of riches, sampling in a desultory fashion that ignores the weight and tradition of Buddhism, Hinduism, Taoism, or Christianity.

Campbell has said that modern civilization is built on the "terminal moraine" of millennia-old mythologies. If so, how do we select the right "fragments of the gods" to build new pathways to spirit?

Ed Tick shows us how. He did so by following that mysterious something that Campbell called "your bliss." What Campbell meant by "follow your bliss" was not an indiscriminate immersion into pleasure or ecstasy, as his critics aver. Rather he meant find the nectar of the gods, something that feeds not just your head, but your heart, and more importantly, your spirit. This is what you follow. The invisible trail may require you to find a new synesthesia of your spiritual senses. It will lead you ultimately to a personal relationship with the *transpersonal* world; in short, you may find that that you are living that intriguing oxymoron, a "personal myth."

Practitioners and teachers a generation right behind Campbell have developed this concept for us: Jean Houston, in *A Mythic Life* and many of her other books; Sam Keen in *Your Mythic Journey*; David Feinstein and Stanley Krippner in *Personal Mythology*. My own contribution from a slightly different slant is *The Mythic Imagination*.[5]

In a related vein, it is the unique formula of the personal genius that James Hillman has written about in *The Soul's Code*.[6] We flourish grandly if we stay true to our soul's inner code, but wither if we try to live out someone else's. We must, as Tick models for us, find ever new ways of flowering, while our roots draw nourishment from ancient wisdom.

And ancient wisdom is truly there to be rediscovered, but neither must we become hypnotized or overawed at its antiquity. Rather, modern seekers must ask, What would it be like if we brought this particular mythogem to modern life? How do we treat it respectfully without groveling before its literal form?

"Mythology is man's representation of himself," writes Kerényi in a comparison of the human creation of mythology to the singing of birds, "and also a revelation of the world. In mythology man's own being and the reality of the being that enfolds him are expressed simultaneously in the modality peculiar to mythology, which is not that of music or of any other art, or of philosophy or science."[7]  The primordial existence of mythology, he says, is "man's song of himself."[8]

This book, then, is Ed Tick's unique "song of himself." At the same time, it offers a path to follow that is not a literalistic or historical one. It reveals the face of myth as something that "never was yet always is." More importantly, the ancient mythic form of the Asklepian tradition shows, by its principle of incubation, an enduring apprenticeship to living, rather than to static wisdom. Set up the ritual structure, a "frame of reverence" as it might be called, and await the revelation of the god.

The Greek world of classical times was beset by war, famine, and plague. It needed most urgently a healing "mask of god," to focus the human sufferer's attention and belief. Likewise, our own modern world seems to have lost the healing face of the divine and yet labors to find some spiritual dimension to illness. "The significance of a god specifically characterized as a god of healing," says Kerényi, "is that he, in a manner of speaking, is the fountainhead . . . his manifestation is the cure, or to put it the other way round, every cure is his epiphany."[9]

It is quite clear that Ed Tick not only loves Greece and her ancient lore, but in the Asklepian tradition has found that archetypal image of the physician that our culture so desperately needs. Incuba-

*Webster*

tion involves a daring act of trust in the unknown; the ritual prepara-
tions are a necessary but not sufficient condition for the
healing to take place. Beyond them lies what we can only call the
action of the god, that transpersonal aspect of the sentient universe
that seems to be interested in our well-being and in our healing.
This power may be propitiated, but never bidden.

There are heartwarming stories of healings and spiritual
awakenings, for Tick's students and himself as well, for he does not
leave himself out of the equation. It is probably this, more than any
other single quality, that will establish this book as a classic in the
lineage of Asklepian lore. Tick does what others only talk about: He
places himself into the sacred landscape, brings his heart and mind
together, composes his spirit—and then invokes the secret power
and waits patiently.

In this way the religion of the healing god can be reborn in our
time. "It may be the Fates who send us our trials," writes Tick at the
very end of this fine book. "He sends us their remedies through
which we may unfold our destinies. We do not know what to call
him. We may as well call him Asklepios."

# PREFACE

Dreaming was once both a mystery and a method for exploring the Great Mysteries. In the ancient world dreams were not shadow plays that really meant something else. Rather, dreaming was a primary activity of the soul. Dream stories were events that occurred to the soul in a living, otherworldly dimension. Interpretation did not tell what dreams really meant. Rather, like unraveling an oracle, interpretation provided guidance for utilizing in daylight what had happened to the soul during the night. Thus dreams were central to people's lives.

One of the most important uses of dreaming was a ritual form of healing by which people suffering from physical, psychological, or spiritual ailments could travel to a healing center where priest-physicians practicing a combination of physical and spiritual medicine could help them prepare for a dream visit from Asklepios, the god of healing. Modern medicine and modern psychotherapy derive directly from this ancient practice.

This tradition is alive and available to us today. We can still seek and experience healing dreams. We can still attain healing or learn what we must do to heal ourselves from transpersonal powers encountered in dreams. Moreover, our medical and psychological healing disciplines could be profoundly improved were we to incorporate the ancient techniques of dream healing into their practice, a change that would benefit millions of suffering people.

Since this book attempts to encounter an ancient Greek god at the crossroads of his world and our own, where it is not awkward for the reader, I have chosen to replicate the Greek rather than use the more familiar Latinate spellings for the names of gods, people, and places, and to define and repeat key classical and modern Greek words. In a general sense, becoming familiar with Greek spelling and a little vocabulary can intensify the experience of immersion in the mythic world that this book seeks to provide.

I wish to express my deepest gratitude to people who gathered around the vision and practice of dream healing in order to help create this book.

For many years, my agent Susan Schulman has believed in and fought for my work with a devotion that goes far beyond any possible material reward. My publisher Sharron Dorr is a person of great spiritual and worldly vision and commitment. My editor Brenda Rosen integrates a rare combination of compassion, sensitivity, vision, and accessibility with the courage and skill of a word surgeon. Stephen Larsen generously provided the Foreword to this book and Louise Mahdi first brought this work to the attention of Quest Books. More importantly, for years both have been inspired and inspiring brother and sister pilgrims and elders on this path.

The American Academy of Psychotherapists and its journal *Voices: The Art and Science of Psychotherapy*, the Earth Tribe and its visionary and compassionate leaders William Taegel and Judith Yost, and my own regional Crow/Hawk Medicine Lodge have, over many years, supported and encouraged the unfolding of my experiential healing work and provided welcome and audience for my experiments in healing.

Numerous colleagues and all those travelers and students journeying to Greece and studying the Greek tradition with me over the years have contributed immense amounts of dream and growth material, insight, courage, and support. I wish especially to thank Nancy Gardener, David Miller, Betty Levin, Michael Mauldin, Shirleyan Ebert, Lynette Bowen Post, Lucy Abraham, Elizabeth Lefton, Ginny Hoops, Bill Hoops, Martha Walrath, Carole Evans, John Berninger, Mary Nicolaou, and Gail Konis. In the academic world, Professors

Steven Katz, Paul Wortman, Camille Wortman, Francine Frank, and Steven Leibo, and in the medical and mental heath fields, Phil DiSorbo, Harris Brieman, John Rhead, Peter Minucci, David Barstow and his journal *Pilgrimage,* and Doctors Robert Wickiewicz and Simon Spivack have all provided generous support, inspiration, guidance, and friendship, and have shared exciting journeys both abroad and within.

The friendship, generosity, and hospitality of the Greek people can never be repaid adequately, and I love and thank them all. I especially thank these Greek friends who have shared their passion for life, love of the guest, and knowledge that the ancient powers are alive and well: Harry Patelos, Leftheri Zabeles, Stathis Papalexandros, the Lambrakis family, Panagiotis Milonakis. With their help, I am always in Greece.

Deep love and gratitude go to Mia Dallas and her family. Mia has been my Greek language teacher and journey assistant for many years, as well as my most enthusiastic student of Greek studies. Mia endlessly nurtures the Greek spirit that dwells in me. I make a special offering on the altar of the god of friendship for Alan "Max" Metrick who has been sharing the passion of mind, creativity, and activism with me for four decades.

Finally, it is impossible to express the love and gratitude I feel toward my wife Kate Dahlstedt and my children Jeremy, Gabriel, and Sappho. They have made innumerable and incalculable sacrifices so that I could follow my creative and visionary path. If the gods thank and bless anyone for the work in these pages, it should be them.

# PART ONE

# INVOCATION AND CALL

*Doctor of our ailing, Asklepios, I begin your praise...*

—Homeric Hymn to Asklepios

Asklepios statue at Epidauros

# THE WOMEN OF TROY

## EPIDAUROS, 1987

In ancient times, for a span of a thousand years, pilgrims seeking health and healing would travel from all over the Mediterranean world to Epidauros, the site of the ancient theater and sanctuary dedicated to Asklepios, the ancient Greek god of healing. Today's three-hour bus ride from Athens to the sanctuary was once a long and arduous journey by ship, donkey, or on foot. But people came, and still do, for at Epidauros, as Henry Miller wrote, "there was a stillness so intense that . . . I heard the great heart of the world beat."[1]

Epidauros is on the eastern Peloponnesian coast near the Saronic Gulf. Immediately upon my first arrival there, I quickly sensed why the Asklepian center of healing had been placed on this site. Epidauros snuggles on a wide, lush, green plain encircled by the highest mountains on the Argoloid peninsula. I wandered among the long, low ruins, passing in and out of old bath and massage rooms, temples, dormitories, and fountains. I examined archaic psychotherapy rooms where seekers had reported their symptoms and dreams to priests of Asklepios, attendants of the soul who, in sworn service to the god, listened in absolute confidentiality and responded soothingly.

The air was thick, warm, and sweet, as though my lungs could gulp it and be restored. It was replete with birdsong, as if young flutists wandered the ruins to give ease to weary hearts. And everywhere there was a breathing, a rustling. The shades of the ancients, unseen, seemed to throng the ruins. In the healing god's sanctuary between the green mountains, I felt that I was as low as I could be on earth. There could be no falling lower. I felt cupped in the palm of some giant, hidden hand.

The kind of healing that occurred at Epidauros was called dream incubation. We can think of it as "dream questing," for it has strong similarities to vision questing as practiced in Native American culture.[2] People from all over the ancient world who sought healing through dream incubation in Asklepian sanctuaries had severe physical, psychological, or spiritual ailments that had proven intractable to other treatments. At Epidauros, they were purified; then they awaited an initial dream that called them into the *abaton* of Asklepios.

The abaton was the sleeping chamber; the name literally means "the place not to be trodden." The word has been translated as "the place not to be entered by the unbidden" by C. A. Meier.[3] In ancient Greek, the name also carried connotations of an asylum: a place "difficult to enter, difficult to leave," a place from which "people with problems could not leave until they were healed."[4]

The ancient word *abaton*, in its origins and original meanings, helps elucidate the principles of holistic healing and the attainment of spiritual experience. In both ancient and modern Greek, βατος *batos*, means "passable, capable of passing through by foot." Thus, *abatos* literally means "impassable by foot" and an *abaton* is "an impassable place." In ancient times, the word was applied to impassable mountains, unfordable rivers, unridable horses, a plague that rendered one incapable of walking, and holy places not to be trodden or trespassed. Metaphorically, it meant "pure or chaste."[5]

Patients seeking healing from an encounter with divine powers must thus go through a period of purification and enter into a state of cleanliness and chastity before approaching those powers. Further, such powers can only come to the seeker in such a place as is re-

4

moved, not passed through by ordinary traffic, not easy to access. Thus, such a place is a sanctuary, preserved from the mundane, set aside for physical, psychological, and spiritual purification and, if the healing enterprise is ultimately successful, for divine encounter. World myths and the practices of traditional peoples attest to this necessary purification and removal from the mundane in order to achieve an encounter between humans and the divine.

Upon entering the abaton, the seeker was put into a narrow, womblike chamber. There the seeker waited, for hours or days, for a healing dream or vision in which Asklepios in any of his guises— god, bearded man, boy, snake, or dog—appeared. The god touched or treated the afflicted part of the person, or provided instruction or advice. Thus a cure was effected. It was the epiphany, the visit of the god through a dream, that healed.[6]

Asklepian dream healing occurred throughout the Mediterranean world. If one could not travel to the principal sanctuary at Epidauros, a priest of Asklepios could be consulted at numerous other sanctuaries at Athens, Korinth, Krete, and throughout northern and middle Greece, the Peloponnese, and the islands. Asklepieia (the temple or sanctuary of Asklepios was called an *Asklepion*; its plural is *Asklepieia*) were found as far away as Spain and Italy to the west, Bulgaria to the north, Asia Minor eastwards, and south to northern Africa.[7] In fact, there are 320 documented Asklepieia.[8] To offer a more complete picture, Asklepian healing is portrayed in this modern fictionalized account set in Athens during the Peloponnesian Wars. This narrative dramatizes what actually took place in sleeping chambers first cut into, then housed in, an abaton built regally against the great stone mountain beneath the Akropolis.

> I went to the little shrine in the cave, in the rocks of the High City, just below the walls . . . A fading sunlight fell upon the pillars of the porch, but it was dark inside; the dripping of the holy spring sounded solemn and loud. The priest took the honeycake I had brought, and gave it

5

to the sacred snake in his little pit. He uncoiled and accepted it; and the priest asked why I had come . . .

The priest of Asklepios interviewed and examined the man, then:

He brought me a cup and said, "Drink this, and sleep; and when you wake, remember what dream the god has sent you." I took the draught, which was bitter, and lay down on a pallet in the porch. There was a man sleeping on another pallet . . .

The supplicant, an athlete, had a dream in which the god appeared to him and extended an olive crown on the point of an arrow. The priest listened intently, "threw incense on the altar, and looked at the smoke," observed the behavior of the sacred snake, then delivered the message from the god, as revealed through the dream, in words the supplicant could understand.[9]

In some accounts, Asklepios was originally a mortal prince and physician who learned the healing arts from the kentaur, Chiron. In others, he was the son of Apollo, the god of light, medicine, and music, and Koronis, daughter of the king of Thessaly. The pioneering ancient physician Galen called him the first psychiatrist.[10] Pindar declared that he carried out healing "with the words which can alleviate men's tormented souls."[11]

Epidauros, the principle sanctuary of Asklepios, began its dream healing around 600BCE. Its magnificent 14,000-seat amphitheater was built around 400 BCE with fees and gifts collected from healing, and tragedies were staged there from that time on.[12] The manifest purpose of my first visit to this sanctuary in 1987 was to attend the ancient theater festival performed there every summer in order to view classical tragedy—that masque of our suffering that reveals our shadow and dream selves.

The complexity and expanse of the ruins at Epidauros emphasize their ancient importance. As I wandered, I wondered about the connection between the ancient tragedies performed at Epidauros and its service as a healing sanctuary. There must have been a strong relationship between viewing such plays as *Oedipus Rex, Antigone, Medea,* or *Agamemnon,* and physical, psychological, and spiritual healing. The obvious connection lay in the dramatic goal of catharsis. *Catharsis* is the powerful emotional, psychological, and physical process that consists of bringing to the surface, intensifying, and purging emotions. According to Aristotle, the goal of tragedy is catharsis, especially the purging of pity and fear. Catharsis is necessary for the psychological healing we strive for in depth psychotherapy.

I would seek clues to the connection between tragic performance and Asklepian healing from my own attendance at the theater. It seemed like an impossible search for someone who, at the time, spoke only a little Greek. But I wished to experience Greek tragedy and its goal in as primal and undefended a manner as possible. Such an open attitude might, perhaps, give me an experience akin to that of the ancients.

As a modern man with my fair share of neurosis and angst, I was in need of the cleansing and releasing of poisonous emotions. Beyond this general purpose, I, too, had traveled to Epidauros with a compelling need. I was on this particular journey specifically to seek renewal and new directions after practicing eight years of intensive psychotherapy work with Vietnam veterans suffering the chronic shell shock and lifelong debilitation through terror, mistrust, alienation, anxiety, and addictions that we now label as "post-traumatic stress disorder." I needed to purge a decade of accumulated "pity and fear." The play that coincided with my visit was Euripides' *The Trojan Women,* the story of the sacking of Troy after the ten-year war.

I decided not to reread the play before the performance, nor did I have a translation in front of me. Rather, I attended, in both emotional and linguistic senses, almost naked. As the light drained from the sky, the stones of the huge amphitheater carved into the mountain surrounded me. I felt transported to another dimension where emotion and thought were carried not by semantics but by voices, oratory, mime, movement, and costume.

The great amphitheater, surrounded by pines, rose out of the mountain as if the stone itself had grown seats. The half-circle of benches rapidly filled with Greek people of all ages, including families with small children—five- and six-year-olds coming to see Euripides. The amphitheater has perfect acoustics still unexplained, so that a whisper or the crumpling of a piece of paper on stage can be heard without the aid of mechanical devices on the uppermost of the fifty-five tiers. I took my seat in the front row. I wanted the full impact with no audience between the players and me.

In addition to being a great playwright and a student of philosophy and poetry in his younger years, Euripides had a distinguished military service and was elected general in the Athenian army. *The Trojan Women* is considered to be the greatest anti-war play of antiquity and perhaps the greatest ever written. It was first produced in 415 BCE as a cry of outrage one year after Athens committed its greatest atrocity by laying siege to the island of Melos. Athens defeated Melos, then slaughtered all its men and sold its women and children into slavery. By writing *The Trojan Women*, Euripides shrove.

*Shrive* is a verb that has become archaic. Deriving from the Latin *scribere*, "to write," it means "to make or hear confession, impose penance, call for absolution." In old and medieval English, it referred to written judgments and penalties in both religious and legal enterprises. It is significant that this word has disappeared from our modern vocabulary, with the exception of the rare idiomatic expression "to give short shrift," by now emptied of its original moral and spiritual meaning of making confession before punishment. It is critical that we note these linguistic changes, for when a word disappears from the language community, the concept it carries weakens and may even disappear as well.

Especially with the Gettysburg and Second Inaugural addresses, our President Lincoln shrove during the Civil War. But we Americans are unused to generals and public figures who shrive. Generals MacArthur and Eisenhower made late-in-life anti-war speeches that are all but unknown to the American public. Our generals from Vietnam have refused to shrive, apologize, or grieve. Such refusal had disastrous consequences for developing American male psyches at the time,[13] for it left the young people who fought or resisted the war carrying the moral and spiritual pain and stain of responsibility. And more recently, the American public seemed to ache for a shriving from President Clinton after the revelation of his sexual indiscretions. The failure to shrive constituted the failure to achieve a moral cleansing, both for the president and the nation.

In contrast, in the biblical story, when reluctant Jonah finally confronted the king of Nineveh, that king and his people shrove, and the city was saved. The great possibility here is that leaders can guide people in the call for public, communal confession, grieving, and cleansing. However, in our contemporary moral vacuum, public figures seem to see it as their duty to resist and deny the need for shriving.

Classical Greece so praised the martial spirit that the conquest of Troy, the source of the *Iliad*, gave Greek culture its models of manhood and warriorhood. But Greece also created possibilities for shriving through the use of tragedy, oratory, and sacred rites for communal rituals of grieving and cleansing. Aeschylus, the first tragedian, was a veteran of the Persian Wars and fought at Marathon, where his brother was killed. He shrove the pain of war and its cost to women and children in his play *Agamemnon* and others. And in Euripides, the Greeks produced a general who shrove. Euripides' composition of *The Trojan Women* might be likened to a major American military or political figure writing a lament for the My Lai massacre in 1969, a year after it occurred. That this play was in performance upon my arrival at Epidauros was another of those life events that seem beyond coincidence. The play seemed to be chosen as if by gods or priests for my personal healing and learning.

When the light from the sun had faded, footlights came on to illuminate the stage, not brightly but rather in a soft, shadowy way, so that I had the feeling of being with the shades, the Greek spirits of the dead. Then the ever-living shades of the play, the Trojan Women's Chorus, came on stage, dancing, gesticulating, groaning their grief at the defeat and sacking of their beloved city, Troy.

The chorus of dark-robed women writhed a snakelike dance of their agony, begging the gods and Greeks for mercy, surrounding each other with gestures of consolation. Hekabe, the queen of Troy, led them in a dance torn between standing up and collapsing under the terrible loss of husbands, fathers, sons, and home. The conquerors, with stiff battle gear and hearts, and their messenger Talthybius, torn between compassion for their victims and the coldness necessitated by military conquest, gestured with and against the women.

Hekabe's daughter, the seer Kassandra, went mad. Her grandson Astyanax, son of the Trojan hero Prince Hektor and heir to Troy's throne, was torn from his mother Andromake and put to death by the Greeks. In the midst of this relentless slaughter, Hekabe cried out from the pit of her stomach, her soul, from a depth out of which I had never before heard human sound, "A-na-the-ma, A-na-the-ma," over and over again. Anathema. It is one of our words, too. I understood it, not with my mind but with my body and soul, for the first time, the way some linguists say we first learn language by attaching raw emotion to sound.

Something in me from pre-memory was wrenched free. I shuddered. I felt nauseous. Pity and compassion and revulsion surged up from my heart and flooded my body. Anathema.[14] Cursed. Wronged. Against the theme. Against the way. Against the grain. Against the order.

Anathema—this was what war was and what war did. It was against the natural order of life. It caused a moral inversion, a reversal of values and purpose, as I had observed in the war veterans I treated in psychotherapy.[15] It made us agents of destruction rather than creation. It was opposite the forward and growing movement of life gifted to us by divinity. Whoever perpetrated war was anathema.

Veterans knew it with their whole beings. It was their "moral trauma," a major component of their disability. They felt spiritually cursed and condemned, a condition Hekabe was calling down upon the Greek conquerors. There could be no healing from war without the lifting of this curse and some kind of setting things right again with the way of life, with the order of the universe, with God.

Anathema. As I left the theater, I had a strange, shuddering, uplifting, inside-out feeling throughout my body that lasted for days. How had Hekabe learned to make that cry?

During this first visit to Epidauros, I had not literally seen a manifestation of Asklepios in a dream. That would come later. But my heart was flooded with combined pity and terror. The structure of *The Trojan Women* was perfect for this. The suffering women surviving the destruction of their city aroused pity, while the punitive conquerors aroused terror. Euripides directly juxtaposed two pure, archetypal representations of these core emotions on stage. The calling up and releasing of these emotions reordered my conceptual frame and washed me clean so that language and life shone anew. Such an experience constituted catharsis. How was my experience related to Asklepian dream incubation, the purpose of this sanctuary?

Greek tragedy, as in *The Trojan Women*, parades our archetypes and their core conflicts and struggles before us. We see the forces and characters of our cosmos personified in gods and goddesses, kings and queens, their messengers and helpers, soldiers and prophets, and the chorus of ordinary people like ourselves. All these are portrayed in masks, through highly stylized mime, gesture, dance, oratory, and music, showing the drama to be, in essence, a dream or a great rite. Greek tragedy enacts not a personal story, but a story out of our collective unconscious. Tragedy is a collective dream or rite, not merely in terms of narrative content, but also in dramatic process— how it is staged, how it appears to us. When we view Greek tragedy, watching cloaked and masked gods, heroes, ghosts, mothers grieving for every child who ever died, in the light of flickering torches, against a backdrop of virginal mountains, we are in a powerful archetypal world.

According to Nietzsche, Greek tragedy presents the perfect balance between the Apollonian presentation of the dream picture—constituting the play and its performance—and the Dionysian state of drunkenness—the surrender to emotions that sweep us out of ourselves.[16] We are at once given the dream and the ecstatic experience in the dream world.

In my experience at Epidauros, viewing the tragedy felt akin to being in a dream. It was night in the sanctuary. Archetypes of war and its suffering paraded before me, as if stirred out of my own accumulated emotions and stories regarding my generation's war. The tragedy itself provided me with the dream state and its experience. Perhaps viewing tragedies at the sanctuary was sometimes a means of preparation for healing, putting the seeker into a dream state and purging emotions related to the wound. Perhaps viewing the tragedy sometimes constituted the beckoning dream itself.

Joseph Campbell observes that tragedy is "precisely the counterpart, psychologically, of the purgation of spirit effected by rite." Both effect catharsis. Both "transmute suffering into rapture by altering the focus of the mind." Where tragedy dissolves, Campbell states, myth begins. Healing is the leap out of suffering and into myth.[17]

I watched the archetypes of war dance, gesture, and exclaim, as in the perfect dream to encapsulate my decade of pained work with war veterans. But this dream was outside of me, performed by players who were, mysteriously, part of me, yet independent. It was not just a performance. Rather, it was a customary performance in an ancient style repeated in this healing sanctuary countless times over two millennia. In Campbell's terms, altering my mental focus transmuted my suffering. I was viewing the rite of suffering that occurs whenever and wherever war occurs. The dream-rite-play was performed ritually, in the cupping palm of the world, under the eyes of the god of healing. Unknowingly, I had come to Epidauros, not just to see a play, but to partake of the ancient ritual of healing, to be put into the special trance or dream state that occurs through sacred rite where individual suffering is uplifted, transformed, lightened and enlightened by being revealed as the material of myth. At that moment, as I was purged of the personal emotions that kept me attached to history, my focus radically shifted. The Vietnam War became one more modern manifestation of Ares, the eternal god and archetype of all war and destruction.

I had become disordered—out of order—from my decade of exposure to the stories and emotions of war. By experiencing the catharsis occasioned by "anathema," I felt the sickness that is moral inversion, wherein good and evil, creation and destruction, right and wrong exchange places in the soul. By feeling it and seeing it in consciousness, I was cleansed of its pollution and put back in proper balance. This, in the classical Greek view, is the essence of healing.

The balance restored to me was this: To feel moral inversion in myself and know it to be sickening and intolerable. To experience the soul's cleansing and reversion back into moral and spiritual order and balance that my veteran clients needed in order to heal. To see and accept what I had previously and absolutely rejected—that war and its pain were an ancient, perhaps even inevitable part of the human myth.

After the performance, an actress from the chorus told me that she hoped to play the part of Hekabe some day. But she expected it would take her twenty-five years of study and practice to learn to make that cry. This was catharsis, this digging down and then pulling up from the roots of the soul. This was what the melancholic Lincoln had felt and tried to express in the few elegant words of The Gettysburg Address. This was what he had called on our country to do after our Civil War and what we failed to do then and in every war since. But without such catharsis, there could be no purification, no transformation, no rejoining of the community, and no homecoming.

For a psychotherapist or other healer, as for an actress, catharsis was the difficult goal of a demanding art. At Epidauros a taste of it was possible for a non–Greek, and language mastery was not required. Rather, what was needed was a visit to this healing landscape occasioned by some inner urgent imbalance, immersion in the Asklepion and its tragic mythology and spirit, and hunger for and surrender to a primal process of winnowing and cleansing.

In our culture and times, healing catharsis occurs only rarely. It often occurs only one person at a time through the arduous digging through defenses that constitutes depth psychotherapy. More commonly, pain that might be released through catharsis is drugged or denied, while dream epiphanies are given little credence or go unrecognized. But catharsis was unquestionably what Euripides had sought and what Hekabe demanded to expedite healing. Catharsis was what I had felt twisting and turning in my body and heart. I had been given my first conscious Asklepian dream healing experience through my nighttime attendance at the tragic rite deep in the healing god's sanctuary.

And I was called to a journey. This first instance of archetypal healing given me in the Asklepian sanctuary propelled me into a search to discover how this god and his practices operated in ancient times, and how they might still serve us today. Catharsis through tragedy at Epidauros was only my first step in immersion and initiation into the living presence of the divine healing powers and practices the Greeks encapsulated in the name and story of Asklepios.

Epidauros was attended as a healing sanctuary from approximately 600 BCE to 300 CE. Asklepios "appears to have carried on his healing activities for over a thousand years."[18] Catharsis and healing dreams are two of the necessary experiences we afflicted modern people need to help lift the moral and spiritual scourge that permeates our beings and culture. Whether through modern psychotherapy, dreams and visions, art that transcends time, or transformational adventures brought about by our immersion in the wilderness or in remnants and ruins of ancient practices, the sanctuary of healing can function for us today.

# PART TWO

# MYTH, METHOD, AND MEANING

*Son of Apollo, awakened through Mother Koronis
Of the Dotian Plains, daughter of King Flegion...*

—Homeric Hymn to Asklepios

Head of Asklepios, National Archelolgical Museum, Athens

## Chapter Two

# THE MYTH OF ASKLEPIOS

Asklepios was a Christ-like figure, profoundly compassionate and deeply loved. His name, according to mythologist Robert Graves, means "unceasingly gentle."[1] Graves's interpretation echoes Pindar, who called him "the most gentle bestower of painlessness and health."[2] Other scholars say that his name derived from the ancient Greek verb ασκω or ασκεω—*asko* or *askeo*.[3] This verb had two sets of meanings in ancient times, both of which give insight into Asklepios's nature. On one hand, *askeo* meant "to form by art, decorate, or adorn, to work out with skill." On the other, the word meant "to practice, exercise, or train,"[4] in particular, to make the body strong by exercise and the mind strong by study. Combining both meanings, Asklepios was one who healed by his art and his gentle ways, using his skill to work out the riddles of our illnesses. Further, he was one who made himself and guided us to make ourselves strong in body and mind through exercise, study, and practice.

Like Jesus, Asklepios was born of a divine father and mortal mother. He, too, spent his time clad in simple robe and sandals, walking through the countryside followed by his disciples, offering healing and succor to anyone who asked. Like Jesus, he was a manifestation of the archetype of the wounded healer and savior who knows our suffering because he has experienced it.

Let us make our way slowly through Asklepios's myth,

17

contemplating, associating, and relating it to other myths, to see what mysteries this god's story can reveal regarding healing. Here, in summary, is the story.

Apollo, the god of light and truth, medicine and music, fell in love with "lovely-gowned Koronis,"[5] princess of Thessaly. Koronis was unfaithful to the god after he impregnated her, having a love affair or even marrying a mortal man, Ischys. Her unfaithfulness was reported to Apollo by the crow, one of his traditional messengers. The crow was originally white. In a fit of rage, Apollo turned the crow black. Then "he sent his strong and stormswift sister" Artemis to slay Koronis with her "golden arrows."

Seeing his beloved on her funeral pyre awakened waves of grief in Apollo. He said:

> "I can no longer
> bear in soul to kill my seed
> with horror in the grasp of its own mother's death."
> The flames gave him ingress, and in a stride he pulled
> the child out of its mother's corpse.

Apollo named this baby Asklepios and gave him to Chiron, "that idyllic kentaur, that friend to man." Chiron was the wisest and kindliest of the horse-men originally known as kentaurs. He was "the hero in hostility to all disease," well learned in the healing arts, especially the use of herbs and incantations. Chiron also suffered from a wound that would not heal, accidentally inflicted upon him by Herakles.

Chiron passed all his knowledge of the healing ways to his charge Asklepios, who in time surpassed him in skill. Asklepios not only mastered the use of herbs and healing waters taught by Chiron, but he also was said to have instituted psychotherapy by healing "with the words that can alleviate men's tormented souls" and by giving mortals the gift of healing dreams.

Apollo was the god of both medicine and prophecy. His own father Zeus had given him the ability to determine the nature of diseases. Apollo also provided divine guidance to mortals through his oracle at Delfi. This divine father Apollo passed on his gifts of diagnosis, healing, and visionary insight to Asklepios, who developed them into high healing arts that he gave to mortals. Asklepios was also given healing gifts by Athena. The goddess gave him two vials of blood taken from Medusa, the gorgon whose look turned mortals to stone. The blood from the right side of her body healed, while the blood from the left side of her body slew.

Asklepios became renowned as the greatest healer in the Mediterranean world.

> And all who came to him for treatment
> of malignancies or wounds
>    from shining spears
> or bullet stones
> or ravages of summer heat or win-
>    ter's cold he healed accordingly:
> some with soothing incantations, some with
> beneficial potions, some with ointments
>    rubbed on limbs, and some
> he brought to health by surgery.

So great was Asklepios's success and fame as a healer that people came to believe he could raise the dead. But when Asklepios revived someone who had died, Zeus slew Asklepios with a thunderbolt.

After death, Asklepios was greatly honored on earth. His temples and healing sanctuaries grew throughout the Mediterranean world. Their influence radiated from his principal sanctuary at Epidauros and the other major Asklepian sanctuaries in Pergamum on Asia Minor and the island of Kos, as well as additional Asklepian sites throughout the Mediterranean world. Eventually Asklepios was elevated to "the god of healing" and brought to live among the immortals.

After his ascension to Mt. Olympos, Asklepios's healing powers continued to grow. People from all over the known world visited his sanctuaries seeking healing, especially through dreams. Asklepios's main sanctuary at Epidauros operated from approximately 600 BCE to after 300 CE. His healing tradition dates from as early as 1300 BCE and continued until completely destroyed around 600 CE after the Roman Empire became Christianized. Thus major Asklepian sanctuaries provided seekers with the means for receiving his healing dreams for a period of almost one thousand years, while the tradition itself was active for almost two millennia.

The god, whose face as depicted in classical sculpture radiates compassion, wisdom, gentleness, and mercy, was greatly loved and often given gifts. His three sacred animals were the snake, the dog, and the cock. Snakes were used ceremonially in his sanctuaries. Cocks were often offered as payment or sacrifice. The last words of the great philosopher Sokrates, as hemlock poison numbed his body and released his soul from the trials of mortality, were, "Krito, we owe a cock to Asklepios. Don't forget."

Considering the myth more deeply, we notice first that Asklepios was son of the god of truth and light and a mortal woman. In this detail, we see a key mythic pattern of birth origins. A healer and savior is often born of a divine father and a mortal mother. A healer must be born of woman; a savior must experience incarnation. He or she must know the birth struggle as one who has experienced it, must know in bones and blood all the agonies, struggles, joys, and sorrows of being human, bring this richness of experience to any healing process, and remain eternally in touch with the nurturing feminine.

Asklepios's father, Apollo, who gave us music and medicine, was also the god of reason. He is aloof, distant, dispassionate, and analytic, even as he provides great boons. Apollo is the repository of medical wisdom, but he lacks the personality to deliver it effectively. We might say that he has know-how but lacks bedside manner.

The archetypal healer, planted and grounded in the human feminine, must partake of both mortal compassion and the dispassionate reason provided by the god. Too little humanity makes a healer unavailable to the relationship that heals. But err on the side of being "too human" and the healer may be so overwhelmed by feelings and personal issues that he or she is unable to heal others effectively. Asklepios, as archetypal healer, is "the divine physician, who combines light and helpfulness in his personality. [A]ncestor and prototype of all mortal physicians,"[6] he was born of the balance, midway between divine and human.

Apollo gave his son prophecy and dream visitations as divine gifts. But in an uncharacteristic fit of jealousy, the usually rational Apollo had Koronis killed. Thus Asklepios inherited a primal wound that he had to learn to master. Conceived of both god and mortal, he was immediately wounded by their clash. He was saved from dying flesh by an act of god, saved from the decay of the earthly by the heavenly, the immortal. Further, like other divine figures to which his pattern is related, by being snatched from his dead mother's womb and the devouring flames of her funeral pyre, he experienced a resurrection.

So many healers—therapists, ministers, physicians, guides—come from dysfunctional families, feeling as though they would have been destroyed in the family womb were it not for some miracle or unexpected intervention, some "act of god." Later they strive to save other stunted lives from dying in the family-of-origin womb.

The future healer was given by his father Apollo to be raised by Chiron. This transfer from powerful but inadequate birth father to accessible mentor is another necessary aspect of the healer's development. Robert Bly likens a mentor to "the male mother." Asklepios, abandoned by his father and with his mother dead, was raised by his male mother, the half-man and half-horse who had the knowledge of healing herbs.

Chiron, too, had a wound. Herakles accidentally inflicted it during a fight with other kentaurs over a vat of wine. Chiron's wound would not heal and kept him in perpetual pain. Thus the mentor as well as the apprentice was a wounded healer. In fact, the wound that refuses to heal, and is even unjust or undeserved, is often a necessary motivation for becoming a healer. "Physician, heal thyself!" is not just a corrective cry against incompetent healers. It can also be heard as the mythic birth cry of all healers. The future healer must be driven to seek healing for him or herself. The search for healing must be successful so that the healer later knows how to conduct others down a healing path that works. Asklepios's birth was half-divine, half-human, but under Chiron, he rejoined the earth powers. Thus his rearing and education as a healer was half-nature, half-human.

There are several Greek myths demonstrating the wildness and destruction that can occur when the horse components of kentaurs dominate their personalities and behavior. In fact, kentaurs may originally refer to fierce, savage, unrefined mortals. In the *Iliad*, they are such a tribe, "wild things of the mountains."[7]

Chiron as archetypal mentor demonstrates that nature and human must be joined in a single being. Nature provides the legs and torso—the grounding, the power and access to instinct. The human provides the upper torso and head—the reach and guidance through arms, eyes, and reason—in order to effectively direct the powerful energies of nature.

Greek author Nikos Kazantzakis sees the kentaur as an expression of the uniquely human position as midpoint between nature and spirit: The human being is a kentaur; his equine hoofs are planted in the ground, but

> his body from breast to head is worked on and tormented by the merciless Cry. He has been fighting, again for thousands of eons, to draw himself, like a sword, out of his animalistic scabbard. He is also fighting . . . to draw himself out of his human scabbard. Man calls in despair, "Where can I go? . . ." And the Cry answers, "I am beyond. Stand up!"[8]

Did Chiron have two hearts or two souls—a horse's and a man's? Healers must feel, experience, and tend to both the animal and the human. Healers must integrate both nature and spirit and be their intermediary. And healers must learn, like kentaurs, to live in, work with, and harmonize the inner tensions that threaten to pull them asunder. As Kazantzakis says, "All things are kentaurs. If this were not the case, the world would rot in inertness and sterility."[9]

Asklepios mastered Chiron's teachings on the use of herbs and incantations—the healing arts derived directly from nature. To these, Asklepios also added the gifts of his father Apollo, the diagnostic powers of medicine and the oracular powers of prophecy. As the capstone of his healing skills, Asklepios added words, the uniquely human dimension of expression, bridge building, and healing.

In any therapeutic practice, Apollo's gifts translate into understanding of the inner disease-and-healing process itself and the germinating and reading of dreams. Diagnosis and understanding are the healing arts derived from reason; dreaming and reading their mysteries are the arts derived from spirit. Thus, Asklepios reclaimed in his own maturity as a healer the gifts of the wounding and abandoning father. The healer heals him or herself by reconciling with and reclaiming the gifts of the previously alienated parents. Further, Asklepios became the greatest of healers by successfully embodying in his art the gifts of both father and mentor as well as his own innovations. Asklepios the archetypal healer successfully integrates the three fields of our being—natural, human, and spiritual.

When traditional societies come into conflict with cultures that interrupt their older earth-based practices, the childhood patterns and conflicts of the shamans and healers-to-be often embody the conflict between cultures. One modern example tells of an African shaman whose father was Catholic and mother traditional Zulu. The young boy was first "torn from his womb," separated from his mother, village, elders, friends, and traditional schooling by his father and educated in Christianity. He was then "resurrected," pulled back to his earth roots and given a traditional education by his mother.[10]

This developmental pattern replicates what we see in the myth of Asklepios. The father-god representing the newer and more rational Olympian culture kills the earth mother and tears their child from her womb. Then the child returns to his roots through the male mother—the mentor. In his maturity, the healer does not merely revert to his earlier earth-based culture, but successfully integrates the gifts and practices of healing arts derived from each of his parental/cultural influences.

All cultures based in earth spirituality are replete with animal and plant spirits that are recognized and utilized by healers. The animals and plants are at one with nature and closer to the divine source of nature than we are. They serve as messengers of the sacred through which divine and natural energies are transmitted to the intermediate human world.

Asklepios's father Apollo, upon receiving word from his own messenger the crow that Koronis had betrayed him, turned the crow from white to black. Those who are called to approach the healing enterprise can not pretend to themselves that they are all "white"— good, pure, of the light. Rather, they must encounter their own shadows, their unconscious and hidden aspects, traditionally represented by darkness, night, and the color black. The crow's transformation highlights this necessary discovery and presages the journey of descent all healers must make into the individual and collective unconscious through incubation.

Asklepios the healer has three totems, his animal helping spirits—the snake, the dog, and the cock.

The snake is the representative of Mother Earth and of transformation. In all traditions except the Judeo-Christian, the snake has been seen as the carrier of beneficent and desirable powers.[11] "Only in Christianity, the Bible, is the once-sacred snake the object of curses."[12] Snake worship and healing practices were widespread in the Mediterranean region. Asklepios was an advanced practitioner of snake healing, particularly the inner transformation of poisons and identity transformations symbolized by shedding one's old skin. Asklepios the healer is represented as carrying a staff around which a single great snake winds.

Our well-known medical symbol is the caduceus, the staff around which two snakes wind themselves, originally carried by Hermes, the messenger god and guide of souls. Some ancient sources say that the bite of one of these snakes was poisonous; the bite of the other healing. Similarly, Asklepios carries blood from the snake-haired gorgon Medusa. "And through the ministry of Athene, Asklepios . . . secured the blood from the veins of Medusa, both from her left side and from her right. With the former he slays, but with the latter he cures and brings back to life."[13]

The psychological meaning of these twin powers—whether snake or blood of the snake-haired woman—points to the ambiguous nature of both the unconscious and the healing process. Psychologically, "the unconscious has a double quality to it. One can never know in advance whether it will be beneficial or harmful, since this depends on the circumstances and also on the attitude of the ego that is relating to the unconscious power."[14] Whether the surfacing of unconscious material will help heal or further wound us depends heavily upon four variables: our ego's attitude toward the material; the gods and guides who transmit it to us and help us utilize it; the environment and community that serves as container for the material; and the manner of its release—whether through accident, traumatic event, dyadic encounter, religious ritual, or sacred event.

Spiritually, the two snakes and two vials teach a key healing lesson. As homeopathic and other therapeutic practices know, the administration of a little poison can bring healing. A Vietnamese proverb states, "Poison cures poison." In ancient snake healing traditions around the world, snake priests and priestesses allowed themselves to be bitten by their poisonous charges. This practice propelled them into altered states of consciousness while, over time, allowing them to build up immunity to the poison. Then they were able to utilize the snakes and their poison in sacred and healing rituals and treatment. This may have been the case in Asklepian practice.

The healing principle here is this: What poisons us can also heal us; what heals us can also poison us. The ancient oracle of Apollo declared this same wisdom: "He who wounds also heals."[15] Again we see that attitude, motivation, intention, practice, containment, dosage, timing, administration, guidance, and community all determine whether a psychotherapy, a medicine, an experience in the wilderness, a ritual participation will bring about a healing or worsening of any condition or dilemma from which we suffer. Here is where the healer's art is of utmost consequence. Though he carries two vials of blood, and though Hermes' caduceus and our medical symbol have two intertwined snakes, Asklepios's staff has only one giant snake twining up its length. The god's snake has been identified as a harmless tree snake of southern Europe that can grow to a length of more than four feet.[16] In addition, Hermes' staff is a hand-held wand, while Asklepios's rod is of nearly body length. Rather than rely on Freudian interpretations of snake and staff as phallic symbols, "It comes close to the myth to interpret the staff as a symbol of fertility and power, since it was the symbol of a god, who had the power to decide between life and death. The staff can also be interpreted as a shepherd's crook or as a walking stick, since the god himself and his disciples were always walking."[17]

In beholding the giant snake climbing the body-length rod, we may be contemplating a classical Greek portrait of the archetypal condition often represented in the mandalas of the sacred art of the East. This condition, well known to Eastern healing, is of kundalini energy climbing the spine through the energy centers of the body. The single harmless snake may indicate that Asklepios integrated both the restorative and destructive elements of the two vials or snakes into one successful healing enterprise. Further, it may hearken back, as Joseph Campbell suggests, to the earlier matriarchal systems in which supposedly contradictory powers of life and death, good and evil, light and dark, body and spirit, were all united in "the primal, one and only, ultimate reality of nature, of whom the gods themselves are but functioning agents."[18]

We turn to Asklepios's other animal totems. The dog is "man's best friend," the animal most loyal and compassionate to humans. Even more, dogs can serve as messengers from and intermediaries to the animal world. A Seneca legend expresses the depth of this relationship. According to the Seneca people, after humans acquired the taste for meat, all animals fled from a common community and developed their own languages. Only then did the Creator make dogs and give them to people as a gift so that there would be an animal intermediary between humans and the natural world.

Asklepios was concerned with accessing the healing energies of nature and putting people back in balance with the natural order. The dog, as an animal intermediary loyal to humans and anxious to communicate with us, could be a great helper in such an enterprise. One of my clients and students, a man named Dave, traveled with me through Greece to seek healing from a life-threatening illness. Dave had a strange dog adopt and accompany him every step of the way on a difficult daylong climb up to the mountaintop fortress of Akrokorinth. This occurred the day before we arrived at the major Asklepian sanctuary at Epidauros where he would pray and dream for healing. (We will hear more about Dave's modern Asklepian healing later.) Dave's dog was a sign the ancients would have recognized that he was accompanied by transpersonal powers and called to enter the god's healing sanctuary.

In ancient practice, the dog was not only concerned with our relationship to nature and the animal world. Meier says that dogs were considered to be guides into the other world among Indo-Germanic peoples. They are especially suited for this role of guiding us to the spirit world, as Dave's strange dog did, because of their ability to follow a trail and their intuitive natures. Thus, they also demonstrate qualities necessary to the skilled healer.[19]

There is a further use to which dogs were sometimes put in

ancient practice. They were sometimes used as sacrifices to the dead. Dog remains with offerings of beef bones and oil flasks have been found around Greece. Recent excavations in central Athens unearthed a dog buried with a collar of semi-precious stones.[20] Homer confirms this type of sacrifice. He tells us in the *Iliad* that as Achilles built the huge funeral pyre for his beloved friend Patroklos, killed before the walls of Troy,

> Nine hunting dogs had fed at the lord's table:
> Upon the pyre he cut the throats of two.[21]

Thus dogs were not only used to guide the living. Dogs also served as offerings to propitiate the departed soul, as companions in the soul's travels beyond life, or as guides in the underworld.

Asklepios's third animal, the cock, was "the preferred animal" of sacrifice to this particular god,[22] and in fact was sacrificed to no other god but him. The cock, and occasionally other animals, was given in thanksgiving for healing, as were votive reproductions of the body part that had been healed. This tradition is still part of Greek Orthodox practice today. In times of need people vow before a saint to give or do something in return for divine assistance. The object of appeal—an arm, a leg, an eye, a child, a ship—is often replicated in small metal rectangles hung in church on an altar or before icons. This offering is called a ταμα, *tama*, meaning both "the vow" and "the votive."[23] Greek people go to great lengths and expense to fulfill their vows, and it is considered dangerous to forsake them. The gift of the tama traces directly back to the Asklepian offering of a votive to the god's sanctuary for the person or body part that had been healed.

The cock is the animal that straddles yin and yang, darkness and light, day and night. It calls us to consciousness, crying at the break of dawn to awaken us from dreams. Asklepios healed through dream visits that would bring the core affliction to the dreamer's consciousness. The cock, sounding the clarion call to awaken after

28

dreaming, symbolizes this potent aspect of the healer, helping bring both the affliction and the encounter with divinity out of the darkness and unconsciousness and into the bright morning light of awareness and availability.

As reported by Plato in the *Phaedo*, Sokrates believed in the healing powers of Asklepios. Though a beloved disciple, Plato was ill and thus could not attend Sokrates at the time of his execution. The day before the execution, Sokrates told Plato that he must go "to the temple of Asklepios to be cured and not forget to offer a cock in sacrifice to Asklepios when he wakes up cured."[24]

Sokrates spent much of his last day in dialogue with his followers attempting to convince them, and himself as he says, that death is nothing more than the separation of body and soul. For philosophers death may be a great good, a longed-for freedom. The wise old philosopher left life telling us that death could be a healing from the pain of life. His very last words, addressed to his older bosom friend and disciple, were, "Krito, we owe a cock to Asklepios. Don't forget."

Sokrates' tragic execution has come to be a healing for our civilization. He has become a model for all time of the life completely devoted to the inner calling. Certainly Sokrates was speaking out of great and hard-won wisdom of the potential goodness of death. He was also clearly affirming his piety before the gods and his belief that in accepting death and freeing his soul, he was achieving a great healing. Remember that Sokrates was a dedicated servant of Apollo and that Apollo's son Asklepios appeared in dreams to those seeking healing and guidance. Sokrates also tells us that in prison he had a dream instructing him to practice the gift of the muses. It is conceivable that in his last days in prison or even in his last moments of life, Sokrates had a dream or vision of the god that supported his great awareness, guided his soul out of its mortal cage, or brought him further wisdom that yet remains a mystery to us.

The manner of Asklepian healing was through dream incubation. Those suffering intractable illnesses of body, mind, or spirit traveled to Asklepian sanctuaries to be given rest, music, and drama, healthy diets and exercise, as they awaited the call into the sanctuary. When a dream or natural event showed that the god called them, they entered into the abaton, the untrodden place. There they were put in cocoon-like underground chambers, fasting and unable to move until the god came in a healing dream and effected or pointed to the cure.

In this, too, the elements of healing are demonstrated. This part of the healing process is especially demonstrated in contemporary psychotherapeutic practice, but is applicable to any complete form of therapeutics. First there is the compelling need to seek a form of therapy because "nothing else has worked." Then there is the period of nurturing and bonding, lingering in the sanctuary grounds in order to improve the details of living, seek relief in a safe place, and strengthen and prepare both psyche and soma for the more difficult healing work. Finally there is the call to descend into the unconscious and return to the womb where the original wound is festering, awaiting a healing visit. Then in kairos, the sacred time of therapy and of dreaming, the archetypal god of healing touches the client in modern or ancient manifestations.

Entering the dream chambers of classical times was both a descent into the unconscious—the dark underground—and into the womb—at once nature's cocoon, the birth mother's womb, and Mother Earth's womb and tomb. To heal our intractable wounds, we must return to the womb of our wound. Asklepios was born out of the womb of his slain mother Koronis. His supplicants had to return to the womb to be reborn out of the place of the original wound. To become a healer, Asklepios had to be raised by his nature teacher and "male mother" Chiron. For a full healing, we must also descend into nature, the great mother's body, for the energies and holding that can truly bring rebirth.

Asklepios as archetype is both a model for us to study, interpret, and emulate, and a psychospiritual energy pattern for us to awaken, feel, channel, and bring to life in ourselves. Asklepian healing dem-

onstrates the great challenge and progress of transformational healing. The literal Greek meaning of psychotherapist is "attendant of
the soul." Through the guidance and intervention of spirit, and with
the guidance and attendance of the soul, the supplicant descends into
the womb of the wound, the place where the primal wound occurred and has festered. There the supplicant needs to experience
awareness, touching, catharsis, and purification of the original wound.
The supplicant also needs a guided descent into the great Mother
Earth's womb, where through her incubation, nurturing, and touch,
often by way of dreams and animal helpers, the supplicant can experience a return of the primal, life-giving energies of nature and spirit.

In pursuit of what brings about transformational healing, the
myth and model of Asklepios teaches that to be an effective attendant of the soul in its quest for healing every healer—and every
person seeking healing—must:

- know and attend to their own primal wounds
- integrate the wounding and the gifts of their parents
- accept and work with the primal marriage of creative and
  destructive forces that is at the core of the human condition
- seek mentors to guide and complete their personality development
- surpass their mentors by adding their own unique ingredients to the healing process
- create sacred time and space within and beyond the treatment room
- support and guide the descent into the womb of the wound
- support and guide the descent into the renewing womb of
  Mother Earth
- watch for and encourage connections with helping spirits
  from the natural and spiritual realms

- foster and maintain utmost respect, concern for, and attention to dreaming in its broadest sense, to any and all material surfacing from the personal and collective unconscious

- give and encourage giving the appropriate sacrifices for the seeking and receiving of aid

- maintain or attend a sanctuary that maximizes the possibility that these healing conditions can be met.

These necessities of the healing process as modeled by Asklepios include but go far beyond the core requirements of the therapeutic or doctor-patient relationships. The empathic, containing, positive-regarding healing relationship is a necessary building block for inviting clients into a modern form of the sanctuary of Asklepios. However, Asklepian healing passes far beyond dyadic encounter. Asklepian healing does not treat the individual as an isolated unit. Rather, it immerses the afflicted person into a complete healing environment. Only in some form of sanctuary connected to both nature and spirit can the descent into the wound and the womb of life, long and deep dreaming, and a visit from energies and powers beyond the human safely occur.

When Zeus slew Asklepios with a thunderbolt, he acted as king of the gods and guardian of cosmic justice to preserve the limits set by natural law. Healers can assist the powers of nature and spirit but cannot alter or surpass the natural order or our own human limits.

How striking is the analogy between Asklepios raising a man from the dead and Jesus raising Lazarus. As healers and saviors sent to relieve our suffering, both figures confront the ultimate cause of suffering—death. But Jesus raising Lazarus is taken as proof of his divinity, while Asklepios raising the dead man stands as an act of hubris and represents the line over which healers must not trespass, the place they must not tread.

In both cases, the raising of the dead demonstrates the divine powers each healer had at his command and the human hope for triumph over suffering and mortality. Yet there is a critical difference in the fate of the healers. In the Greek worldview, there are absolute limits that may not be transgressed by either gods or mortals. In contrast, in the Christian view, Jesus transcended mortal limits by transcending death, both death for the common person by resurrecting Lazarus, and his own death when he achieved resurrection after crucifixion. The promise of the Greek view is that we live in a universe ordered along ultimate principles that rule all things; balance and serenity can come to us if we live in acceptance of these principles. The promise of the Christian view is that even these ultimate principles can be transcended.

Clearly, both myths teach that it is not for mortals to transcend the limits of life and death. Leave that to the gods—and perhaps not even to them! As a mortal healer and guide, I have felt the agony of not being able to save, resurrect, return from the dying, clients I had come to love. I have also felt the pain and agony of helping to bring clients "back from the dead" only to return them to a Zeus-ruled world that slays.

Healers may channel or partake of divine energies, but they are not gods. Rather, like Asklepios, they need to be the meeting place of nature, humanity, and spirit. They must never forsake or surpass their human limits. They must grieve and accept the killing and the dying, even as they aid and affirm the living. Otherwise, the primal forces of nature will turn against them. They must strive to work with the order of the universe and accept their allotted limits and ends, including the finality of death itself.

## Chapter Three

# DREAM, MYTH, AND RITUAL

Dreams are created by individuals; myths, by cultures. As human experience accumulates over vast stretches of time and layers of civilization, history, and nature, cultures create collective dreams that eventually become their myths. They repeat in us, as individuals and cultures, as we repeat the ancient, enduring human journey in its contemporary manifestation. When we interpret myths, we are interpreting the dreams of the ages.

In the modern age, Freud first reminded us to take our dreams as serious messages from unconscious sources, and many explorers and commentators on the dream life have followed in the last hundred years. Freud's reminder came after centuries of neglect of such nonrational phenomena as dreams. In fact, he rescued dreams from the realm of nonsense and restored them to the psychological.

While Freud located the source of dreams in the unconscious, the deeply personal, other theorists beginning with Jung saw that dreams also have collective or transpersonal dimensions. In fact, ancient traditions from all over the world support the experience and interpretation of dreams as messages from transpersonal sources. The inheritors of Freud successfully restored the psychological dimensions of dream work, while the inheritors of Jung successfully restored the transpersonal dimensions of dream work. One of the great challenges we face in modern dream work is recognizing and differentiating the personal and the transpersonal, the individual and the collective, the psychological and the spiritual. Then we must knit our processes, interpretations, and guidance received into a gestalt as inclusive, complete, and successful as is the dream itself.

One of the major and most powerful practices of transformational dream work in all of human history is found in the myth and traditions of Asklepios. Asklepios teaches us how we may heal through dream questing what cannot otherwise be healed. According to the Asklepian tradition as well as testimony and practices from numerous traditions worldwide, dreams and related phenomena such as visions and shamanic journeys are not "symbolic of" something in the everyday world. As James Hillman has written, dreams are not "a piece of the psyche along with memory, perception, emotion, and the like. Dreaming is the psyche itself doing its soul-work."[1] Dreams are profound soul experiences in themselves, not to be merely interpreted for meaning and guidance. Since they occur at the foundational layers of our psyches where everything is mythic, they can profoundly reveal, rearrange, affect, and transform the very organization of imagery that has its life at that foundational level. Thus, quite literally, through our souls' adventures in the inner world, dreams can change our minds. When and how to seek and purposefully use dreams for transformational work in our psychic foundations is taught by both the myth and the practices of ancient Asklepian work.

Moreover, the collective dreams that we know as myths can themselves be an endless source of guidance, inspiration, and wisdom. Whether I am guiding a psychotherapy or supervision session; a class, retreat, or workshop; a journey into the wilderness or to an ancient land; or when I am struggling with a dilemma of my own, I approach myths as I do dreams, seeing them only as larger and more universalized. Myths are certainly symbols to be interpreted. But they are also vividly alive experiences that take place in what the ancient Greeks called *kairos,* the sacred rather than ordinary dimension of time,[2] what Jungian analyst Thomas Lavin calls "urging time."[3]

I encourage my therapy clients, students, and traveling companions to treat both their individual dreams and our collective myths as primal experiences as well as symbol systems. This approach helps us fully embrace what happens in our dreams or in our identification with myths. In the therapeutic work of interpretation, we use dreams and myths as guides and aides to understanding waking life. But beyond this interpretive level, we can consider dreams and myths to be forms of actual psychic experience in the inner world. Such experiences reveal the dimensions of the archetypal world that lives eternally within and beyond us. Simultaneously, they offer healing through the awakening and reorganization of psychic energies and structures.

Every one of us repeats the themes of myths that may be found in dramatized form somewhere in world literature or culture. The particular myths any of us enact, through the drama of our daily lives and through dreams and other unusual experiences, reveal the essential aspects of our psychodynamics. Their identification and decoding can be a major aspect of therapy.

The archetypes are living energy patterns and configurations that exist eternally but find living expression through our psychodynamics and creative processes. In short, we live the myths, while the archetypes live us. We must pay homage and embrace the surfacing of archetypes and myths in our private lives, even as we seek understanding, healing, and creative distance from them.

All this is to say that the ancient life as portrayed in myth—of gods and goddesses, ordeals and oracles, heroes and heroines—is eternally alive and well and is accessible to us even today in our secularized and materialistic world. Our task is to recognize, decode, and access the mythic patterns and archetypal presence, disguised as they are in contemporary concepts, images, and experiences. As the ancients said, the gods live forever. All we need do is remember them.

The first way ancient life is accessible today, rarely practiced but more common than what will follow, is through identification. Following the model of Jungian analysis, we can freely associate to myths as we do to dreams. We can seek themes that resonate with us, images that spark personal images and memories, points of identification, until we realize that "particular myths, at least, will be living themselves out in one's life . . ." and we come to feel that "This is my myth. This is myself I am seeing here."[4]

I commonly introduce mythic stories to my psychotherapy clients struggling with intractable dilemmas. For example, I have often used the story of Odysseus and the Sirens with both men and women struggling with sexual obsessions, fantasies, or acting out. As recorded in Homer's *Odyssey*,[5] on his voyage home from the Trojan War, Odysseus had to sail past the island of the Sirens, who sang so beautifully and seductively that sailors inevitably turned their ships toward the enchantresses, only to be shipwrecked on the rocky shoals surrounding their island. To sail safely past them, Odysseus plugged his crew's ears with wax. But the captain himself wanted to experience their irresistible music. In order to simultaneously listen yet resist, Odysseus had himself tied to his mast.

Contemplating this myth, a sexually compulsive man for the first time saw himself not as a pathological misfit but rather on a universal hero's journey necessitating his need to learn restraint and containment of the power of his sexual drives. A woman after several affairs asked for the first time who it was she was trying to shipwreck and devour, how it was that her femininity had become a disguised weapon of destruction rather than a source of joy, sharing, and nurturing to self and others.

In a similar manner, in my work with war veterans, I use the myths and legends of warriorhood from traditions the world over. I teach my veterans that world mythological traditions honor the returned warrior, wounded or not, defeated or not, and that there are mythic means and strategies for returning them from their sojourn in the underworld. I demonstrate that their shell shock, battle fatigue, or post-traumatic stress disorder can be understood and experienced mythically as a condition of being stuck in the underworld. I invite my veteran clients to undertake the psycho-mythic transformational journey from disabled veteran to healed and returned warrior of honor.

Seeing one's personal struggles mirrored in ancient myths automatically brings a feeling of relief to the sufferer. As Joseph Campbell succinctly put it, "Guilt is what is wiped out by the myth."[6] One's personal drama accurately reflected in an ancient story demonstrates to the sufferer that he or she is not struggling alone and unnecessarily, but rather is in a necessary ordeal with some eternal aspect of the human condition.

The second way the life of the ancients is accessible to us is through our replication of mythic formulae. By studying the myths, legends, and testimonies of ancient traditions closely, we can discern actual formulae for performing rites, rituals, ceremonies, blessings, prayers, oracle seeking, and ordeals. "Every aspect of the myth survives: its formulae, its plot, its place descriptions, and its archaic attitudes from a lost world. Thus, the ancient world is recoverable ..."[7] The myths not only reveal to us eternal themes of the human drama. They also tell us how, when, where, with whom, in what ways these dramas were enacted in ancient cultures. We can then choose to reenact the myths—not in ways that forsake modernity for a flight into the dead past, but in ways that are comfortable, accessible, and adapted to the contemporary world, that revivify and revitalize contemporary life and create a new synthesis of the contemporary with the eternal. As Lao Tzu taught, "Stay with the ancient, move with the present."

There are many ways available to us for such mythic reenactment. We may participate in such Native American purification ceremonies as a sweat lodge, or in such life-guidance seeking ceremonies as a vision quest. We may go on pilgrimage, traveling to sacred sites to seek inspiration, offer prayer, and deepen a personal connection to a divine or human figure. We may take the ecosystem very seriously and immerse ourselves in nature to the extent that we reenter the living web from which we have become alienated. We can watch for the ways the web responds to us and take these responses as personal, reading them as signs and oracles. We may identify with a mythic tradition to such a degree that we undertake a journey that replicates the mythic hero's journey as recorded in ancient sources. We may pray as the ancients did in their very temples. We may even offer libations and food sacrifices as they did. We may create new personal or communal rituals, marking significant life passages or events, modeled on traditional rituals but constructed out of the familiar material of our own lives and traditions. In all these cases, we go beyond association into a living identification. We do not forget who we are as modern people with a modern consciousness. But we accept and believe that the ancients had access to transpersonal dimensions that we have lost, and that by following their teachings, we may regain and achieve such access as well.

Mythic immersion is possible today, whether through association and identification in the consultation room with a therapist as support and guide, or through identification and replication in nature or around the world, perhaps with a teacher, therapist, modern shaman, or experienced pilgrim as guide, or on one's own. Any way we practice such immersion in myth, the movement is the same. The personal finds its place in the universal. The individual's fear and judgment of psychopathology is transformed into a sense of participation in the struggles of the ages. In the myth we labor not for ourselves alone but for all humanity.

First we struggle and suffer alone. Eventually, with grace or guidance, we identify with the myth. Then we see that we are living the myth and that it belongs to all humanity. Our struggles become ordeals in service to the archetypal dimensions of human life that we, too, are helping into the world. Finally, we accept that the divine is the true power and that divinity's myths are living us. When we enter that consciousness, we gain a true acceptance that there is no way out. There is only the way through. There is only living the myth with willingness and consciousness. Through such living we gain an invaluable and irreplaceable sense of our destiny, purpose, and relationship to our cosmic home and story.

# PART THREE

# AN ASKLEPIAN PILGRIMAGE

*Great to humanity, soother of cruel suffering . . .*

—Homeric Hymn to Asklepios

Pergamum Asklepion

## Chapter Four

# CONSCIOUS MYTHMAKING

Many myths map the paths to adventure, transformational challenges, and healing. To revitalize the healing potentials of myth for ourselves today, it is not enough for us merely to study them or for therapists and other healers to apply them in working with clients. Rather than imprison myth in the consulting room or the classroom, we can take the myths themselves, and the pioneering myth-mapping work of key figures such as Carl Jung, Joseph Campbell, and others, into the realm of action through organized practice. Applied in the psychotherapy setting, Carl Jung called the practice of working with myth "active imagination." Beyond the consulting room, mythologist Stephen Larsen calls it "conscious mythmaking." As Larsen explains, vision quests, dream theater and psychodrama, mask-making rituals, as well as the medicine of Asklepios, "the original therapist," are all examples of conscious mythmaking in that "a symbolic structure or container is made in which myth and consciousness are aligned in a special way."[1]

To practice conscious mythmaking, we educate ourselves in the history, mythology, culture, lifestyle, and practices of the ancients. We may travel to the sites where ancient mythical and historical events actually occurred. Standing on the actual spot where mythic events took place can help us overlap ancient and modern worlds so that we enter kairos, transformed time and space. The distinction between past and present disappears. We immerse ourselves in an eternally present mythic consciousness. Further, the particular landscape of a myth carries the energies and ingredients, the faces and places, the names and images that gave birth to that myth. The return to a myth's home territory offers a radical invitation to that myth to return to life in us.

Pilgrimage can be a form of conscious mythmaking. Traveling with an attitude of serious engagement, seeking a thorough cultural and mythic immersion, knowing that there was a living spirituality here that worked for the ancients and can be accessed by us, invites dreams and unusual events to occur for us. These are likely to feel luminous, charged with energy, or particularly symbolic of life issues and themes with which we are most concerned. When we drench ourselves in the archetypal world, the archetypes are invited to awaken in, return to, and answer us in ways that are neither ancient nor modern, but rather eternal.

I use the term "mythic history" for what we are seeking when we approach a figure like Asklepios in this way. This term is derived directly from the Greek word Μυθιστορεμα. In modern Greek, the word *mythistorema* is translated as "novel" and is used to denote that literary genre. But the word means more than what we have come to understand as a book of fiction. The Greek poet George Seferis, who was awarded the Nobel Prize in 1963, used this word as the title of his first important collection of poetry. Seferis's collection was an interrelated series of lyric poems that attempted to give a complete portrait of the Greek landscape and the soul's experience dwelling in it, past and present. As he applied the term and as I use it, mythic history connotes not just an imaginative narrative, but the unfolding of a sacred story that includes all the elements of myth. In mythic history, a universal design and purpose influence character and action as it unfolds in time and space and shows us the map of destiny.

In the next several chapters, we explore some of the ancient sanctuaries of the god of healing as modern travelers on an Asklepian pilgrimage through the Mediterranean world. Making such a journey, whether through writing, reading, dreaming about, or actually visiting the sites, amounts to the reconstruction of and participation in the mythic history of this god. Through contemplating the mythic history of Asklepios, we can visualize when, where, why, and how this god and his practices came to walk among mortals. We can comprehend where, when, and how dream healing took place. Most importantly, by replicating the mythic history in our imaginations, we make the myth conscious and accessible. We may thus energize an Asklepian awakening in ourselves, no matter where we are.

Among the 320 Asklepieia identified by archaeologists, a few are among the most extensive and impressive of the ruin sites in all of Greece and Asia Minor. These include Asklepios's principal healing center at Epidauros and the two largest and most important of the god's sanctuaries after Epidauros. One is on the island of Kos, near Rhodes and just across from the Turkish coastline. The other is at Pergamum, on the western coast of Turkey and incorporated directly into the modern city of Bergama.

Other remaining Asklepieia are much smaller, yet still clearly recognizable as the healing and dreaming sanctuaries they once were, with much still standing of rooms, altars, even stone couches for dream-sleeping. Such an Asklepion is found at Korinth, on the northeastern corner of the Peloponnese. Still others are merely scattered foundations, fallen columns and rubble demarcating temples, anterooms, sleeping chambers, dormitories, and other types of rooms necessary to Asklepian healing. These sites may be found by themselves or as an important and incorporated public section of a more extensive ruined city.

Such an Asklepion can be found in the remote ruins of Troizen, birthplace of Theseus, the hero who slew the Kretan Minotaur and later was a great visionary and tragic king of Athens. Another is the important Asklepion that was on the Akropolis in classical Athens and was one of the many buildings of dedication and service perched on that high city dedicated to and presided over by Athena, goddess of war and wisdom and protectress of the city. Yet another, with its beautiful mosaic floor of a horse galloping through waves, can be visited on the remote coast of southern Krete. This Asklepion, active in both Greek and Roman eras, is snuggled into the seaward slope of a mountain facing the Libyan Sea and overlooking the tiny village of Lendas.

Finally, other Asklepieia are memories. We know the approximate site. We have records of their existence. We can behold the rock and the landscapes in which they stood. We may have records of healings that took place in these sanctuaries. But the sanctuaries, their temples, foundations, and healing fountains are gone. At these sites we must use our powers of imagination, intuition, and empathy to see and feel where the dream questing and healing took place. Such is the case with the Asklepion at Trikka in Thessaly, reputed to be the birthplace of the healing god himself, where our Asklepian pilgrimage begins.

## Chapter Five

# BIRTHPLACE AND HOMELAND
## TRIKKA, 1300 BCE

We begin our mythic history of Asklepios at the beginning, with the god's birthplace. Some accounts say that Asklepios was born a god as a result of Apollo's union with Koronis. Other accounts, including his mention in the *Iliad*, hold that Asklepios was originally a prince of Thessaly, who became famous and beloved as a highly skilled physician. According to these accounts, it was only after a long period of time and the widespread influence of Asklepian sanctuaries that Asklepios the mortal physician was elevated to the stature of a god.

A third interpretation of Asklepios, much less familiar to the popular imagination, is that Asklepios was one of the *chthonioi*. These were "spirits who live in the dark recesses of the earth" as opposed to the well-known gods of the upper world who populated Olympos.[1] These earth spirits date to a much earlier period than the Olympian gods and were plentiful during the time of the matriarchy. Their earlier origins correspond to Asklepios's early birth date.

To ancient Greeks, chthonioi could be either divine or heroic and, in either case, they could be prayed and sacrificed to for intercession in human affairs. Herakles is one example of such an underground spirit, also born of the union of a male god with a mortal woman. Herakles had many shrines and was worshiped not as a god but as a hero, a being of undying might and influence. Alexander the Great experienced Herakles as a personal spirit guide to whom he prayed and sacrificed and from whom he received dream visitations and guidance.

It is likely that all three accounts of Asklepios's origins merge into a unified mythic history. Asklepios may have originally been a mortal physician-prince whose kindness, goodness, and success as a healer first inspired hero worship. In the pagan world, such successful mortal heroes were worshiped after death as spirits of exceptional and ongoing power, bringing them close to demi-god status. One such late hero from historical times is Alexander the Great. Alexander's fame, popularity, and deeds were so impressive that his history, including in his own mind, was transmuted from the personal to the mythic. This son of the mortal king Philip of Macedon came to be regarded as a son of Zeus; Alexander himself suspected that this was true and sought through oracles to validate its accuracy. This great political and military leader became a hero in the divine classical sense. After death he became a demi-god to whom people sacrificed and prayed and at whose tomb they worshiped. Alexander's mythic history is a late example of the process that occurred with other, earlier Greek heroes. It may exemplify the pattern of transformation for Asklepios from Thessalian prince to god of healing.

From the evidence at Trikka, Asklepios's birthplace, it appears certain that he was a very old god or hero, undoubtedly a pre-Olympian originally worshiped as a chthonic god of the earth powers. We can view, built directly into Asklepios's mythic history, the ascension of the patriarchy and its Olympian gods from the Homeric era onward. In the final version of the Asklepian myth that has come down to us, Apollo slew Asklepios's mother just as he slew the great python, the messenger of the earth goddess at Delfi, and replaced her as the god of oracles there. Here we see a distinctly late Greek and rational sky god slaying the feminine principle, the earthly connection and continuity with the matriarchy. Also in the myth we have inherited, Zeus himself slew Asklepios. Then Zeus permitted his transformation from an earth god with powers over life and death into a sky deity suited to the Olympian company and ruled by its laws, including the inevitability of death.

It is clear that Asklepios was well established and accepted as a hero, messenger, teacher, savior, and earth god of healing long before the classical era. His origins may or may not have been in an actual historical personage. Nonetheless, he was humanized and presented as a heroic healing prince during the Mycenaean and Homeric eras and is present as such a figure in the *Iliad*. He became an Olympian sky god during the early classical period, from which we have ample evidence of the widespread influence of his worship and practices at Epidauros and other sites.

In ancient Greece, temples and sanctuaries of a deity were thought of as homes to which that god could return again and again. Mortals built such homes in order to call the god to them for protection, guidance, healing, special blessing, and personal and community patronage. Greek deities also had their particular homes, their birthplaces with which they were associated, by which they were sometimes named or surnamed, and to which they might return again and again. For example, Apollo is often called Delian Apollo after his sacred island of Delos, on which he was born and later worshiped. While Epidauros was the sacred center of Asklepian worship, home of the god in his mature healing guise, Thessaly was both his birth home and the place of origination of his healing cult.[2]

In the wisdom of mythology, harmony and balance are portrayed by the presence of opposites. It is noteworthy in this vein that the other great mythic-historical character whose origins were in Thessaly was the most fearsome and savage of warriors to fight for the Greeks during the Trojan War. Achilles, like Asklepios, was from Thessaly and was mentored by Chiron. Thus, Thessaly gave birth to figures who embodied the complementary archetypal characteristics of war and peace, savagery and healing, rage and gentleness.

Thessaly is a mountain and plain region of central Greece, today about six hours northwest of Athens by car. The Thessalian plain is the fertile breadbasket of Greece, producing the greatest quantity of grains that this rugged mountain-and-sea country can muster. Thessaly has many precipitous mountains with curvaceous slopes and steep drops. It has lakes and rivers, forests and scattered villages, where the lifestyle is simple and age-old. This region was already famous by the time of Homer for being a land of horses and expert horse rearing.

Throughout ancient Greece, heroes and deities of the underground were often worshiped in caves going into the earth rather than temples rising above it, often built on mountaintops. It is significant, as we have seen, that Asklepian dream questing took place in womblike chambers carved into the rock. Early dream chambers are likely to have been caves, such as were native to the home mountains of Asklepios and served as early natural places of worship of the chthonic powers. Thus, going into the dream chamber was not only going into the earth mother's womb. It was also returning to Asklepios's territorial womb and to the underground chamber of chthonic powers. Supplicants of Asklepios crawled into narrow rock openings much as did the god's sacred snakes. It was not only the dream, but the dream procured in this snakelike way from deep in the earth with its mysterious powers, that healed.

Strabo, who wrote the geography of Greece in the first century BCE, cited the belief that Asklepios was born by the river Lethaios at Trikka.[3] We also have this poetic excerpt from Herondas dating to the third century BCE, who addressed Asklepios as "Thou who rulest over Trikka and dwellest in sweet Kos and Epidauros."[4]

About half a millennium earlier, Homer referred to Asklepios's home as Trikka, for he says that one contingent of thirty ships among the Greeks going to Troy was from Trikka and "over these two sons of old Asklepios held command—both skilled in healing."[5] Here are further examples of the tension of opposites unified in mythology: Asklepios's two sons, Machaon and Podalirios, were both warriors and physicians of the Greek army during the Trojan War. The name

Machaon derives from μαχομαι, *machomai*, meaning "to fight, combat, slaughter." The son of the "everlastingly gentle" is "the warrior," "the slaughterer." The same figures, offspring of the original healer, were simultaneously skilled in ruling, killing, and healing.

Early in the *Iliad*, the Greek commander Agamemnon calls on Machaon to heal Menelaos, wounded by an arrow. The passage shows the influence on Machaon of both his healer-father and his father's kentaur mentor:

> "Go quickly as you can and call Machaon,
> son of Asklepios, the great healer . . ."
> He found him standing ready, troops with shields
> In rank on rank around him—companies
> Of his that came from grazing lands in Trikka . . .
> Machaon . . . pulled the arrow
> Free of the belt and clasp . . .
> When he saw the arrow wound, he sucked it
> Clean of blood, then sprinkled it with balm,
> A medicine that Chairon gave his father . . .[6]

Assuming about forty years to a generation, as many ancient writers did, and taking the date of the Trojan War as 1260 BCE,[7] we can date Asklepios's time in Trikka at about 1300 BCE. This date closely corresponds with the ancient belief that Hippokrates, the Greek physician called the Father of Medicine, born in 460 BCE, was eighteenth in succession after Asklepios.

Thessaly is not only the site of Asklepios's birth. It was also said, not surprisingly, that here in the region famous for horse rearing, those half-human, half-horse figures, the kentaurs, had their homes. Asklepios's teacher, Chiron, "that idyllic Centaur—king of Pelion's woods, that friend to men,"[8] lived in a cave on the Mt. Pelion range. In ancient times, Pelion was famous as a source of healing herbs. Today, the cave of Chiron as well as a sanctuary of Zeus can be visited by a three-and-a-half hour hike and climb from the Thessalian village of Portaria.

In this cave, Asklepios lived and studied with the wise old kentaur. Here is a modern fictionalized portrait of Chiron:

> The shadows stirred in the cave, and a man came forth from it . . . He was kentaur all over, grizzled and old. He paused at the cave's mouth, and I saw his wide nostrils snuff the air like a dog that had been indoors, his eyes following his nose . . .
>
> I gazed long on his face. Whatever wild shape his guardian god had put on to beget him, some god was there. You could see it in his eyes. Dark and sad they were, and looked back a long way into the ancient days of the earth, before Zeus ruled in heaven . . .[9]

On these mountains, in these forests, with this teacher, Asklepios gathered healing herbs. These mountain glades continue to be a major source of healing plants, with well over a thousand plants with medicinal uses native to the region even today. In Thessaly horses thrived, kentaurs galloped and played, healers sought the cures for ailments and sufferings. Such a region was the healing god's classroom. To enter a cave seeking a dream healing was also to enter Asklepios's schoolroom.

Records say the original site of the Asklepion at Trikka contained the characteristic inner dream questing sanctuary. However, the site has not been excavated.[10] Yet we know of the healing practices here from carved Asklepian inscriptions. For example, one inscription dating from 300 BCE declares the importance of honoring the father god before seeking help from his son and offering a gift to the god before seeking a cure: "Not even in Thessalian Trikka would you attempt to go down into the Abyton of Asklepios unless you first sacrifice on the holy altar of Apollo Maleatas."[11]

Beyond archeological evidence, something of the nature of Asklepios can be intuited, too, by viewing the thick, healthy mountains and sweet flowing rivers of Thessaly, or the old, simple, unadorned and utterly beautiful potholed, winding, unlit streets of the modern town of Trikala that is ancient Trikka.

Asklepios was beautiful, gentle, soft, deeply loving of and loved by the common people. The healing influence of nature, the womblike, embracing and replenishing quality of Mother Earth, the steadiness of ancient rhythms and an ancient people content to live by them, are all communicated by the god of healing whom Homer called "blameless." It is also communicated by the people and landscape that belonged to the healing god and that Homer called "rocky terraced" and "horse-rearing." Beauty, harmony, fertility, and simplicity seem to reign there even today. On the grain-yielding, horse-rearing plains of Thessaly and in its mountain streams and caves, we can perceive, if not a sanctuary itself, an Asklepian spirit.

## Chapter Six

# Healing Sanctuary

## Epidauros, 600 bce

A sklepios and his healing practices wandered south from the mountains and plains of Thessaly. It was said of the godly physician that he walked everywhere, his snake-wrapped staff in hand, his disciples following him. Finally, his followers, the carriers of his religious and healing cult, reached the verdant valley on the Argoloid peninsula of the Peloponnese. Here the major healing sanctuary of the god was established by 600 bce.

There is a lapse of six or seven centuries between Asklepios's rulership in Thessaly and his completed establishment of a sanctuary at Epidauros. During this time, the god's disciples had successfully established a healing cult from which came the priest-physicians of the ancient world. They were wandering, establishing smaller sanctuaries, practicing herbal healing and dream incubation, teaching and serving as had Asklepios their master. By the sixth century bce, the god's healing ways were established throughout the Mediterranean world, radiating from Epidauros with both major and minor sanctuaries elsewhere.[1]

According to Apollodorus of Rhodes, who wrote the oldest surviving handbook of Greek mythology in the first or second century bce, Epidaurus was originally the name of one of the sons of

55

Argos. Argos was a son of Zeus and Niobe, the first mortal woman with whom the king god slept. He became the ruler of the Peloponnese. The city of Argos on the Peloponnese is named for the father and ruler; nearby Epidauros for one of his sons.[2]

We have visited Epidauros in a previous chapter. We have felt its spirit and examined its power as a center of healing, respite, and artistic expression. Imagine the god first emerging in mythic time as a god-born and kentaur-bred healer from distant mountains. Imagine him wandering throughout the Greek world for six centuries, teaching and practicing his dream incubation. Imagine him finally arriving in the magical, mountain-surrounded valley of Epidauros, where the theater teaches that, if we practice aright, we can indeed hear perfectly. Imagine his influence so large by this time, his technique so popular, his countenance so loved, that he could successfully establish a sanctuary as magnificent and influential as Epidauros. Imagine the people so hard-pressed by plague, war, illnesses, and crises that the influence and popularity of the healing god exploded.

It is not only the beauty of the Argoloid and its natural healing powers that established Epidauros as an Asklepian sanctuary. In the ancient Greek world, the place where a god or person died or was buried and from which his or her shade moved on was considered an especially sacred site. The greatest honor an ancient warrior could receive was to be buried on the battlefield where he fell. The noblest tomb of a sailor was beneath his oar on the shore overlooking the seascape on which he died. It was the same with gods. They were especially worshiped at their places of death or entombment.

According to some ancient accounts dating from 400 CE, Asklepios's tomb is at Epidauros.[3] If the god is buried there, it would make Epidauros an especially powerful and sacred crossroads.

According to another version of his myth, Epidauros was the place where the infant Asklepios was both born and exposed to die. In this version, Koronis's father migrated from Thessaly seeking land. He brought his daughter, who was pregnant by Apollo, with him. She gave birth to Asklepios in Apollo's temple. But fearing her father's anger, Koronis exposed the infant to die on Mt. Titthion, which means "nipple" in Greek. A goatherd working his flocks on the mountain lost a goat and a she-dog that guarded his herd. He found them suckling an infant by turns. He was about to lift up the infant, but suddenly saw the child drenched in divine light and retreated from the presence. Thereafter, Asklepios was left to his father Apollo who, as in other versions, turned him over for rearing to Chiron.[4]

As both the cradle and tomb of Asklepios, Epidauros was a meeting place of this world and the next. It was a place where the living could travel to encounter the god and his animal powers. It drew power from its position near the mountain whose animals had suckled the god. Nearby as well was the sepulcher of the god who had the powers to restore life, as his own had been restored in infancy, and to transcend death.

It was not only the efficacy of Asklepios's healing methods that attracted so many supplicants and led to the great size and influence of Epidauros. Asklepian medicine contained a fundamental principle that was both enlightening and healing. The loss of this healing principle is at the core of our modern crisis in health care and must be restored if true healing is to be available to people who are suffering.

Epidauros was a sacred sanctuary, a place permeated by the spirit of the god. Patients were not "treated" as in the modern sense, and physician-priests were not the principal characters in the drama of healing. Rather, patients were immersed in a complete sacred ecology. Physician-priests guided the process, but the nature of the process itself guaranteed that afflicted people healed themselves through their own hard-won meeting with the god. As mythologist Carl Kerényi explains:

> [A] place for incubation served for the most direct possible method of healing. The patient himself was offered an opportunity to bring about the cure whose elements he bore within himself. To this end an environment was

created which, as in modern spas and health resorts, was as far as possible removed from the disturbing and un-healthful elements of the outside world. The religious atmosphere also helped man's innermost depths to ac-complish their curative potentialities. In principle the physician was excluded from the individual mystery of recovery: the patient sought out the deity in a much more personal way than in the great mysteries of the archaic and classical period. It is therefore to be presumed that at Epidauros the physician remained intentionally in the background.[5]

At Epidauros, both priest-physicians and seekers practiced, in Kerényi's phrase, "a religion of the patient." The priest-physician was a guide to a process, not an authority figure who instigated the pro-cess. The seeker needed to enter and directly experience mythic consciousness in order to achieve that which heals—a meeting with the god.

This interpretation and the boons that derive from Epidaurian Asklepios are strengthened by a consideration of the god's children. We know of his sons Machaon and Podalirios from Trikka, princes, warriors, and healers. But his three daughters originated from Epidauros.[6] They were Hygieia, Panaceia, and Iaso.[7] Their names mean Health, All-Curing, and Healer. In Greek art they are often portrayed as accompanying their father in his healing work. They sometimes appeared with him in healing dreams. Hygieia, his most important attendant, also had a healing cult of her own at Titane.

Though the Asklepios of Epidauros seems to be the first instance of the god having daughters, the daughters themselves are much older manifestations of healing powers deriving from the earth itself. Long before the Epidaurian Asklepios, Hygieia and Panaceia, Health and All-Healer, were titles given to the earth mother goddess Rhea Koronis at her shrine at Titane. These names were given to the Great Mother's breasts, from which flowed the two great balms of humanity in our suffering—the milk of kindness and of healing.[8]

Later, these healing principles were personified as Asklepios's daughters and ultimately included as medical deities in the Hippokratic Oath.

In the sons of Asklepios we have the ambivalence found in masculine energy deriving from the healing god. His sons are both healers and warriors, as the masculine gifts can be equally directed toward creation or destruction. But in the daughters of Asklepios and his wife Epione, in the spirit of Epidauros, we view the feminine components of healing derived from nurturing, care-giving, and gentle tending. His daughters personify these traits and their gifts—good health, well being, curing, and healing.

Stand in the theater of Epidauros and listen. Stand before the god's temple and pray. Drink the pure healing waters that still arise from an underground spring as they did in Asklepios's day, not only at Epidauros but also at every one of his sanctuaries. Imagine structured dream-seeking as a ritual of such import that many thousands of ill or suffering people turned to it as a means for healing what otherwise was intractable and inconsolable. Imagine dreams being of such power and importance that they were not only clues to one's unconscious life, but were direct messages or visits from divinity that could forever alter and rearrange both spiritual and physical health for the better.

Imagine this and you perceive the history of a god and his millennia-long influence. Imagine this and you stand at Epidauros, an earthly shrine whose divine influence radiated to the far corners of the known world with genuine power, compassion, hope, and divine encounter, such as we long for today.

## Chapter Seven

# EARTH-WALKING SAVIOR

## KORINTH, 480 BCE

A bus or car ride from Athens heading west takes us first through crowded, noisy urban sprawl. We leave Athens behind, and the severe, stony hills of Attika dominate the landscape. We roll through countryside that has been baked and tanned by many centuries of sunlight and history, feeling a curiosity and aliveness of spirit that opens in us with every mile we penetrate into this ancient region.

Soon we roll through fertile regions punctuated with groves and orchards of sinewy trees and vines. We are approaching the city of Korinth in a region that has been a great producer of currants and raisins for over six hundred years.

Modern Korinth is a modestly sized provincial capital situated at the northeastern corner of the Peloponnese, about an hour and a half west of Athens. It is a rather plain, early twentieth-century city situated on powerful and temperamental land. Korinth was destroyed by earthquakes in 1858 and 1928 and by a huge fire in 1933, and rebuilt after each. It is also kept small and commercially unimportant because of the success of the canal that cuts through its nearby isthmus, allowing ships to pass from the Gulf of Korinth directly to the Aegean Sea.

The streets of Korinth are flat, wide, and dusty. A central park and plaza area provides some greenery for relaxation. Small hotels, coffee shops, grocery stores, and tavernas line Korinth's main street. Here, too, buses gather for destinations all over the Peloponnese. One of these buses takes us on the twenty-minute ride through fertile countryside and narrow village streets to the important ruin site with its small host village that is *archae Korinthos*, ancient Korinth.

Once the isthmus of Korinth was a site of great military, political, and social importance. The ancient city of Korinth commanded heights that looked down on the gulf and isthmus, guarding land and sea passages between the Peloponnese and Athens. Its great mountain, called Akrokorinthos, exploding upwards out of the plains, provided both lookout and defensive fortification. The ancients said that this crucial strategic position was one of the two horns of the Greek bull; possess these horns, and you control the entire Peloponnese. The Korinth of preclassical and classical times held this huge mountain stronghold and grew into a great city. It was once third in importance of all the Greek city-states, surpassed only by Athens and Sparta. Emissaries from all over the Greek and Mediterranean worlds came here seeking a Korinthian alliance. Near here the sanctuary of Poseidon of the Isthmus was located. The Isthmian Games, after the Olympics second in importance in the Greek world, were held here every other spring in honor of the god of the sea.

We disembark in the Old Korinth village square. It is wide, with tavernas, kaffenions, a grocery store, gift shops, and an immaculate, modestly sized Greek Orthodox church with a small garden courtyard. A robust old man greets us in Greek. He invites us to sit and have refreshments at his coffee shop. He bustles gaily, offers to watch our bags for the day, and shows us where to stash them behind his shop. He serves us quickly, then launches into storytelling. He asks us where we are from and why we've come. He pulls out photographs of the village as it was when he grew up here seventy years ago. He shows us a forty-year old photo of his father along with Aristotle Onassis and the prime minister of Greece sitting and sipping coffee together under the very tree, at the very table where we sit.

We walk through the village, past its neatly scattered houses with orange and lemon trees, bougainvilleas, and cats. Almost immediately we pass out of the village to arrive at the lower site of the ancient city. Seven massive and stately white columns of the 540 BCE temple of Apollo stand before us, above the steps and foundation, built to replace another temple two centuries older. This temple feels like Apollo—dignified, aloof, looking down on this site and us with cool reason, wisdom, and guidance, sending waves of music and artistry through the landscape, touching everything around us with calm beauty. Through the temple portico we can see the agora, the public marketplace, and the great mountain fortress behind it. We turn into the city to feel its ancient life beating in us.

The lower site of Old Korinth consists of a wide, busy, packed agora whose remaining stoas, houses, stores, temples, and podiums date primarily from Roman times. Korinth was first settled about 1000 BCE. Over the centuries it grew in prominence until the Roman general Mummius destroyed it in 146 BCE. Caesar rebuilt it in 44 BCE, and Korinth grew in importance again, so much so that the Apostle Paul lived, taught, and preached here in 51-52 CE. In the center of the agora, halfway along the southern line of shops, is the great stone Bima, the platform from which speakers addressed the assembled rulers and people. Paul addressed the Roman governor from here in words probably close to those contained in his Letters to the Korinthians. "Where is the wise man? Where is the scribe? Where is the debater of this age? Has not God made foolish the wisdom of the world?"[1] We wander this agora, visiting the temples of Apollo, Venus, Poseidon, and Herakles. We see the large number of shops and the fine paving of the streets. We imagine the preaching and debating between Greeks, Romans, Jews, and Christians that occurred right on these stones. We sense the active, busy, artistic, social, intellectual, and religious lives of the Greek and Roman eras.

We proceed from the agora and temple grounds north along

the Lechaion Road, which once ran to the old harbor, two miles away and now completely silted in. Six hundred yards down this road, just inside the city and up against its old walls, situated just west of the gateway that led to the harbor, is the Asklepion.

During the time of Korinth's prominence, Asklepios arrived here, too. As the influence of the god and his healing ways spread from his main sanctuary at nearby Epidauros, the followers of the god established a sanctuary in this thriving early city. "In a relatively short space of time, the new Savior God became extremely popular. He thus needed suitable lodgings."[2] The Asklepion of Korinth dates from about 480 BCE and remained in operation until 370 CE, 850 years later, when it was destroyed by the Christians of Korinth and its hill turned into a Christian cemetery. The location, longevity, and the richness of the finds relating to Asklepian cures on this site all attest to its early and sustained importance as a sanctuary of healing and medicine.

The healing god's new lodgings were built on a flat rock hill atop the old foundations of a temple of Apollo. Apollo's worship in Korinth was moved to his temple near the agora, while the new temple built for Asklepios was larger and greater. The son's temple was erected on the father's and grew on a grander scale. This is one indication of the degree to which people eventually turned to Asklepian worship, finding the healing god compassionate and accessible, unlike the more aloof and distant Apollo. Here is another parallel to Jesus' story. The son of a divine father born of a mortal mother, and not the father god, is the earth-walking savior. His worship and the accessibility and healing he offers transcend in popularity the worship of his father. The son of god and mortal mother moves into the father-god's temple and replaces the father-god as favorite deity.

Korinth's Asklepion is designed and built in the manner characteristic of many of the healing god's sanctuaries. We first encounter a temple and altar to the god. Next there is a large abaton, the sleeping chamber. There is a sacred fountain that gushed forth some of the particularly fine, sweet, nourishing water for which, according to Pausanias, Korinth was famous. This Asklepion also had six water reservoirs for storage and recycling. Finally, it had houses for the priests and guest rooms for pilgrims seeking cure.

The Korinthian Asklepion survived for many centuries. When Korinth was destroyed by the Romans in 146 BCE, the Asklepion was hardly hurt, and it is likely that Roman troops used it for their own healing needs. It was fully restored about a century later and remained active until its complete destruction in the Christian era.

The extent of successful healing that occurred at this Asklepion is evidenced by the great collection of votive offerings to the god and his temple that have been found on this site. They are now housed in their own locked room in the adjoining museum and can be viewed by request. The offerings at Korinth were made of terra cotta and were often life size. Votives depicting eyes and ears, half torsos, hands, arms, legs, feet, and heads have been found. One of the hands shows an unusual tumorous growth. A similar case is known from an Asklepion on Krete, where "a woman was cured of a painful ulceration on her little finger by Asklepios's appearance before her in a dream."[3] Most numerous at the Korinthian Asklepion are votives of the sexual and generative organs—especially breasts and male genitalia. This has led to the speculation that male and female sterility, female breast diseases, and other generative organ disorders were treated here.[4]

Based upon our own treatments, we moderns might expect surgery to be performed on some of these conditions, such as tumors and hardening of the breasts. However, no surgical tools have been found at Korinth as they have at later Asklepieia. We do know that the supplicants slept in the abaton to seek dream healing from Asklepios. We also know that hydrotherapy from the springs and psychotherapy with the priests both before and after dreaming contributed to their healing. And just as we know from inscriptions and monuments found at Epidauros, Athens, and Krete that large numbers of cures occurred at those Asklepieia, we also know from the large number of votives found at Korinth that many cures occurred here.

Little remains of the Korinthian Asklepion. It lies outside the archeological site of the ancient city. It is almost an afterthought to a visit to Korinth unless the modern pilgrim specifically seeks it. But discussing Asklepios with the local residents or asking their directions, one experiences the excitement and influence the god's tradition exerts even today.

"You know about our healing god?" one villager asks in answer to my query. His face glows with shared recognition. "You must visit his temple. Let me draw you a map."

"Asklepios can show us the way to heal today. Doctors can't do it without the god's help because medicine alone doesn't heal people. Doctors must learn again to use this god," a museum guard tells me.

We follow the map and the enthusiasm to the site of the Asklepion. It is surrounded by orchards and thick with weeds and wildflowers. The agora is not far behind us. The mountain fortress looms up behind us. We stand on the flattened top of the stone hill. We wander the extensive foundations of the temple and abaton, white marble set into the hard ground, carved white stones, a few columns sitting above ground. We view the area of the altar, where the sacrifices of cocks took place. We view a stone couch, a few upright columns, and entrances to underground passages. This Asklepion today is quiet, remote, carpeted and buzzing with active beehives tended by villagers.

In this overgrown field, in ancient times, many supplicants dreamed and were cured. Though the patients are gone, their thanksgiving offerings remain, telling us what was stricken and what cured by a dream visit from the god.

We leave the Asklepion to climb to the mountaintop fortress, formidable and daunting beyond imagination. Thick stones form walls, bastions, palaces, homes, and temples. They snake along the dips and rises of the high mountain overlooking the entire valley and gulf nearby. We climb and climb, legs aching, hearts pounding, to breath-grabbing vistas of plains and waters beyond. We see both the beauty and the security that was provided by this horn of the Greek bull. We see, in landscape, why a temple of Aphrodite, goddess of beauty, crowned the highest hill of Korinth. We stand, with a 360-degree view, bathed in the beauty of the Greek landscape. And we look down, far below, at the tiny shapes that mark the Asklepion of Korinth. Up here, at the very pinnacle, the goddess of beauty stops us at the single white marble column marking her ancient temple site. Here she reduces us to silent awe. But down below, among the stricken, Asklepios walked.

## Chapter Eight

# RAISING THE DEAD

## TROIZEN, 480-428 BCE

We take a small caique across the narrow strait of azure waters that separates the Saronic Gulf island of Poros from the Peloponnese. Or we take a bus south from Epidauros. Or we take one from Nauplion, the sparkling seaside town that in 1828 became the first capital of modern Greece. Whether arriving by land or water, we disembark in the village of Galatas, named for the sweet milk produced by its mountain grazing cows. Here we rent a moped for our trek into rolling hills and remote mountains.

We ride through the few narrow streets of Galatas, stopping for freshly baked bread, tomatoes, olives, cheese, and some lemons from the huge grove south of the village that perfumes this air with its scent. Leaving the village, we zip along the road that follows the Peloponnese coastline, watching pine-forested Poros across the way. Fishing boats bob, and sunlight glimmers off dancing waters.

Four miles from Galatas, we turn inland and travel west. We climb. The sea drops off behind us. Brown and green mountains beckon ahead. Soon we reach the village of Trizin, built into the slopes that keep climbing beyond. Our sputtering mopeds slowly climb the steep village streets, passing whitewashed houses with lush gardens of flowers and fruit trees, a few tavernas and small stores. We could park our cycles and hike along a footpath that, in half an hour, would bring us to our destination.

Instead, quickly in the countryside again, we roll ahead on bumpy roads past orchards and farms, grazing donkeys and goats. We are looking for two small dirt roads, each barely marked by small rusting metal signs. Each gives us access to a part of the site of ancient Troizen. The first leads to a wide agora with ruins from the town's many ages: Roman baths, an early Christian church, an akropolis with a temple to Athena. But on this Asklepian journey, we want the second, smaller site.

The road is rough and bumpy. It takes us past scrubby pastures and small gardens. Then it ends abruptly in the midst of a field, beside a small house. An elderly Greek woman is hanging laundry in the strong sun. She waves gaily. We bid her good day and ask her where the ancient site is. She smiles and makes a strong waving motion with her hand, telling us to go still further. The "old place" is beyond where anyone lives.

We park our mopeds among the rough weeds, as if they were modern steeds left to graze. We walk through brambles, around thorns and fencing, over stones, around olive, pine, and plane trees. Suddenly we cross a line of old town walls. A large spread of marble foundations opens before us. We walk through what must have been a great building and sanctuary grounds. We pass more marble foundations, then wander amidst walls, arches, rooms, passageways made of thick brown stones, appearing to be much older than the glittering marble of classical times. We are in an ancient city, unmarked by signs, museums, or guides. Tall and craggy mountains surround us. We must plow through thick bushes to explore the full extent of this old city. Today it is all ours. Only dragonflies, songbirds, bees, lizards, and snakes baking on the sun-splashed rocks share the space. We feel history. We feel the shades breathing.

Troizen was once an important town. It was the birthplace of the Greek hero and early Athenian king, Theseus. He grew to manhood here, hunting boar and deer in these mountains. Here he lifted the stone, still pointed out by local people, that hid his father's sword and sandals, revealing to him his true identity as son of Aegeus, king of Athens. He left here to rid the Korinthian isthmus road of bandits and then to take his place as the heir to Athens' throne. From Athens, he went to Krete with other sacrificial youths to dance in the bullring of Knossos and ultimately to slay the Minotaur. Some of these heavy brown stone walls appear typically Mycenaean, possibly dating from Theseus' time.

Here, too, Theseus' son Hippolytos died. Hippolytos was the only child of Theseus and his wife, the Amazon queen Hippolyta. Their wedding is celebrated in Shakespeare's *A Midsummer Night's Dream*. After Hippolyta died in battle, the Kretan princess Phaidra became Theseus' wife. Phaidra attempted to seduce Hippolytos. When he rejected his stepmother's love, she committed suicide, leaving a death note blaming him. Under his father's mistaken curse, the young man fled to Troizen. Here, in his father's birthplace, the curse of Theseus came true. Hippolytos was dragged to death by his chariot horses.

The locals here worshiped the tragic youth. It is his fourth-century BCE temple and sanctuary we enter first upon crossing the town walls. Euripedes tells us that in ancient times a ritual honoring this youth and his tragic death was observed at this very place. The ritual was a gift from Artemis, whom Hippolytos had served. The goddess tells the dying youth:

> To you, unfortunate Hippolytos,
> By way of compensation for these ills,
> I will give the greatest honors of Troizen.
> Unwedded maids before the day of marriage
> Will cut their hair in your honor. You will reap
> Through the long cycle of time, a rich reward in tears.
> And when young girls sing songs, they will not forget you,
> Your name will not be left unmentioned,
> Nor Phaidra's love for you remain unsung.[1]

Today, in the ruins of the Temple of Hippolytos, solemn and silent in its remote beauty beneath the mountains, we feel the sorrow of all unfairly cursed and doomed youth, torn by contradictory forces of love, eros, devotion, independence, morality.

It was this same dead Hippolytos, many ancient sources say, whom Asklepios tried to bring back to life. But "Zeus, who viewed the wide world" and protected its justice, would allow neither the reversal of tragic destinies nor the transcendence of the natural laws of life and death, even when a mortal's death was unfair and undeserved.

Historical novelist Mary Renault reconciles myth with history by suggesting that it was a priest of Asklepios from nearby Epidauros who attempted to raise Hippolytos. In her account, a chief priest of the healing god unsuccessfully attempts the resurrection that he knows is forbidden. "The priest-king died soon after, suddenly, struck down as he worked, the swift death of Apollo; and it was said that the god was angry with him, for trying to raise the dead."[2]

However, other ancient sources say that Asklepios was successful. "Local legend said that he [Hippolytos] did not die ... but became the constellation Auriga."[3] Roman mythology also had Asklepios successfully restoring the youth to life, to become identified as an obscure male deity associated with Diana. Here is Ovid's report, in the words of Hippolytos:

> You might have seen my soul slip from my body,
> But body itself was like a lake of blood ...
> I saw the dayless land of death below me
> And sinking down I washed my ragged body
> In dark waves ...
> There I would be today, but Phoebus' son
> Restored my life with medical attention:
> Fine magic weeds and strange life-giving waters
> Which were against the power of Death himself.[4]

It may be that, from the tragic perspective of the Greeks, Hippolytos's death was tolerable. The belief in Hippolytos's resurrection may have developed later. Hippolytos's resurrection in the Roman myth may reflect the hubris that accompanied Roman power, the belief that any enemy, even death, could be conquered. Or it may parallel the cultural evolution from the Roman into the Christian worldview. At that time, the archetype of the god who dies and is reborn, and that god's ability to transcend death, began to enter popular consciousness.

Troizen thrived as an active settlement into classical times, remaining an ally of Athens. When the Persians invaded Greece in 480 BCE and threatened Athens, the city was evacuated. A large number of its refugees, women, children, and old people, fled here, while some Athenian soldiers defended the Akropolis, and most others took to the ships to fight at Salamis. As the influence of Epidauros spread, the followers of the healing god's cult came to Theseus's city and established a healing sanctuary.

Wandering the ruins of the ancient town, just northwest of the temple, we cross a flat area baked brown by the sun. In front of us is a fair-sized rectangular formation of stones and column bases above a marble foundation set into the hard ground. Here the town ends, for beyond this site, the land leaps abruptly upward, and the mountain is covered by a thick growth of forest. These ruins mark the spot where afflicted people came for help and where the god returned—not to raise Hippolytos, but to visit supplicants in their sleep. This building was the Asklepion of Troizen.

Here the god was worshiped. Here, as at other sanctuaries, sacred springs gurgled down from the mountains above to cleanse and purify supplicants. Here, too, cocks were sacrificed to give thanks and to cry for awakening. Here, too, the spirit of the land combined with ritual practice, faith, and urgent need to call the god into the dreams of those seeking healing.

We have records of some of the dream cures that took place at this site. Here is an account of the healing of Aristagora, a woman of

Troizen who slept in this very temple. It dates from about 350 BCE.

> She had a tapeworm in her belly, and she slept in the
> Temple of Asklepios at Troezen and saw a dream. It seemed
> to her that the sons of the god, while he was not present
> but away at Epidauros, cut off her head, but, being unable
> to put it back again, they sent a messenger to Asklepios
> asking him to come. Meanwhile day breaks and the priest
> clearly sees her head cut off from her body. When night
> approached, Aristagora had a vision. It seemed to her
> that the god had come from Epidauros and fastened her
> head onto her neck. Then he cut open her belly, took the
> tapeworm out, and stitched her up again. After that she
> became well.[5]

Aristagora's testimony indicates that, by the classical period, seekers experienced Machaon and Podalirios as dream helpers and healers
along with their father, the healing god. This testimony indicates that
the sons had considerable healing powers but less than their father. In
fact, both these figures had cults. Machaon had a separate cult at
Garenia; Podalirios, at Drion. More generally, they appeared with
their father.[6]

Today, at ancient Troizen, the only signs are provided by nature.
There is no museum displaying votive offerings. The sacred spring is
not enclosed by a church or flowing from a fountain so that modern
seekers may drink. Rather, the healing temple stands silent and fallen.
We must erect it in our minds. We sit there alone, in the buff-colored
grasses. The mountains in which Theseus roamed as a child tower
and hum above us. We close our eyes, feel the hot sun, pray, and
meditate. We feel the presence of shades and the power of a life once
passionately lived. We feel the sorrow of Hippolytos, the doomed
youth, and of Theseus, his grief-stricken father. We feel the fears and
hopes of Athenians and free Greeks fleeing the Persian invasion and
the compassion of Asklepios who visited thousands of ailing commoners. We feel all this in the silence as we watch lizards and snakes

crawl towards us in the sun. We stay still and allow them to come close, for we know the tradition: their proximity, their touch, their lick may be a kiss of healing from the god.

Then we rise and pray in the nearby small temple of Aphrodite for love that does not manipulate or destroy, but renews and heals. We leave ancient Troizen and climb the steep dirt road that leads into the mountains. We follow it until it becomes a footpath leading through the place called Devil's Gorge. On both sides, the mountains climb steeply overhead. Down below, at first, we see only a huge cache of boulders, like a path of debris tumbling down the gorge. We continue deeper into the gorge, past wildflowers, larks, and owls. We hear the gurgling of water and soon see the rippling river, rare in the Greek landscape, as it tumbles over stones and rushes on. Everywhere among the stones there are little waterfalls spilling into small, private mountain pools.

Climb down from the path into the gorge. Choose a pool of your own in this wild and remote place, out of sight of all others. Like Aristogora, "cut off your head"—that is, suspend rationality. Take off your clothes. Say prayers that "take the tapeworm out," requesting cleansing, purification, release from whatever pollution, whether grief, fear, guilt, or shame, you carry. Then call the god who came in compassion to so many near this place in ancient times. Immerse yourself in the mountain fastness that once bathed Theseus. These waters helped make him strong of mind, body, heart, and spirit so that he could do the difficult work that was demanded of him as a prince and young king for the liberation of Athens and unification of Attika. Pray for such strength to meet your own destiny, whatever it is. And immerse yourself in the waters that once flowed directly from the heart of these mountains and down to the sanctuary of healing to give pure, sparkling drink and a cleansing bath to those who ailed.

## Chapter Nine

# BEAUTIFUL AND BESIEGED

## ATHENS, 429-420 BCE

The cult of Asklepios, with its worship and healing practices, arrived in Athens during an exceptionally tumultuous period of the city's history. Athens was at the center of Western civilization and at the height of its greatness. Perikles, Sophokles, Euripedes, Sokrates, and many more of Athens' greatest writers, philosophers, and statesmen were living. Reason and science were on the rise, while religion was becoming institutionalized, its sincere and spontaneous practice among city dwellers declining. It has seemed strange to some students of history that Asklepian dream healing, a practice that combined empirical methods and interventions with those based on faith and structured experiences of the irrational, arrived in Athens at the height of its period of enlightenment.

But the Athens of this time was not only indulging her political and philosophical powers. She had built the Akropolis, produced great works of philosophy and literature, and been the savior of Greece during the Persian Wars. But she had also transformed from a city-state that was "first among equals" into the leader of an empire. She lorded over her neighbors and allies in ways that made enemies and brought disfavor. The era of Asklepios's arrival was one that sorely tried Athens' powers, putting everything Athens had stood for to the test, and ultimately punishing her for her hubris in a way that brought her down from her proud heights.

In 429 BCE, Athens was embroiled in the beginnings of what would be the long, destructive Peloponnesian War. This conflict pitted the power, influence, and resources of the Athenian city-state against those of Sparta and her allies, and ultimately led to Athens' defeat and subjugation. Further, Athens had recently passed through a terrible plague that decimated its population, killing many thousands of people who sought shelter inside city walls that were under siege from without. Plague and war were upon Athens, and with them came pain, loss, terror, grief, and despair. Here is how this period was described by Thukydides, historian of the Peloponnesian Wars, who himself survived the plague:

> In the first days of summer the Lacedaemonians and their allies . . . invaded Attika . . . and laid waste the country. Not many days after their arrival in Attika the plague first began to show itself among the Athenians . . . A pestilence of such extent and mortality was nowhere remembered. Neither were the physicians at first of any service . . . but they died themselves the most thickly . . . nor did any other human art succeed any better. Supplications in the temples, divinations, and so forth were equally futile.[1]

Under the attack of both enemies and plague, "death raging within the city and devastation without," the moral, spiritual, social, civic, and daily living conditions within Athens deteriorated terribly:

> The bodies of dying men lay one upon another, and half-dead creatures reeled about the streets and gathered round all the fountains in their longing for water. The sacred places . . . also were full of corpses of persons that had died there . . . men, not knowing what was to become of them, became utterly careless of everything, whether sacred or profane. All the burial rites before in use were entirely

upset. . . . Perseverance in what men called honor was popular with none. Fear of gods or law of man there was none to restrain them.[2]

This climate, precisely because it was so troubled, was perfect for the arrival of the god of healing. "The pestilence that struck Athens at the beginning of the Peloponnesian War, and the sense of isolation that prevailed among the Greeks with the recession of the team spirit of the city-states era, favored the compassionate, manloving god."[3] His arrival in Athens was one of the first classical era offshoots of the god's cult. It seemed to occur suddenly, with much ritual, celebration, and fanfare. We know of this major event from actual celebratory inscriptions dated 424 BCE that have been unearthed on the southern slopes of the Akropolis, in the location on which the god's sanctuary actually stood. We are told that

> [T]he god arrived in the city from Epidauros during the celebration of the Eleusinia. He brought his sacred serpent with him on a car, and was met by a citizen called Telemachos, who seems to have been responsible for the introduction of the cult. Together with him came Hygieia, and thus was the whole sanctuary founded.[4]

Dream healings had occurred in Athens before. Plutarch tells of one brought by Athen's own patron goddess Athena before the arrival of Asklepios. During the building of the gateway to the Akropolis, the most enthusiastic of the workmen tumbled from a great height and was seriously injured. Physicians gave him up for dead. Perikles, Athen's ruler, was quite distressed. Athena appeared to Perikles in a dream, revealing a course of treatment. Perikles applied it and quickly and easily healed the injured workman.[5]

Asklepios's arrival touched all Athenians. How it affected the people, how important it was to distinguished and common citizens alike, is illustrated by an incident from the life of the great tragedian Sophokles. According to Plutarch, Sophokles had a healing visit, an epiphany of the god, not in the sanctuary established on the Akropolis, but in his own house. Plutarch says that Sophokles "rejoiced in the belief that he was entertaining Asklepios," that he had an epiphany, and "that Sophokles even during his lifetime gave hospitality to Asklepios."[6] In celebration, Sophokles composed a paean to the god which was sung for a long time after the poet's death. It read, in part,

> O far-famed daughter of Phlegyas, mother of the god
> who wards off pains . . . The unshorn Phoebus. I begin
> my loud-voiced hymn . . . accompanied by flutes . . . The
> helper of the sons of Cecrops . . . may you come . . .[7]

This paean was inscribed with the poet's name and set up in public places. Fragments of a second century CE copy have been unearthed in the Athenian Asklepion itself. After his death, in honor of this incident, Sophokles was given the nickname Dexion by the Athenians. *Dexion* means "he who receives . . . for he received the god into his house and set up an altar to him."[8]

In addition to Sophokles and Plato (as we saw earlier) receiving cures by way of Asklepian intervention, the comic poet Aristophanes apparently experienced a cure in this manner. The evidence for his complete familiarity with Asklepian healing is recorded in his play *Plutos*, first performed in 388 BCE.

In *Plutos*, Aristophanes recounts a story of the god of wealth, Plutos. This god was blinded by Zeus so that, in spite of his best efforts, he was never able to distribute his bounty fairly. Chremylos is a righteous old man who is upset at life's injustices. He particularly dislikes how the wicked are given money and power, while the good suffer. He sets out to cure Plutos of blindness. In return, Plutos promises to benefit the old man and refrain from rewarding the unjust.

In Aristophanes' tale, Chremylos' slave witnesses the dream healing. The slave reports the priest of Asklepios telling all supplicants to go to sleep. During the night, the slave observes the priest clearing the altars of food offerings that were given to the god during the day.

But later, Asklepios and his attendants appear. The healing god touches Plutos' head and wipes his eyes. Then his attendant wraps his head and face in a red cloth. Asklepios makes a sign. Suddenly, two snakes slither out of the temple and glide under the cloth to lick Plutos' eyelids. He awakens, cured of his blindness.

Both the satire and wisdom of this play survive in the Greek folk tradition to this day. Eighty-year-old Charalambos Patelos, from the island of Ikaria, tells this story with twinkling eyes:

> In ancient times, the priests would dress in white robes to disguise themselves as gods. Then they would steal the food the patients brought for the god, swoosh, right from their pillows. The priests got a free meal, while the patients thought the god took their gifts. Very funny. But later, when everybody fell asleep, that's when the snakes and dreams came. That's when the miracles occurred![9]

The story of Plutos was, in part, Aristophanes' comic answer to eternal questions of injustice, greed, and evil. It is satirical up to the priest's theft of food offerings. But then it accurately portrays dream healing through incubation, the application of ointments, and the use of incantations and sacred snakes, important components of Asklepian practice. To further demonstrate that Aristophanes' version of a cure, though in his comic play, is not imaginary, compare this historical record of a cure inscribed on a tablet from Epidauros. This record is of blindness healed through an epiphany during sleep combined with surgery and the application of ointments. It is startling in its similarity to Aristophanes' comic rendition and includes some divine comedy of its own:

> Ambrosia of Athens, blind in one eye. She came as a suppliant to the god but . . . scoffed at some of the cures as incredible: it was impossible that the lame and the blind should become whole simply through seeing a dream. Then she went to sleep there and saw a vision . . . the god

81

stood over her and said that he would cure her, but he required her to set up in the temple as payment a silver pig, in memory of her stupidity. When he had said this, he cut open her blind eye and poured in ointment. And when it was day she went out cured.[10]

Many inscriptions recording cures have been unearthed on the site of Athens' Asklepion, dating back to the fourth century BCE. They resemble these in their key elements of recording a cure through a dream or vision, sometimes accompanied by medical or surgical procedures. Thus, Aristophanes' play, Sophokles' epiphany, Plato's healing, and the numerous inscriptions unearthed in the various Asklepieia of cures, ceremonies, and paeans to the god give us a full picture of the extent and practice of Asklepian worship in fifth- and fourth-century Athens and Epidauros.

Though the Asklepion of Athens does not stand today in grandeur and beauty as does the Parthenon of Athena or the sanctuary at Epidauros, we can visit what remains of its temple and sanctuary grounds. These are nestled into the southern slope of the Akropolis, the high city and sacred precinct of classical Athens. Such a visit provides us with a compelling vision of the honor and importance once afforded to the healing god by classical Athens, at once great, powerful, and beautiful, but also besieged, over-proud, and suffering.

The Athenian sanctuary of Asklepios stands at the base of the great wall of rock that supports the Parthenon and the sacred precinct of Athena. It can be reached today by climbing above the Theater of Dionysos.

The great semicircular theater dedicated to the god of ecstasy, wine, and rebirth, once seated 17,000 spectators and was the stage where many of the great tragedies of classical Greece were first performed. The theater itself evolved over centuries from an original shrine to the dancing god where his annual spring ritual of rebirth and renewal was practiced. Just as classical tragedy evolved from earlier Dionysian ritual worship, so his place of worship evolved from shrine to large theater to accommodate the changes in practice. The theater performance itself became the form of worshiping Dionysos and could be closely associated with or even accompany Asklepian healing, as we have seen.

The theater seats rise from the stage and orchestra pit where the chorus performed. The first row contained thrones for priests and judges. The seats radiate outward, in ever expanding yet perfectly aligned rows, looking from above like a glowing stone half-circle of sun, toward the great rock behind them. Crosswise the tight rows are divided in three places by walkways called *diazoma*. The uppermost section of seats, nearly gone today, climbed to the sheer rock itself.

In ancient times, a supplicant, in modern times, a visitor, finds the entrance to the Asklepion from its eastern side by way of the upper diazoma. Originally a gateway and ramp led from the auditorium to the healing grounds. On the western side, this same pathway continued around the base of the Akropolis, above the later Theater of Herodes Atticus, built about 160 CE, and extended to the entrance to the Akropolis itself. One could approach the god of healing either from the west by passing under the keen and watchful gaze of Athena, or from the east by passing through the precinct of rebirth and ecstasy ruled by Dionysos.

[Architecture is poetry in matter.] In these grounds dedicated to deities we can read architecture as sacred metaphor. Here the road to healing is an axis. At its eastern end, its place of origins, it passes through the precinct of drama, dance, ecstasy, passion, and rebirth. [At its western end, its place of crisis, it passes through the precinct of intelligence, wisdom, guardianship, assertiveness, and excellence. The urge to healing can be awakened in us through the wounding revealed and the catharsis achieved in viewing or participating in the drama, dance, and passions of our lives. Or we can enter our search for healing from the place of crisis, where we call upon the powers of mind, stewardship, and striving for excellence and use these powers in service to our healing.

Once down the ramp, the supplicant passed along the rear wall

*architecture is poetry in matter* "    Edward Tick, PHD.

83

of a *stoa*, a roofed colonnade that served as a multi-use public building. He or she then arrived at the columned gateway into the sacred grounds. Entering this sanctuary, the supplicant saw two buildings. To the right was the longest and largest, the two-story abaton, each story independently and evenly supported by rows of columns. To the left was the Prostyle Stoa, shorter than the abaton and used as either priests' quarters or an extension of the sleeping chambers. A beautiful garden stood in front of the stoa, while an altar and four-columned shrine of Asklepios stood in front of the abaton. Further to the west, beyond the stoa, stood several small buildings looking like temples. And within the abaton was a site found at all Asklepieia and critical to their work. Inside the abaton was the *bothos*, the sacred spring of healing waters that flowed out of the rock of the Akropolis itself.

This, then, was the classical Athenian sanctuary of Asklepios: a grand, two-tiered sleeping chamber behind a shrine and altar to the god; a smaller but striking house for priests or additional sleepers behind a beautiful and peaceful garden; several small but noble and handsome temples to related deities; a sacred spring streaming from the great rock of Athena itself and pouring its healing and restorative waters directly into the dream chambers. All this on the southern slope of the Akropolis, in the traditional direction of warmth, passion, connection, and relationship, presided over by the compassionate healing god and all gathered under the watchful gaze of the great goddess of wisdom, warriorhood, excellence, and stewardship herself.

Today, we visitors to this Asklepion climb through the Theater of Dionysos. We pass statues and carvings in honor of the god of fertility and drama. We cross the orchestra pit and choral floor, climb past the half-standing throne seats. We climb through steep tiers of seats until we reach the upper diazon. We turn left, careful of our footing on the steep slope and amidst the rubble of ages.

We circle the upper tier of theater seats, feeling the passionate mime and ode singing of the ancient chorus. We leave the theater behind and cross into a rarely visited section of ruins crowded with rubble—columns, stones, bases, carvings, many in disarray, some being reassembled, with a few hoists and lifts to help the patient masons and archaeologists.

We stand in front of a low wall that is the remaining first-floor foundation of the abaton. We stand before a large circular stone that is the remaining base of the shrine. We meditate before a modest squarish flooring of stones that constitute the remains of the temple of Asklepios. We wander amid fallen and unplaced stones, many numbered and organized, many still missing their homes, that now cover the area in front of both old buildings, once a pristine garden and sanctuary grounds. We wonder at the fact that this half-organized collection of foundations, walls, and thickly scattered marble was once a beautiful temple dedicated to and successful in the pursuit of healing through rituals organized to provoke an epiphany with the god.

We return to the *bolos*, the small altar of rectangular stone. Here prayers and sacrifices to the god were made. Here, no doubt, many a cock gave his final cry. We pray, we question, we seek a presence. Then we look to the left, into the wall of rock. Set against the rock is a twenty-foot-high wall of thick stone blocks that were once part of the abaton. And set into that wall is an arched gateway, intact, with a metal gate blocking access. The gate is locked. To the right of this archway is a six-foot-tall rose bush, in full and glorious bloom even during a November visit. To the left is a low, neatly trimmed tree. Near the roses is a small sign that tells us we have arrived at the sacred springs.

Behind the locked gate the sacred springs still flow. There is a small Greek Orthodox church built inside that archway, incorporating the sacred springs into its worship. The local people say that, even though the springs are blocked off to our access, these waters pour and heal just as they did in ancient times. This Asklepion may no longer function as it did in fourth-century Athens. But its waters still gush. Their source is still included in religious worship. And the people still believe in the healing powers of these waters that flow with seeming eternal presence from the god's and goddess's sacred rock.

85

## Chapter Ten

# THE FATHER OF MEDICINE

## KOS, 400 BCE

From the northeastern tip of the Greek island of Kos, Turkey looms up out of the sea just two miles to the east. Standing on this point of land in the early morning, or watching from anywhere along the hilly eastern coast of the island, we see the sun dye the Turkish coastline shades of gray and purple. Layers of mountains stretch into the distance. The sky, a short while ago black and diamond studded, glows in rose and blue as it brightens and whitens. Finally, as though heralds should announce its arrival, the golden chariot of Helios peeks over the tops of the mountains. First we see a single brazen rim. It grows and blazes until, quickly, steadily, it becomes a fireball perched on the tip of the purple mountains. It seems so close and looks so solid that we feel, with just a few strokes of our oars or the right tailing wind, we might arrive at its perch and climb aboard. Our hearts are about to leap toward the chariot's car, but too soon the titan cracks his whip, and the chariot of living fire launches on its daily gallop across the velvety blue field of sky.

Growing up on this island during the time of the new classical enlightenment of his age, Hippokrates, now called the Father of Medicine, watched these same sunrises. He was born on Kos in 460 BCE during the era in which the sun, and the rest of nature and

87

human existence, were being emptied of the mythological and coming to be seen as natural phenomena to be understood with our rational faculties.

Perhaps the clearest illustration of this enormous change is provided by Sokrates, a contemporary of Hippokrates. Sokrates swore by Apollo, the god whose oracle had given him his mission by saying that he was the wisest of mortals. Sokrates did not doubt that the gods existed and that he was Apollo's servant. But the philosopher rejected the myths of the gods as though they were superstitious fairy tales. "Isn't that perhaps why I am being attacked, Euthyphro? Because these stories about the gods are something I can't take? As for me, I can only say that I know nothing whatsoever about all that. Tell me, by the name of Zeus, the god of friendship, do you really believe these things happened?" Sokrates asks in the *Euthyphro*.[1] This statement shows both Sokrates' reverence toward Zeus and his doubts about the truthfulness of the myths. Instead, he insisted that all experience, including Apollo's oracle, be subjected to rigorous examination. Truth, including divinely revealed truth, must be arrived at and confirmed through rational reflection, debate, and discourse.

Hippokrates lived in the same changing ideological climate as Sokrates. His mind "was typical of the Periklean time spirit—imaginative but realistic, averse to mystery and weary of myth, recognizing the value of religion, but struggling to understand the world in rational terms."[2] He applied the same rigorous intellectual requirements to the theory and practice of medicine as Sokrates did to the philosophical search for truth. These two thinkers were leaders and cohorts in transforming the paradigm of the day, and of the Western world, from the mystical/mythic to the rational/scientific. As Steven B. Katz, a scholar of medical and scientific rhetoric, summarizes the shift:

> Myth was pushed out of medicine at the same time that it (and rhetoric) was pushed out of philosophy. The Hellenic period of Hippokrates, and a little later, Plato,

witnessed the rationalization (but ironically, also the re-
tention) of mystical science within the logic of the
framework of newer scientific and philosophical systems.[3]

In medicine, Hippokrates fueled this movement from myth to
rationality by rejecting divine causation as the source of disease.
Instead, he searched with analytic rigor for natural cause, symptomatology, processes, and treatment. All these, in Hippokrates' view,
were natural events, to be understood and treated within the ecolo-
gies of nature and the human mind.

The gods did not disappear for Sokrates and Hippokrates. Rather,
they were removed to a greater distance from human life and nature.
The gods were the powers behind all things. Humans might seek
harmony and balance with divine forces and be respectful and reverential. But these pioneers of the classical enlightenment no longer
believed that the gods were responsible for our psychological or physiological conditions. Human life might be religious, but it was no
longer mythic. Sokrates and Hippokrates, each in his sphere, strove
for a balance between faith and reason, belief and rationality. Perhaps
in his boyhood Hippokrates had viewed the sun as a god's chariot. In
his manhood, he was more likely to view it as a natural phenomenon, as the movement of elemental fire in the sky kept in balance
and motion by the unseen forces called gods.

Hippokrates was the son and grandson of Asklepian priests. He
grew up and first practiced "among the thousands of tourists and
invalids who came to take the waters in the hot springs of Kos."[4]
Hippokrates

> acquired his first medical notions from his father whom
> he would follow during the therapeutic rites to the sa-
> cred oak wood, to the incubation rooms of the temple of
> Asklepios where dreams were interpreted, and to the foun-
> tains where patients were plunged into purifying basins.[5]

Further, Pliny tells us that Hippokrates learned medicine by writing down the successful cures that had been recorded by patients on the walls of Asklepios's Koan temple.[6] His training and early influence were Asklepian, even as his intellect surged forward out of the mythic and religious frames of his ancestors' calling and tradition.

A visit to Kos readily reveals the extent and influence of Asklepian practice on the island before, during, and after Hippokrates' time. The extensive Asklepion is situated in the hills about four miles southwest of the island's main town, also called Kos. The sanctuary sits amidst the lush trees and wildflowers produced by Kos's perpetually mild and hospitable climate. It is built across three terraces in the hillside, demonstrating the popularity, growth, and spread of the healing practices at this site over a period of at least six centuries.

Step out upon the terraces of the Koan sanctuary of the god of healing. Numerous columns in aligned rows stand tall, their foundation stones and cross columns proud and strong against the sharp blue sky. Cypress, plane, and oak trees surround the terraces and speckle the distance, creating a lush green circle with a variegated crown line that surrounds the sanctuary with peace. Wildflowers abound, sprouting at the feet of the columns. As each terrace rises to a higher level, the views are broader, more extensive, the temples set more firmly against the blue sky. The atmosphere in this sanctuary of the healing god is of serenity in natural beauty, pride in accomplishment of healing, sincerity of service to the afflicted.

The entrance to the Asklepion is on the north. We walk past Roman baths to arrive at the lower terrace. This terrace was built in the second century BCE to accommodate the large numbers of people arriving to seek healing. It was about the size of a football field and surrounded on three sides by colonnades. Living quarters and treatment rooms were in the rear. Walking across the long terrace, we sense how many people sought healing or attended the afflicted here. Cross to the uphill, south side, and we find the stairway leading to the middle terrace, purification fountains on either side.

Treatment and healing were practiced on this lower terrace. As we climb the stairs, we approach the oldest of the terraces. A reverential air settles on us as we approach the sacred grounds of Asklepian worship. Here, in a cypress grove sacred to his father Apollo, stood an altar of Asklepios erected around 350 BCE. An Ionic temple, built to house the treasury, was built here more than half a century later. At the top of the stairs we see, opposite us, the great altar. It was first built in the fourth century BCE, then rebuilt on a grand scale five hundred years later and modeled on the great altar of Zeus at Pergamum. Also facing the altar are the two columns of a temple. Adjoining this temple are the remains of the abaton housing the sleeping chambers. A stoa and second century CE temple stand in the east.

We climb up a broad and grand staircase that carries us up another thirty-six feet, onto the third terrace. Here, atop the hills, distant mountains stare back at us. Another temple, completed around 160 BCE, looks out into the distance, dominating the entire sanctuary. We look down on the complex that for centuries thronged with the afflicted seeking healing and the priests and physicians who attended them. Here the boy Hippokrates watched his father and grandfather conduct the healing rituals of the god. Here the man Hippokrates inherited the god's tradition and charge. Here his intellect strained to observe, analyze, record, and predict the progress of diseases as aspects of nature and personality rather than as afflictions sent by gods. And here the physician founded the first modern medical school in the Western world, setting in motion the philosophy and practices that lead directly to our modern medical tradition.

The ruins from all three terraces post-date Hippokrates' time. One surprising revelation offered by this sanctuary is that the "glory of Kos, the fame of its Asklepion [occurred] after its ancient glory had been secured for all time by Hippokrates and his school of medicine."[7] That is, this extensive healing sanctuary was built and visited by multitudes of the afflicted after the more rational and scientifically based medical approach of Hippokrates had been established and had made Kos famous.

The medical history of Kos provides a fascinating window into the dialectic between sacred and scientific healing in the ancient world and the resulting evolution of healing principles and practices. Carl Kerényi speculates on the probable historical progression of medical practice on the island of Kos and its impact on the ancient world.[8] Ancient sources tell us that Hippokrates came from a line of Asklepian priest-physicians and learned their form of medicine by observing temple cures. Religious healing was practiced in a smaller, more humble Asklepian sanctuary or temple on Kos long before the time of Hippokrates, perhaps stretching back to the tradition of the practices of the sons of Asklepios, as recorded by Homer. Hippokrates reinterpreted this older tradition along naturalistic lines. According to his teaching, the gods were alive and well, but they no longer caused or cured diseases. Rather, in cooperation with nature, human beings did.

The history of medicine that followed the early religious period on Kos, as reconstructed by Kerényi, may have been as follows. Under the leadership of Hippokrates,

> the school of physicians at Kos achieved a high level of medical science; next, a turn toward religious depth, originating at Epidauros, spread to Kos itself; finally, in the early imperial age, the medical element regained its predominance, even at Epidauros. The pre-Epidaurian period at Kos was not necessarily irreligious; it was merely characterized by a different kind of religion—a religion not of the patient but of the physician, who accordingly played the leading role.[9]

So on Kos we had early Asklepian temple healing practiced on a humble scale. We do not have the ruins of these early sites; they may be under the extant ruins, as it was common in ancient practice to build newer sanctuaries atop older ones occupying the same hallowed ground.

After early Asklepian practices came the influence of the classical enlightenment. In medicine the enlightenment was led by Hippokrates, which made Kos famous throughout the Mediterranean world as a healing center. In fact, Hippokrates' fame was such that he was credited, at least as far back as Galen, with ridding Athens of the plague. This he accomplished by purifying the air throughout the city by burning fires constructed of the sweetest garlands of flowers.[10] This fame coupled with the spreading influence of Epidauros so that a major Asklepion was built on Kos in which divinely inspired dream questing was practiced. Thus, both religious and scientific medicines were practiced there, and thousands of the afflicted flocked to Kos for cures. Finally, divinely inspired medical practices faded in influence, and the healing sanctuary of Kos, as well as others, including the great center at Epidauros, gravitated toward more rationalistic and scientific practices, without abandoning their lineage or loyalty to Asklepios. Today, a visit to Epidauros and some other Asklepian centers may impress us as much by the statues of the healing god and altars for the sacrifices of cocks, as by the collections of scalpels, forceps, probes, and catheters found at some of the sites[11] that look much like medical tools in use today.

The paradigm shift from mythological to naturalistic thinking evidenced in medical practice applied as well to other natural phenomena. For thinkers like Hippokrates, the gods caused neither earthquakes nor epilepsy, mountainslides nor madness, thunderstorms nor pneumonia. As Hippokrates stated in his treatise "The Sacred Disease," epilepsy as well as all other illnesses and ailments have natural causes. In his treatise "Regimen," he argued that ailments caused by nature are best healed in cooperation with nature. Thus, as holistic medicine is beginning to do today, Hippokrates stressed natural means, such as diet, exercise, fresh air, hydrotherapy, massage, and various forms of fasting, cleansing, and purgation, as treatments of choice for illnesses. Prayer was advised as an aid to healing, but attention to restoring the natural powers of the body was his foremost cure. Divine dreams and dream healing still took place, but Hippokrates

differentiated between divine and physical dreams. He left the interpretation of divine dreams to the priests and diviners.[12] Rather, he
observed, recorded, and guided disease processes over time, did not
seek miracle cures, and did not himself lead the practice of Asklepian
dream healing.[13]

Hippokrates was a great organizer and systematizer. He studied
the clinical facts reported on the tablets of the Asklepian temples,
assembling, arranging, and codifying them until he successfully produced "the first clinical document of Western psychiatry," transferring
psychiatric interpretation and practice from the sacred to the secular
realm.[14] In temperament and method, he seems more like Aristotle
than Plato, more analytic than mystic. Inheritor of a great tradition,
he was most interested in careful observation and classification of all
the facts pertaining to that tradition, while being suspicious of too
much philosophizing or theorizing that takes leave of the observed
facts. The voluminous writings he and his followers left behind include many medical and psychiatric case studies, the first such in the
Western tradition, in observational and descriptive form very much
like case studies of today.

An additional parallel between Sokrates and Hippokrates is
found in their shared sense of ethics. Sokrates was a moral philosopher attempting to inspire and instruct the people of Athens to care
about the good of their souls. Hippokrates, in his sphere, was profoundly concerned about the ethical practice of medicine. Part of his
movement away from the religious and toward the natural was to
prevent abuse of the patient by religious authorities. Regarding epilepsy he wrote, "Charlatans and quacks, having no treatment that
would help, concealed and sheltered themselves behind superstition
and called this illness sacred in order that their complete ignorance
might not be revealed." He wrote essays on such topics as "Decorum," "Treatment," and "Regimen," in which he spoke as master
teacher to physicians, instructing them in proper professional bedside manner, serving as ethical mentor and guide to the physician's
practice.

Hippokrates' best known contribution to medical ethics is the oath that bears his name. The Hippokratic Oath, written either by the master himself or followers in his school, is noteworthy in its amalgamation of religious, ethical, and practical considerations. It begins as a vow to the gods, showing the divine origin of the physician's art, calling, and practice: "I swear by Apollo, Physician, by Asklepios, by Hygiaea, by Panacea, and by all the gods and goddesses, making them my witnesses." This invocation is a priestly vow meant to be taken at the moment of initiation into a new sacred status. It demonstrates Hippokrates' reverence for the gods and affirms the sacred origins of medicine in the earlier Asklepian priest-physician tradition.

Other notable ingredients of the oath include vows to honor one's teachers and to provide mentoring without fees to one's sons, one's mentor's sons, and others who have taken the oath. These practices, too, hearken back to the temple tradition of priestly mentoring, in which a seeker responds to a calling, vows allegiance, and is mentored in the sacred practices by one already initiated.

Refraining from doing harm, including not assisting in suicides or abortions, maintaining personal purity and holiness, and maintaining respect and confidentiality are additional hallmarks of the oath. Hippokrates, we recall, was said to be in direct line of succession from Asklepios. All Greek physicians of his time were called *Asklepiads* and were considered to be direct descendants of the healing god. The oath shows that physicians were direct inheritors of the god's practice, in his lineage, and bound to honor and continue that line of inheritance. This belief replicates the shamanic pattern found in many traditional cultures and reinforces the notion of the chthonic origins of the Asklepian tradition. In the old pattern, healers, visionaries, and medicine people often come from the same families or clans, and their traditions and training were passed down from parents to children over the course of many generations. In his own family, Hippokrates could trace his physician-priest lineage back several generations, and he passed this inheritance on to his sons as well. As

Homer records, the priest-physicians' calling and practice was in the nature of a family cult passed down from Asklepios to his descendants since prehistory.

The Western tradition has long credited Hippokrates with turning medicine away from the religious and superstitious and toward scientific practice. We must, however, seek to understand Hippokrates' thought and practice in context of the world in which he lived. Sokrates rejected the factuality of the myths, but that does not mean he did not believe in the gods. Likewise, though Hippokrates rejected the mythological origin of illnesses and maladies—plague as punishment for the bloodguilt of the royal house, for example—he nevertheless believed in and worshiped the gods, and his medical practice was full of faith and reverence. We are in danger of glorifying Hippokrates from our own perspective, seeing him as one completely freed of religious thinking and practice, rejecting the ancient gods, not because he did, but because we ourselves reject divine intervention in human affairs.

Hippokrates, who swore by Apollo and Asklepios, might more accurately be thought of as a teacher and healer standing in an extraordinary balance and tension between the mythical and naturalistic paradigms, partaking of both in his theory and practices. "All is divine and all is nature," Hippokrates wrote. For the ancient Greeks, nature was divine. To study natural processes was not to reject divinity but to study and seek to discover divinity's secret workings. Kerényi stresses that the achievement of such "clarity and purity of mind" in the classical era was not a rational as opposed to a spiritual achievement. Rather, it was precisely a spiritual achievement, using reason as a primary tool, in the tradition of the sun god Apollo.[15]

> When the author of the dissertation on the "sacred malady" professes that for him all diseases are human and divine, this does not mean "natural and supernatural," but "natural and for that very reason divine." And these physicians' awareness of the divinity of their art must be understood

in the same sense . . . [O]n "Decorum" shows this same sense: "transplant wisdom into medicine and medicine into wisdom. For a physician who is a lover of wisdom is the equal of a god." The power to help, unless accompanied by the inner clarity of knowledge, or for that matter the knowledge of the philosophers without ability to help, would not make a physician godlike. The divine physician, who combines light and helpfulness in his person, is Asklepios, ancestor and prototype of all mortal physicians.[16]

Hippokrates the Asklepiad, physician and descendant of the god of healing, consciously labored to continue this tradition. All things revered, including nature, science, and one's art, were divine in origins, essence, and practice. Hippokrates swore to the gods from whom he was descended, indebted, and devoted. He expected and inspired other physicians to do the same. He called not for the abandonment of spiritual and religious principles and practices in medical healing, but for their serious and sincere practice in rational, reasonable, practical, and natural ways. As Professor Katz observes:

> Hippokrates' medical-ethical treatises and aphorisms can be understood as a rational distillation of sacred beliefs and healing practices that had gone on before. That is, in both Hippokrates and Plato, philosophical-scientific "ethics" is a condensation of the divine.[17]

We may have arrived at the final and greatest parallel between Hippokrates and Sokrates. Listen to the background music, the oath taking, the piety, and high ethical standards preached by these two wise elders. Hear the reverential and devotional music in their words and teachings. These two seem to be saying: Do not seek the gods in mystical stories or rituals that take us away from the world. Rather, seek them in everyday lives, practices, and professions, in the water we drink and the discussions we have, in the ways we think and help. Walk with the gods, down here, on the earth. Live and work in a way that reminds us that everything is holy. Seek to inspire the holiness that resides in harmony, balance, respect, clarity, and moderation. The gods are not far away in some mythical sphere. They can be seen, known, felt, and worshiped right here.

Hippokrates did not reject the gods in favor of science. Rather, scientific inquiry was divine methodology. Simultaneously, by reducing the power and influence of divine forces on human illnesses, he elevated the status of the physician to that of reigning expert on human illnesses. While bringing us closer to nature by showing us how to seek the sources of our illnesses and cures in nature, Hippokrates also encouraged elevation of the power and influence of the physician into the position of central importance in the healing process. Hippokrates took an axe to the centuries-old tradition of the Asklepiad in which physician and priest had been one and the same person and role.

In the first years of the Common Era, the Roman encyclopedist Celsus declared that Hippokrates separated medicine from the study of philosophy.[18] From the time of Hippokrates onward, these disciplines and their associated roles evolved separately and as specialties. Medical healing, after Hippokrates, became physician- rather than patient-directed. It also became a physician- rather than physician-priest-facilitated activity.

Hippokrates of Kos, the Asklepiad, brought the gods closer to the earth and its people. And by establishing the supremacy of physician over priest, he gave physicians previously unknown power, importance, and centrality in the healing process.

## Chapter Eleven

# To the Imperial City

## Rome, 291 BCE

Greece faded as supreme power in the Mediterranean world, but its gods continued to rule. Zeus reigned as the Roman Jupiter. Hera, queen of heaven, became Juno. Ares, the terrifying Greek god of war, had never had a Greek city-state brazen enough to appoint him as its patron. In accord with Roman military power, Ares became much more powerful and terrifying. In the Roman pantheon, the god who delights in slaughter was second only to Jupiter in importance, command, and allegiance.

Under the Roman eagle, Asklepios became Aesculapius. He was still the god of healing and was welcomed into the Imperial City itself. "Asklepios was one of the first foreign gods to be admitted to Rome. His temple was dedicated as early as 291 BCE. In its importance this event may be compared only with the entrance of Asklepios into Athens. It set a pattern for the attitudes of Roman citizens and officials of later centuries."[1] Under the right conditions, archetypal powers that manifest to us as deities within a particular cultural context provide not just succor and vision to the afflicted or the pilgrims of a culture. Such powers, for good or ill, can transform an entire society.

The story of how Asklepios came to Rome was a famous

source of wonder in the Empire, recorded in literary and historical works by Ovid, Livy, and others. Asklepios's arrival in Rome and his immediate influence testify to the transpersonal healing powers of this archetype and the means by which such powers may be present to an entire culture. It also provides a fascinating example of the overlap of mythical and historical events and of the penetration of the worldly by the transpersonal within a well-documented historical period. This story was of such import and influence that some early Christian writers such as Augustine went to great pains to refute it and to ridicule or disparage the divinity and influence of the healing god that it celebrates.

Asklepios was brought to Rome for the same reason that he had been brought to Athens more than 130 years earlier. Periodically, a civilization may be overwhelmed with internal and external crises that far exceed human abilities to solve. At such times, people long for divine intervention. Their need may evoke a period of spiritual hunger and soul-searching such as we experience even today. Human longing may open up, as it were, vacuums in the individual and collective psyches that call forth and mobilize the energies of the healer archetype to enter the culture. This is how it was in Rome.

In 295 and 293 BCE, plague erupted in Rome. "For three continuous years our community had been troubled by a pestilence, and it seemed impossible either through divine grace or through human aid to put an end to such a long-lasting evil," wrote Valerius Maximus at the beginning of the Common Era.[2] As Ovid describes it:

> Long, long ago a plague walked through the city
> And Roman air was death; one saw pale bodies
> Sink into wasting sickness everywhere.
> Spent with continual rounds at funerals,
> And knowing that physicians could do nothing,
> Men looked to heaven for a sign of cure.[3]

Despairing of human solutions, "the priests consulted the

Sibylline Books," says Maximus, a form of seeking Apollo's oracle. In Ovid, this consultation is dramatized as a visit to Apollo's shrine at Delfi. The seekers were instructed, "Look to Apollo's son and not Apollo." Consequently, the Romans dispatched a trireme carrying their ambassador, Q. Ogulnius, to Epidauros, still the principal Asklepian sanctuary, to beseech aid—in fact, to ask the sanctuary to give the god to Rome! Epidaurian elders disagreed about how to respond. Some believed that aid must be given when asked; others that neither the god nor the city's source of wealth should be surrendered. Night fell, leaving all in doubt.

We know from numerous inscriptions that a representative of an ailing patient might sleep in a temple of Asklepios as a proxy. The visit to Epidauros by the Roman ambassador can be seen as such a representative visit. The patient who had come to Epidauros was the entire citizenry of Rome; Ogulnius was their proxy seeker. Just as the god often brought healing to an individual supplicant through a dream, so he brought a dream to the Roman ambassador on behalf of his beleaguered city. In the dream, Asklepios appeared before the ambassador exactly as he did so often before supplicant dreamers:

> And then, as if he came within a vision
> The god of health stood at the foot of Roman beds.
> As though he were at ease in his own temple,
> He held his flowering wand in his left hand,
> And with his right he smoothed his length of beard,
> The kind physician speaking to a patient:
> "Let all your worries lie at rest, my dears,
> I'll journey with you across the open sea.
> Take notice of the serpent on my wand
> Who coils around it, and you must know him well,
> For he shall be myself tomorrow morning.
> Larger than life as heavenly beings are."

The next day the troubled Epidaurian elders gathered at Asklepios's temple to beg for signs. They saw "a golden serpent with a gold crown that glittered round his head." It hissed as the entire temple "shook with the coming of a god on Earth." Then the serpent stood upright. The priest knew the god within the snake and led Greeks and Romans alike in praise and prayer. The god bowed, hissed, glided down the temple steps, looking backward and saluting his ancient home in farewell. He then spent three days winding his way through the city to the harbor. Reaching the shore, he seemed to bless and dismiss his followers and then wriggled up the gangway to coil peacefully within the Roman ship at the spot of Ogulnius's tent. The joyous Romans sacrificed a bull, "dressed the ship in garlands of gay flowers," and cast off.

The ship sailed for many days, finally reaching Antium, site of a temple either to Apollo, according to Ovid, or to Asklepios. There

> ... the great snake uncoiled his godlike size
> And glided where his father's temple opened
> To greet the pilgrims on its yellow sands.

The snake took refuge in a tall palm tree, not typical for this terrain but the tree under which Apollo had been born on Delos. For three days the snake remained in his father's tree, fed and watched over by the Roman ambassadors. Finally, he climbed the ship's rudder, rested his head on the stern, and the crew sailed to the mouth of the Tiber River.

> And all along the river crowds came cheering
> Elders and young, good wives and girls, and O
> The Trojan virgins who keep fires burning ...
> One saw altars rise on either side ...
> One almost heard quick fires speak their gladness.
> Then came the sacrifice in sparkling blood.

As the ship entered Rome, the serpent raised his head and scanned the banks, as if looking for his proper new home. At one point, the Tiber separates into two arms around a mole of land. The serpent

chose the place that people call an island . . .
And here it was the serpent came ashore
To be the son of Phoebus that he was,
And not a serpent but of godlike features
To clean the city of its deadly fears
And wake good health among the Roman people.

The snake god did not choose the island in the Tiber by chance. Kerényi gives its history.[4] The island was quite low lying and so never healthful; often it was nearly a swamp. But it already had a powerful established religious tradition that Asklepios joined, altering it in significant ways. Mythologically, the island had originally been formed of wheat cast by the goddess of agriculture Ceres, the Roman version of Demeter. It was consecrated to Faunus, the Roman wolf god, roughly equivalent to the Greek Pan, but more savage and beastly. It was also sacred to the early Roman god Vediovis, "the underworld Jupiter who took the place of Apollo and sent plague and its cure." Another nearby god was called Soranus, also associated with wolves and purifying fire. Kerényi summarizes:

> Thus an Italic Apollo—an ambivalent god who killed and healed—had his place on Tiber Island . . . Here, side by side with Faunus, the snake of Asklepios was to glitter in a wolflike nocturnal world and yet with its cold body symbolize as it were the warm light of life . . . In the cult of Asklepios, as the Romans knew it on Tiber Island, the limits between chthonic darkness and solar radiance are effaced in a way that is almost terrifying—terrifying to those who cling to the romantic conception of the Greek gods, but less so to the physician who . . . is accustomed to a certain twilight realm between light and death.[5]

The Asklepion on Tiber Island was carved and shaped, with a retaining wall carefully built, such that the entire sanctuary resembled a ship. A relief of the god and his snake, along with sacrificial bulls' heads, were carved into this wall and are still visible today. Shaping the island into the form of a ship was meant to commemorate the voyage of Asklepios from Epidauros to Rome. We shall see, in a case of modern Asklepian healing, that it has additional meanings even today to the unconscious and to those seeking cures.

Finally, Ovid tells us, on January 1, 291 BCE, Asklepios's temple was dedicated on the island:

> [O]n this day, the Senate dedicated two temples. The island, which the river hems in with its parted waters, received him whom the nymph Koronis bore to Phoebus. Jupiter has his share of the site. One place found room for both, and the temples of the mighty grandsire and grandson are joined together.[6]

It was not only in Rome, but also at Pergamum and other places, that Asklepios was worshiped as mystically connected to Zeus or Jupiter; the ruler and the healer of the universe becoming coequal.

The snake is the god's perfect symbol for travel between the underworld and the world of light and for achieving a balance of their powers in one being. The elders at Epidauros, intimate with the god's ways, did not believe that they had lost their god to Rome. Rather, their god's power and presence could travel or be transferred by way of his totemic animal without that god abandoning them. Thus Asklepios the Gentle remained strong in Epidauros and simultaneously arrived in savage Rome to take as his home a fetid island populated with dark powers. On this new home island, in the midst of plague, and throughout the Empire, the mild, compassionate light and warmth of the healer thus balanced the darker, more savage powers loosed and worshiped in Rome. As Kerényi summarizes, in the cult of Asklepios that now came to Rome "what is most deeply hidden in man is raised to the gold, ivory and marble upper world of the Greek temples."[7] Thus, the arrival of the god in Rome accomplishes the essential healing goal of classical medicine: achieving balance and harmony between and moderation of primal energies whose conflicts may manifest in physiological, psychological, cultural, or spiritual realms.

Under Roman domination the god remained a favorite of the common people. The Asklepion of Rome remained busy and active, and healings occurred there for many centuries. For example, inscriptions from the second century CE tell of the healing of four commoners: A blind man named Gaius was given back his sight by being told to prostrate himself before and then touch the base of Asklepios's statue and then touch his own eyes. Lucius was cured of pleurisy when the god told him to mix a poultice of ashes from the altar with wine and lay it on his side. Julian, spitting blood, was saved by being instructed to mix the seeds from a pinecone from the altar with honey and eat them for three days. And a blind soldier, Valerius Aper, also had his sight restored. The god told him to create an eye salve made of the blood of a white cock mixed with honey.[8]

Asklepios's influence and healing powers were of such importance, and the belief was so strong that this god belonged to everyone, that his boons and protection were offered and extended even to slaves. During the second century CE, Suetonius tells us,

> When certain men were exposing their sick and worn-out slaves on the island of Asklepios because of the trouble of treating them, Claudius decreed that all who were exposed should be free, and that if they recovered, they should not return to the control of their master; but if anyone preferred to kill such a slave rather than to expose him he should be liable to the charge of murder.[9]

Not only in Rome did the healing god's powers manifest. There were hundreds of sanctuaries throughout the domain.[10] The god was especially popular with the military. "Most of all it was the Roman soldiers who contributed to the extension of Asklepios's reign. They took him to all the regions that came under Roman domination, to the farthest corners of the empire, to the ends of the inhabited world."[11] Roman soldiers, often wounded, bloodied, or fallen ill during their marches of conquest, worshiped Asklepios in outlying districts and regions. They sometimes established his sanctuaries where there were none. Often when the legions conquered, even as they razed towns and cities, they protected Asklepieia from harm and used them for their own healing needs. Such was the case, for example, during the Roman conquest of Korinth. Though the central city was demolished, the Asklepion on its outskirts was preserved and protected.

And it was not only among the common people, the soldiers and slaves, that Asklepios was popular, not to them only did he minister through healing dreams. The god's influence spread to the nobility, so much so that he is known to have brought dream healing to emperors. Marcus Aurelius, who reigned 161-180 CE, in an early section of his *Meditations* in which he thanks the gods for various boons in his life, thanks them also for "remedies that have been shown to me by dreams, among other things, against blood-spitting and dizziness."[12]

Marcus Aurelius, as well as the common people whose healings were mentioned above, received instructions for remedies and practices from Asklepios. They did not receive dream surgeries or other procedures that produced the desired healing immediately. As the dominant culture of the Western world changed along with its values, beliefs, and practices from Greek to Graeco-Roman, there was a significant shift in the types of dreams that supplicants received. Roman era dreamers had "pharmacological dreams" in which they were directed to make and take potions, poultices, and mixtures, and "prescriptive dreams" in which they were directed toward various regimens for cleansing, exercise, and lifestyle changes. This represented a "shift in the pattern of Asklepian dreaming from supernatural surgery to more earthly kinds of physical therapy . . . [T]he dream kept pace with changing cultural circumstances."[13]

Thus Asklepios, now called Aesculapius, was admitted into the Roman halls of the gods and healed many thousands, from emperors to soldiers, common people to slaves.

## Chapter Twelve

# HARMONIZING SCIENCE AND SPIRIT

## EPHESUS, 100 CE

Following Hippokrates' influence, medicine continued to develop its rational and scientific dimensions during late Hellenistic and Roman times. By and large, medical thinkers did not abandon their religious beliefs. Rather, their understanding of divinity and its presence in the world altered along with philosophical developments. Nature was divine. Thus, Plato and Hippokrates had declared, since they were parts of nature, the human body and soul, as well as their health and disease processes, were also divine. Logos, the divine order of the cosmos that so fascinated Greek philosophers, was seen to be replicated in the human psyche and body. Though physicians were increasingly dedicated to a skeptical and naturalistic outlook and to empirical methods of investigation, nonetheless they upheld that the essential goal of medicine, as the Greeks had believed, was to restore order, or Logos, to the body-soul system. To accomplish this "logical" restoration, they tried to discover the natural, rational, and psychological causes and cures of ailments, in a way that did not conflict in outlook or methodology with their perception of divinity.

In the wider culture, the figure of Asklepios transformed and enlarged so that he was worshiped as both savior and healer.

Beginning in the classical era and continuing through Roman times, Asklepios evolved beyond his perceived role as a healing god into a more comprehensive savior god. This development paralleled the spread of early Christianity. For a few centuries, even as Christianity collided and conflicted with paganism, both religious traditions awakened to the worship of the savior archetype, and both Christ and Asklepios were honored as saviors.

One of the famous early collisions of the new Christian savior with established pagan worship occurred in the great city of Ephesus in the first half of the first century CE. Originally built directly on the coast on a deep and fine natural harbor, Ephesus expanded seaward as its harbor silted in. More than five hundred years before the Common Era, Ephesus was a major city, home to renowned poets, sculptors, and thinkers. It was, for instance, the birthplace of the great philosopher of change, Heraklitos. By the first century CE, Ephesus, already over a millennium old, was the second largest city in the eastern world, with a population of over 200,000, superceded only by Alexandria.

"Many-breasted Artemis" was the goddess worshiped at Ephesus. Her temple, four times the size of the Parthenon, was one of the seven wonders of the ancient world. Its 127 columns spanned a length longer than a modern football field. In this temple, and in the great amphitheater carved into the side of Mt. Pion, which seated 24,000 spectators, annual spring ritual festivals to the goddess took place, with pageantry ranging from choral performances to sacrificial rites.

St. Paul came to Ephesus as a missionary. During the spring festival to Artemis, he burst into the temple to denounce her: "The temple of the great goddess Diana should be despised," he declared, "and her magnificence should be destroyed, whom all Asia and the world worshippeth."[1] Hearing these words, the Ephesians rioted. Paul had to be imprisoned to save his life.

Later Paul lived in Ephesus from 55–58 CE. His teachings denigrated the goddess in favor of the new male son of God. Paul's larger message of Christian worship and the lifestyle he believed should proceed from it, along with the story of the Ephesian riots, are recounted in Acts 18 and 19 and in Paul's Epistle to the Ephesians. The collision between Christianity and paganism which this event represents would continue to intensify over the centuries, leading eventually to disastrous consequences for both religious and scientific medicine.

The city of Ephesus was an ideal location for such a conflict to occur. Ephesus was one of the renaissance cities of the Roman era. Its ornate, three-story Library of Celsus contained 150,000 volumes. Its harbor was perpetually busy with trade; its sidewalks resplendent with mosaics. The city was filled with lavishly decorated temples to gods, goddesses, and emperors. Among its public buildings, gymnasiums, smaller theaters, large private homes for the wealthy, and apartments for common citizens were numerous brothels, both sacred and profane. In its public restrooms, nobles and slaves sat as equals. Its fountains flowed with sweet waters from the surrounding mountains. Its simple, rational code of laws was inscribed on a large wall, erected at the central crossroads of the city, so that no one could claim ignorance.

Today, Ephesus is one of the largest ruin sites in the world. It lies fifty miles south of Izmir, attached to the modern Turkish town of Selcuk, and ten miles north of the harbor city of Kusadasi. Walking the miles-long stretch of avenues that comprise the ruins today, we are overwhelmed by the show of success and wealth, by the commercial, intellectual, artistic, and religious refinement that the city had achieved. We stroll slowly through the ruins, sit in the small theaters where intimate performances occurred, or in the great amphitheater which once served this teeming human colony. We walk through the magnificent library as Mark Antony once did. We contemplate the statue of Excellence personified as a beautiful cloaked maiden that adorns its entryway. We sit on the cool marble carved toilet seats in the public restrooms in the center of the city, hearing the echoes of gossip millennia old. We imagine daily life in this city that once was one of the centers of civilization.

As we walk, we pass a thigh-high marble slab set into the ground.

Looking closely, we recognize on its gleaming white face a single snake curling up a staff. It is the caduceus of Asklepios. On this ancient street paved with mosaics, surrounded by houses and temples, we realize, a hospital once stood. Like Kos offshore to the south and Pergamum a hundred miles to the north, the Ephesus of Paul's time was a major center of scientific and religious medicine.

A visit to the Archaeological Museum in nearby Selcuk helps us further appreciate the comfortable blending of the two branches of ancient medicine. One room of the museum is dedicated to the medical center and school that thrived in Ephesus during the reigns of Trajan and Hadrian, between 98-138 CE. Though the medical center is gone, the museum's medical room gives us a sense of what might have taken place there. Numerous statues of Asklepios, from half-size to life size, line the walls. Most show his characteristic snake-wrapped staff, his supple robe-cloaked body, his hands extending in gentleness and compassion, as if he were handing to a supplicant the healing requested in prayer. Side-by-side with the statues are cases full of medical and surgical instruments. There are probes for extracting and forceps for grabbing arrow and spear points. There are large clamps for stemming blood flow. Alongside these, we see extracts from scientific treatises on medicine by Rufus and the other ancient physicians of Ephesus. These artifacts demonstrate that by the first century CE, Ephesus was a major center of medical practice, and that the religious side of medicine continued to be practiced side by side with the scientific.

Perhaps the greatest physician and teacher of the Ephesian medical center, Rufus practiced there at the end of the first and into the beginning of the second century CE. He was an expert in dietetics, anatomy, and pathology, about which he wrote numerous books, of which at least five are preserved. Among his many achievements, Rufus was one of the earliest physicians to investigate and write about the psychology of patients and the psychological factors in illness. He taught that through the clinical interview, physicians might come to know the whole person, so as to properly understand and treat a disease. According to Rufus, it is not enough to observe and treat the illness:

> The patient must be interviewed. By means of these questions, it is possible to learn a great deal concerning the illness, which enables a better treatment. The time that an illness begins is also important. In addition, one should inquire as to the patient's attitude toward life and general mental state. In this way, the patient's mental health can be assessed.[2]

Rufus practiced medicine at a time when human dissection was outlawed. In order to teach anatomy to his students, he substituted animals for humans. But he protested the ban, declaring that anatomy was most correctly taught through human dissection.[3] This view demonstrates his empirical preference and method. Simultaneously, however, Rufus believed in and affirmed the efficacy of Asklepian dream healing. To Rufus, as to Galen later on, dream healings were not inexplicable miracles. Rather, they were specific wise interventions by the god in response to disease conditions.

Here is a case study that Rufus declared "is worth telling." It demonstrates Rufus's style of careful clinical observation of the progression of diseases and their cures. He also notes, however, Asklepian epiphanies, the conversations that occurred between Asklepios and his supplicant, the bargaining and cooperation between the god and an ailing human, and the divinely-mediated healing that resulted.

> How it happened to Teucer the Cyzicenean [ca. 100 CE] is worth telling: when he was afflicted with epilepsy he came to Pergamum to Asklepios, asking for liberation from the disease. The god appearing to him holds converse with him and asks if he wants to exchange his present disease against another one. And he said he surely did not want that but would rather get some immediate relief from the evil. But if at all, he wished that the future might not be worse than the present. When the god had said that it

would be easier and this would cure him more plainly than anything else, he consents to the disease, and a quartan fever [i.e., characterized by convulsions every four days] attacks him, and thereafter he is free from epilepsy.[4]

Rufus also observed and recorded clinical data that included dreams in which the god promised specific treatment and observations of that treatment, sometimes in the form of another disease process. One generation later, as we shall see, Galen observed the same divine treatment methodology. Because he had observed such healings, according to Edelstein, Rufus believed that the god could perform miracles. Thus it was impossible that religious medicine would ever be wholly replaced by human medicine. As Rufus himself said, "If somebody were so good a physician that he could provoke fever (as the god can), there would be no need for any other procedure of healing."[5] In religious medicine according to Rufus, we need physicians to do for us what we are able to do for ourselves. What we can do, the god does not. Simultaneously, we need religious medical practices to enable the god to do for us that which we can never do.

In the thriving first-century city of Ephesus, and under the guidance of Rufus and his students, the teaching and practice of medicine demonstrated no conflict between the empirical and the spiritual. In fact, Ephesian medicine affirmed that, each in its sphere, both are necessary.

In the early centuries of the Common Era, both the worship and healing practices of Asklepios continued in the old Greek temples and sanctuaries and spread to new locales. Healing sanctuaries and medical centers continued to grow, develop, and thrive. Over the centuries these centers added new buildings and received blessings and offerings from such luminaries as Alexander, Caesar, and Claudius. In the fourth century CE, during this spread of the healer's influence in the Hellenistic and then Roman eras, Pergamum was founded. It reached its height of fame and power in the second century CE. It was at Pergamum that Marcus Aurelius's court physician, Galen, was raised and began his practice.

## Chapter Thirteen

# THE ANCIENT PSYCHIATRIST

## PERGAMUM, 150-170 CE

As Asklepios grew in stature, so did his worship. Services were held in his temples and sanctuaries not only for special healing purposes but also for the general worship due any major god. Songs were dedicated to him; festivals and games held in his honor. Herondas, writing in the third century CE, tells of Asklepian worship on Kos—the morning crush of people at the temple gates, their joyous praise of the god, their sacrifices not just of cocks but of oxen and fattened and stuffed pigs.[1]

By the second century CE, a temple to Zeus Asklepios had been established at Pergamum, a thriving city on the eastern coast of the Mediterranean that had been a center of culture, politics, and commerce for more than a hundred years. There, the worship of Zeus, the father god, and Asklepios, his beneficent son, blended into one. To his worshipers during this era, Asklepios "has every power, and not alone that which concerns human life."[2] The god's influence was such that the Platonic philosopher and scientist Proclus, writing at the end of the fifth century CE, declared that "he who causes everything to act according to nature is Asklepios who keeps the universe from falling sick or growing old, and the elements from relaxing their indestructible bonds."[3]

Thus, from his beginnings as an individual and specific god of healing, Asklepios had grown to become the embodiment and keeper of the universal principles that ancient philosophers and scientists had observed in nature and believed were necessary to both human health and cosmic wholeness—balance, interconnection, and eternal regeneration. Aristides, the ancient writer who recorded many dream healings in the Pergamum medical center, reports a dream in which he saw a companion pointing to the sky and declaring, "This is the one that Plato calls the soul of the universe," to which, Aristides responds, "I look and I see enthroned in the sky Asclepius of Pergamum."[4]

During this era of Roman domination of the Mediterranean world, the scientific-rationalistic and mystical-divine dimensions of Asklepian healing were maintained in a dynamic balance. Medicine had evolved into two branches, religious and human. Physicians took pains to distinguish who and what they could treat. The untreatable were not forsaken, but were directed to the temples.[5] Thus, scientific and religious medicine, which we in the modern world view as competing, each had its purpose and prescribed clientele. Ideally, these branches were held in dynamic tension by physicians who recognized their human and scientific limits and affirmed the value of prayer, studied dream healings scientifically, and believed in their efficacy.

From inscriptions and other evidence found at sanctuary ruins and the writings of physicians of the time, it is clear that scientific and mystical aspects of healing were often practiced by the same healers. Some of the most effective and influential physicians may, as in earlier days, have functioned as priests, expert in both the medical and spiritual arenas. An afflicted person could go to sanctuaries of Asklepios to receive both medical treatment and psychospiritual ritual, a combination that often led to astounding healing experiences.

Galen, the great Roman-era physician and the ancient world's "greatest representative of clinical psychiatry,"[6] achieved such dynamic balance as a scientific physician whose calling, practice, and healing site were all built on priestly foundations. Galen was born in Pergamum around 129 CE. Educated at Pergamum's Asklepian center, he practiced there between 157-162 and 166-169. While there, Galen earned a great reputation as a physician to gladiators. He then spent much time working in Rome, becoming the personal doctor of the Emperor Antoninus and his family and securing the high position of court physician to Marcus Aurelius.

The ruins of the great city of Pergamum are located today in modern Bergama, on Turkey's Mediterranean coast. Galen's practices, the voluminous writing he left behind, the testimony of Asklepian fragments from the sanctuary, and the extensive Asklepian ruins that still stand in Bergama all provide evidence of a religious culture that yet allowed the intellectual freedom necessary for the unfolding and development of the new rational scientific worldview.

Bergama today is a busy Turkish town with a population of about 40,000. Just over fifty miles north of Izmir, it rests in a fertile region in which cotton, tobacco, and vine crops flourish. We walk the bazaar that straddles the main street of the city, weaving between the crowds and the many pushcarts vending fresh and dried fruits and nuts. We pass carpet, leather, and textile shops, restaurants, and a few electronic goods shops. Dozens of men stand in large and small clumps, talking, bargaining, arguing, or joking about politics.

Small hotels or pensions are sprinkled along the main thoroughfare. An archaeological museum stands toward the western end of town. We enter a *hamam*, the Turkish bathhouse at the northern end of the main avenue. There we are served *elma*, sweet apple tea, as we wait for a traditional sweat and massage. Nearby are the great mosque and the famous Red Basilica. Hadrian originally built this Basilica as a temple a generation before Galen's time. Like so many religious sites of Asia Minor, it was converted into a church in Byzantine times, then destroyed by the Arabs a few centuries later. With the passage of centuries, a smaller church was built on top of the wreckage. Standing in ruins in this part of the world, we stare down through the levels of the collective psyche, viewing layers of religion and culture rolled over and layered again by successive boulders of time and fate.

Bergama is capped on both northern and southwestern ends by important and extensive ruins. A tour of both sites erects in our imaginations the busy commercial, political, social, cultural, scientific, and religious center that was once Pergamum. The northern ruin site begins at the high end of Bergama, in narrow cobbled streets where small, attached houses are decorated in flaking and fading paint. A century ago, this was Bergama's Greek neighborhood. Here, until their expulsion, generations of long-established Greek families lived and died.

The streets begin to climb. A hike up the steep castle hill takes us to the Greco-Roman akropolis that stuns us with its grandeur and beauty. Our thighs aching, we climb successive levels of ancient Pergamum built by Hellenistic Greeks during the third century BCE. We climb marble staircases, pass under archways and tunnels built into the hillside that take us through several layers of defensive walls. We make our way through high weeds and brambles. We stroll through a lower second-century BCE *agora*, the public marketplace, among the scattered ruins of small and large shops and public buildings. We walk through a large gymnasium complex, built on three terraces, one for children, a second for teens, and a third for young men over age sixteen. It had a stadium and flat practice fields surrounded by athletes' facilities built into the hill. The remains of Roman baths stand near the uppermost gymnasium.

We continue climbing ancient streets, turning now and then to admire the ever more expansive view as Bergama shrinks below us. The old path winds its way like a gigantic rock- and weed-strewn snake around the curves of the mountain. We leave the lower city, pass through another line of defensive walls, and pick our way over stone steps and building blocks placed and fallen thousands of years ago. Halfway up, around another face of the mountain, we arrive at the sanctuary of Demeter.

We walk between two columns that mark the ancient *propylon*, the gateway. We descend the wide, regal stairs leading into the temple. Before us stretches a long, marble third-century sanctuary complex where the Eleusinian Mysteries were once practiced. Here, in one of the oldest buildings of Pergamum, the abduction, descent, and resurrection of Persephone were reenacted in a ritual that initiated thousands into a spiritual consciousness that embedded human life in a grander vision of the eternal cycles of death and rebirth. We sit on the stairs at the near end of the long terrace. We imagine priests and priestesses guiding initiates through hymn singing, storytelling, and psycho-dramatic reenactments of loss, death, and nature's eternal return.

As we sit and listen to the ancient echoes, a child appears at the far side of the ruins. Boy or girl we cannot tell. The child rises through the rubble until we see its mount, a black horse. Black horse and olive-skinned child emerge from the rocks. We stare as they cross through the sacred precinct. The clopping of the horse's hooves reverberates through the ruins and sounds to our ears like the drumming of our hearts, like the ticking of time in the heart of the universe. The horse mounts the stairway, clomping loudly as it passes us and moves on through the ruins. We shake our heads to break the spell. Was it a modern horse and child that we saw? Or a glimpse of Persephone as eternal youth, forever riding the black horse of Hades, the steed of devouring time?

The path continues to curve and climb, and we with it. We make a wide arc and circle to the south, where we have vistas of the town below. Soon we pass through an upper agora to arrive at the massive theater built into the mountain's incline. The rows of seats are carved so steeply into the mountainside that a permanent tension is created. We seem to view a perpetual landslide of rock created and counteracted by the stone benches that break into their stiff upright positions off the fierce incline.

Above the theater, we pass under and around huge retaining walls constructed of massive boulders. They provided defense as well as creating mountaintop terraces for building. Atop one of these terraces was the huge second-century altar of Zeus, famous throughout the ancient world. Around its podium was carved a relief of the victory of the gods over the giants. The size and stature of this altar to the king of gods and the frieze of his pantheon of deities echoed ancient pride in the Greek triumph of rationality over unconsciousness, civilization over barbarism, law over instinctuality, individual over mass identity.

We wander and explore the akropolis, now open to extensive views of the Turkish countryside in every direction. Along the northeastern ridge overlooking a huge lake, we contemplate the sparse remains of half-a-dozen palaces, evidence that even the pride of kings erodes before the onslaught of time. Toward the center of the akropolis, we stand before the foundations of the temple of Athena. Here, the daughter of Zeus had her position as guardian of the city. Here, in these extensive ruins, she seemed to hold court in a center of civilization guided by ideals of refinement and learning.

Adjoining the north colonnade of Athena's temple stood the famous library of Pergamum. At its height, this library contained 200,000 parchment volumes and was the second largest in the Western world, superceded only by the library of Alexandria. Notably, the library was built around 170 BCE, about the same time that Galen achieved such fame as a physician that he left Pergamum for the second time to practice in Rome, this time to remain there for the rest of his career. This library, the famous school of sculpture that developed in Pergamum, and the importance of the Asklepion and its chief physician, all attest to the influence this city once had. The flowering of Pergamum was part of "a wider intellectual renaissance in which medicine, philosophy, and rhetoric were entertained together with equal enthusiasm; particularly notable was the emergence of a close association between medicine, the cult of Asklepios, and oratory."[7]

We walk again to the southern edge of the akropolis. We can just see the Asklepion at Bergama's far end, a wide avenue of columns and walls. At Korinth, in Athens, and here as well, the rulers and sky gods lived in the high city, but Asklepios was down below, close to his chthonic origins in the earth from which his snakes emerged and from which he drew his healing power.

The Asklepion at Pergamum, now on the far southwestern side of modern Bergama, had been active for half a millennium before Galen's birth. It was founded in the fourth century BCE, significantly enlarged in the second, and eventually ranked with Epidauros and Kos as one of the most influential healing sanctuaries of the ancient world. It was destroyed by an earthquake about a century after Galen's time and not rebuilt.

We walk slowly along the wide avenue that passes between rows of columns, some mere stumps, some snapped in half by the ages, others standing tall and proud with their marble scrolls held against the clear blue sky. This is the Sacred Way, the entrance to the Asklepion along which thousands of worshipers and the afflicted walked.

At the end of the Sacred Way, we arrive at a courtyard surrounded by columns. In its center stands a waist-high white marble cylinder. The snakes of Asklepios are carved into its curvaceous sides. Two snakes dance opposite each other, weaving in the heat around and above hanging vines that never whither. The snakes loop over their own writhing bodies, meeting fang to fang in the center of a carved circle, as if in an eternal kiss of healing. On this altar, animal sacrifices were once made. Today, in modern supplication, we pray, meditate, pour water or wine. We then step through a propylon and into the sacred precinct.

Immediately to our south is the temple of Asklepios. Its foundations are low, partially buried in earth that has mounded around their sides. Just behind this temple is the round temple of Telesphoros. Telesphoros was a mysterious mystical figure associated with Asklepios and first worshiped at this site. Sometimes he was thought of as a child-god or referred to as a son of Asklepios.[8] In the fifth century CE, by which time the gods had become, to some, more idealized universal principles than personages, Damascius writes that Telesphoros "supplies the missing element which is not previously present in the Paeonian wholeness of Asklepios . . . and . . . perfects the health of one who admits him properly."[9]

Telesphoros continues to fascinate modern mythologists. Jung carved his image, declaring that "he roams through the dark regions of this cosmos and glows like a star . . . points the way to the gates of the sun and to the land of dreams."[10] Kerényi calls him "the little hooded nocturnal god."[11] In the modern visualizations and dream-work that contribute to conscious mythmaking, Stephen Larsen includes Telesphoros in invocations as the "hooded dwarf" who is an essential assistant to the healing god.[12]

What does this little hooded child-god, this helper of the healer represent? Why in Pergamum did dream incubations occur in the basement of his temple? How does he complete Asklepios and per-fect our health?

The story goes that an oracle commanded that Telesphoros be worshiped in the Pergamum Asklepion,[13] from which his worship spread throughout the ancient world. Kerényi explains that ancient wisdom "ascribed the mysterious process of healing rather to the night and sleep than to the day and waking," and that this nighttime activity was evoked by the "dwarflike, nocturnal figure" whose name meant "The Finisher."[14] Meier translates the name *Telesphoros* as "Perfector" or "Consummator."[15] Alternative translations might be the one who "Brings to an End," "Brings to Completion," "Grants Accomplishment," "Fulfills" or "Brings to Fruition."[16] Anne Maguire observes the similarity of appearance and relationship between Telesphoros and the universally worshiped "little phallic god." As such, he carries the powers of creative eros, generativity, sexual union, and inner transformation.[17]

In considering the meaning of Telesphoros, let us reflect on several dimensions. Asklepios often appeared to his supplicants as a child. Another savior of the time instructed us that, "Except you be as little children, you shall not enter the kingdom." Modern psychological healing teaches us to reclaim the lost inner child. Meier calls Telesphoros "the Boy who fulfilled dreams and prayers."[18] Moreover, modern holistic wisdom stresses the importance of humor to the healing process. Perhaps the dwarf-like aspects of the figure are meant to be amusingly grotesque. Further, Telesphoros's name affirms the importance of the descent into night, the wound and its womb, into nonrational—hooded, dark, underground, childlike, potent—consciousness.

Telesphoros challenges us to surrender to our childlike parts and to sleep, to trust our hidden erotic and creative powers, to trust the cyclical, death-rebirth nature of the disease process, to allow healing to occur rather than to force it, and to look for help in strange, unexpected, unbelievable, even grotesque or humorous forms. When we are desperate, answers may appear in irrational forms. Kerényi thinks that Telesphoros's name may also indicate the presence of death. It might also stand for the accomplishment or completion of the healing process or the fulfillment of dreams. In the dense ambiguity of myth, we are reminded at once that the ending of the disease process may be either healing or death, that death itself may be a healing, and that to heal we must undergo a psychospiritual death and rebirth.

In Pergamum, the temple of Telesphoros was a two-story building. High and thick arched domes beneath the temple support its floor and reveal that as much worship and healing practice occurred beneath the ground as above it. In the temple's well-constructed basement, both hydrotherapy and incubation for dream healing were practiced. We can see the smooth and solid walls and floors that contained the purifying baths.

From this southeastern corner of the sanctuary grounds, a long passageway proceeds in straight underground flight from the temple into the center of the sanctuary. We walk through this darkened passageway as if we were passing down the corridor toward dreams. As we come out into the light, we awaken in an unknown place. Steps ascend from the tunnel, and the daylight seems framed and embraced by the arched entryway. We emerge near the sacred well and springs. A few gleaming marble steps down, a pipe juts from the rock. Here the sweet waters that used to bathe and purify the supplicants still flow. We stoop to drink. Under the high hot Turkish sun, the water is cool, sweet, health-giving. It tastes of the vitality of the fertile earth.

Contemporaneous with Galen, Aristides wrote an oration praising the health-giving properties of this well. He says of this water:

> . . . for many it comes to take the place of a drug. For when bathed in it many recovered their eyesight, while many were cured of ailments of the chest and regained their necessary breath by drinking from it . . . it cured the feet . . . One man upon drinking from it straightway recovered his voice after having been mute . . . For some the drawing of the water itself took the place of every other remedy. Furthermore, not only is it remedial and beneficial to the sick but even for those who enjoy health it makes the use of any other water improper.[19]

Ahead of us, along the northern boundary of the precinct, is a stately colonnade. Its seventeen white columns, cracked and tanned with the ages, stand erect on their long foundation and steps. At the eastern corner of the colonnade was the library. At the western end, set into the hillside, is the semicircular theater. Here, during Hellenistic and Roman times, catharsis and laughter were encouraged as aids to healing. Today, the theater is kept in repair and used, as are the ancient theaters in Epidauros, Delfi, and Athens, for an annual festival of classical plays.

This sanctuary of Asklepios was the home healing place of Galen, where he trained and practiced. Galen was

> undoubtedly the most cultivated, capable, and intelligent scholar of ancient medicine. A profound expert in general medicine, in neurology and in psychiatry . . . who completed a unique scientific operation: the unification

of all the clinical, experimental, and theoretical data of neuropathology and psychiatry from a global perspective.[20]

It has been said of Galen and Rufus, whom we met at Ephesus, that "these men were good scientists, keen observers, and interested in the results achieved rather than any religious controversies or beliefs."[21] These men, their colleagues and students, were strict practitioners of the scientific outlook and method. Galen observed, examined, and reported what he actually saw; he drew his conclusions about what worked or failed to work based upon empirical evidence.

Galen's contributions to the development of medicine, particularly in anatomy, physiology, and psychiatry, seem at first to exclude him from the category of physician-priests as in the earlier Greek tradition. Modern interpreters stress his accomplishments as a rational and skeptical scientist, rating him after Hippokrates as the second most important figure in the evolution of modern medicine. They praise his rationality, his empirical method, his rigorous clinical practice and standards, his freedom from religious argumentation. But is this all that he was? Does this reading of the past account adequately for his practice in the Pergamum Asklepion?

Like Hippokrates, Galen was a scientist who was educated in a centuries-old Asklepian sanctuary and tradition. Galen, indeed, left us a large legacy of scientific medical tomes. He wrote between four and five hundred works, of which nearly ninety remain. They are still much studied and admired for their clarity and precision of scientific observation. He was an effective and insightful psychological thinker, understanding the profound degree to which a patient's psychological disposition and experiences affect the causes, progress, and outcome of disease. What is relevant to our study is something that is usually omitted or scoffed at in modern studies of Galen's contributions. This is his degree of reliance upon the spiritual and his integration of scientific and religious medicine.

Galen observed, recorded, studied, and interpreted temple cures based upon scientific principles. Thus, from the scientific point of view, he has left us reliable and definitive testimony that Asklepian temple healings through dream epiphanies were real and that we are dealing with scientifically observable phenomena in the matter of these cures.[22] Here, for example, is one of Galen's case histories:

> Another wealthy man . . . from the interior of Thrace, came, because a dream had driven him, to Pergamum. Then a dream appeared to him, the god prescribing that he should drink every day of the drug produced from the vipers and should anoint the body from the outside. The disease after a few days turned into leprosy; and this disease, in turn, was cured by the drugs that the god commanded.[23]

In this study, Galen observed the origins and progression of a disease and its cure. He diagnosed the ailment as soon as it was recognizable. He affirmed that diseases can transmute from one clinical presentation to another, here during the healing phase. He recorded dream elements as basic clinical facts. These included the beckoning dream that brought the supplicant to his sanctuary, the prescription provided by the god in an incubation, and the use of snake medicine both internally and externally. In this case, we see a comfortable marriage between scientific and religious medical traditions. Expressions with religious themes—the dreams—and religious practices—incubation—were treated as essential and observable clinical facts.

Clearly, for his patients' benefits Galen interpreted, prescribed, recorded, and consulted their dreams. But epiphanic dreams also impacted Galen's life and practice in several personal ways. First, they called him to the practice of medicine as to his destiny. It is recorded that, while still a youth, Galen had a dream in which Asklepios appeared to him and instructed him to become a physician. Further, dreams of the healing god directly affected his research and writing. Galen wrote one of his anatomical treatises on the basis of an epiphanic dream.[24] Dreams also contributed to his diagnoses and sometimes provided Galen with direct instruction on how to intervene, heal, and cure, even instructing him how to perform difficult surgeries:

> Some people scorn dreams, omens and portents. But I know that I have often made a diagnosis from dreams and, guided by two very clear dreams, I once made an incision into the artery between the thumb and the index finger of the right hand, and allowed the blood to flow until it ceased flowing on its own, as the dream had instructed. I have saved many people by applying a cure prescribed in a dream.[25]

Finally, it may be that Galen himself experienced a healing directly from Asklepios. He wrote in praise of "the ancestral god Asklepios of whom I declared myself to be a servant since he saved me when I had the deadly condition of an abscess."[26]

Galen clearly respected the gods and saw Asklepios as the source of health and healing. Though a scientific physician, he considered himself Asklepios's servant and attributed both his own and many patients' healings directly to the god. He referred to himself as the "therapeut" of his "fatherly god, Asklepios."[27] And while he was not himself a priest, but a scientist and physician, he included prayer and invocation as part of his methodology. Here, for example, is Galen's invocation to Asklepios on administering a medicinal antidote:

> Be gracious, blessed Paeon, you who fashioned this remedy, whether the Trikkan ridges hold you, O demigod, or Rhodes, or Kos and Epidauros by the sea; be gracious, send your always gracious daughter, Panacea, to the emperor, who will propitiate you with pure sacrifices for the everlasting freedom from pain which you can grant.[28]

As a man of his times, Galen believed that the body was a complex living system, like the cosmos, each part having a unique purpose. The purposes of the soul, for instance, were reason, feeling, and will.

By Galen's time, the classical ideals of moderation and balance had long been embedded in the philosophy of medicine. Illness and psychopathology arose, he believed, from disharmony and disequilibrium in any part of the human system. For instance, an imbalance in the soul's feeling function might manifest in disease symptoms. Such an imbalance could be caused by an immoderate lifestyle, by predisposition, psychology, experience, or environment.

Galen observed that many of the cures sent or assigned by Asklepios were for the purposes of balancing disproportions in patients' emotional and psychological makeup. Indeed, many Asklepian cures that seem paradoxical, ironic, or humorous can be understood as divine interventions designed to rebalance the passions and humors, as Galen observed:

> And not a few men, however many years they were ill through the disposition of their souls, we have made healthy by correcting the disproportion of their emotions. No slight witness of the statement is also our ancestral god Asklepios who ordered not a few to have odes written as well as to compose comical mimes and certain songs (for the motions of their passions, having become more vehement, have made the temperature of the body warmer than it should be); and for others . . . he ordered hunting and horse riding and exercising in arms . . . for he not only desired to awaken the passion of these men because it was weak but also defined the measure of exercises.[29]

Galen was also keenly aware of the power the divine attributes of wisdom and authority had on his patients. He observed that patients would endure a difficult and demanding regimen when they thought that it had been prescribed by a god and believed it would lead to beneficial results:

> . . . we see that those who are being treated by the god obey him when on many occasions he bids them not to drink at all for fifteen days, while they obey none of the

128

physicians who give this prescription. For it has great influence on the patient's doing all which is prescribed if he has been firmly persuaded that a remarkable benefit to himself will ensue.[30]

In modern psychological terms, the patient makes his transference not to the therapist but to the god. This is a fundamental reason that the patient cooperates with paradoxical or uncomfortable remedies that may appear irrational, absurd, or incomprehensible. A patient who believes that healing comes personally from the god cooperates fully. As a result, the body/mind system may undergo immediate and radical restructuring, leading to a genuine and holistic healing.

For Galen, Asklepios was the ultimate authority. Galen the mortal physician was his grateful, obedient, and cooperative servant. Thus it appears that in Galen's medicine, the religious and scientific coexisted as two forms of the healing god's art.[31] The mortal physician stood in relationship to his god Asklepios as Asklepios the half-divine healer on earth stood to his father Apollo, the sky god of medicine. In this worldview, the scientific practice of medicine, clinically specific and theoretically complete as it was, was one of the honorable ways of cooperating with divinity and helping its powers unfold among mortals.

We cannot leave Pergamum or Galen's era without speaking of another voluminous writer and witness of Asklepian healing. This man achieved fame not as a physician, but as Asklepios's most eager and grateful patient. Aelius Aristides lived from 117-181. From about 145, when he was in his twenties, until his death, he lived near the Pergamum Asklepion and experienced numerous dream healings there. Aristides left an extensive record of his own and others' prayers, practices, dream healings and their interpretations, all in great gratitude and praise of Asklepios.

Aristides was the son of a wealthy and prominent family of Smyrna (modern Izmir). He studied rhetoric and oratory with leading teachers of the day in Athens, Smyrna, and Pergamum. He had intended to take his place in the popular profession of orator, declaiming philosophical speeches before the noble, powerful, and rich, helping shape his world in the public sphere, while bringing fame and fortune to himself.

Fate and character derailed Aristides' plans. From about age twenty-five on, Aristides was stricken with attacks of illness that made him unable to pursue his chosen career or even to function at all. Significantly, Aristides was most often stricken with symptoms in the body parts that he needed most. For example, his throat constricted, his breath became blocked, and he choked on his food when traveling to Rome in 143 to present his oratory at court. About two years after this illness, he went to Pergamum to immerse himself in the intensive practice of Asklepian healing. Commentators agree that his record of diseases comprises an astonishing psychosomatic history.[32] Since his illnesses prevented him from practicing the profession to which he had dedicated himself, he used his oratorical skills in the service of Asklepios, singing the god's praises and recording religious and medical practices and cures, especially his own.

Aristides informs us of poems, odes, and paeans that he and others wrote for the god's festivals and worship. Choruses performed them. Candles were lit, offerings made, sacrifices performed. Aristides tells us of the popularity of the god. Huge crowds of people attended his festivals. Great numbers of supplicants, many from faraway places, came seeking cures. Likewise, philosophers and healers from Krete, Asia Minor, and all over the Mediterranean basin came to learn this god's practices.

Aristides also informs us about particular practices of religious medicine. Purifications were achieved through actual events, such as vomiting, washing, dunking, fasting, and through dream events. Healing waters were used extensively for bathing, cleansing, and drinking. Both actual and dream sacrifices were made to the god. Often, actual and dream events coincided in their particular purpose. For example, Aristides recorded offering religious libations in a worship service and then vomiting at home. Both constituted forms of purification. He also recorded dreams in which he made religious offerings and then vomited, thus imaginally purifying both psyche and body. In these instances, it was as if the unconscious and consciousness were cooperating to give the supplicant a holistic experience.

Aristides records many pharmacological remedies prescribed through dreams, often detailing the specific concoctions. He also says he experienced dream surgery. Other gods as well as Asklepios sometimes helped in the healing. In Aristides' particular healing dreams, Athena, Telesphoros, and the Egyptian deity Serapis, an Alexandrian-era god of healing, appeared.

We learn much about the principles of Asklepian medical practice from Aristides. In scientific medicine, the attending physician might be of paramount status. However, "when he heard the dreams he was wise enough to yield place to the god." Then both doctor and patient "recognized the true physician" and followed the god's prescriptions.[33] In religious medicine, the god was the medical director, and each participant kept his rightful place in the hierarchy.

Religious medicine often proceeded by way of paradoxical cures. When Aristides suffered from catarrh, stomach trouble, and difficulties with his palate, Asklepios told him to bathe in the icy waters of a river, in the middle of winter, with a stormy north wind blowing. After his swim, he reports a rosy hue and a warmth flooding his body and remaining with him, a significant shift in his mental attitude, and "a certain inexplicable contentment" that did not seem of human origins.[34] He reports further paradoxical prescriptions: He raced barefoot in winter; rode horses when he did not feel up to it; sailed across a harbor during a wind storm that endangered other ships; ate honey and acorns and then vomited. He says that Asklepios ordered all these practices during a time when he had an inflammation at its worst.[35]

Elsewhere Aristides told the story of a sick man who was ordered to work so hard that he perspired; it was that willful exertion that broke the man's fever. In all these instances, paradoxical prescriptions balanced the disequilibrium of the body/mind system. They were obeyed because they came from the god. And the god—or the body/mind system of the dreamer giving voice to the god—knew just what intervention to prescribe in order to achieve systemic balance.

Religious medicine, as we learned from Galen, is a medicine of the soul. Illnesses are indications of imbalances in the body/mind system caused by disharmonies in the soul. Aristides left a prayer imploring the god to relieve him of his disease "and grant me as much health as is necessary in order that the body may obey that which the soul wishes."[36] He knew, too, that his soul was the primary object of the god's concern. He thus came to discover the true boon of sickness. Sickness was an advantage because it brought the patient close to the god.

The longer Aristides followed Asklepian practices, the more he was transformed into an enthusiastic student, follower, and devotee of the god. As Aristides himself seemed to realize, he had found his destiny through his illness. That is, though he could not declaim in public, his skills of oration, his desire to praise, his hunger to belong and be seen, were fulfilled by his service to the god.

In the end, Aristides considered Asklepian temple medicine not just a path for healing but a complete religion. He became more than a grateful patient, as Galen was more than a scientific physician. Galen became a familiar with the god who was his medical and spiritual master. And Aristides became an initiate into Asklepian ways as into a mystery religion. Its practice became his life.

*Chapter Fourteen*

# ASKLEPIOS AND CHRIST

## THE ROMAN EMPIRE, 300-500 CE

She gazes at us with piercing, languid eyes. Her lips are full and slightly parted, as if whispering a secret. Her skin is smooth; her neck sleek and long. Her hair is pulled back from a central part, rippling in wavelets to the back of her head where it is gathered in a bun. Tender earlobes peek from beneath the rippling tresses.

But her nose is broken. Only the right nostril and the straight bridge remain. And hammered deeply into the creamy marble skin of her forehead, right in the center where the spirit eye would be, is a large cross. A second smaller cross is etched into the center of her chin. She has been branded in stone.

This bust of Aphrodite is on display at the National Archaeological Museum in Athens. It presents a small yet vivid portrait of the fate of the pagan gods under the new religion that came to dominate the Roman Empire. Statues of all the pagan gods and goddesses, not just the goddess of love, were defaced, beheaded, or toppled. They often had noses, arms, legs and, on statues of males, genitals broken off. This desecration occurred so commonly that, looking at broken ancient statuary today, we cannot discern whether it was devouring time, irascible nature, or some offended early Christian that bears responsibility for the damage. As with Aphrodite, other statues were sometimes branded with the cross. Asklepios survived a long time under Christianity. But eventually, he, too, was toppled and replaced.

The Roman Empire was Christianized during the reign of Constantine between 306–337 CE. Constantine's mother Helena was a Christian who had made the pilgrimage to Jerusalem, returning with a piece of wood reputed to be a fragment of the true cross. Early in his reign, Constantine, though not a Christian, was tolerant of the new faith. Then, in a battle outside Rome that he fought to become sole emperor, he is reported to have had a vision of a flaming cross. He ordered his soldiers to paint crosses on their shields. He believed that the Christian God was fighting on his side.

From this point on, Constantine worked actively to integrate Christianity into Roman life. In 311 he issued the Edict of Milan, which made Christianity equal to all other religions in the Empire. In 325 he called the Council of Nicaea to create a Christian credo regarding Jesus. This statement, now known as the Nicene Creed, unified a previously argumentative and splintered early church. Shortly thereafter, Constantine chose the ancient Greek city of Byzantium as the capital of his Eastern Empire. He adorned it with noble buildings. He erected stronger walls. In 330, the city was ceremonially dedicated to its recreator and renamed Constantinople (now modern Istanbul).

As part of his increasing support of Christian causes and beliefs, Constantine turned against Asklepios as he did against the other pagan gods. Eusebius, an early Christian scholar and bishop of Caesarea, had the emperor's ear and wrote his biography. Eusebius describes Asklepios's enduring popularity during the Constantine era as well as early Christian animosity toward the healing god, who was seen to be competing with Christ for the roles of savior and healer:

> [G]reat was, indeed, the deception of men seemingly wise, with thousands excited over him as if over a savior and

physician who now revealed himself to those sleeping (in the temple) and again healed the diseases of those ailing in body; of the souls, though, he was a downright destroyer, drawing them away from the true Savior and leading into godless imposture those who were susceptible to fraud . . .

Eusebius then describes Constantine's destruction of the Asklepian temple at Aegae in Cilicea:

[T]he emperor, therefore, acting fairly, holding the true Savior a jealous god, commanded that this temple, too, be razed to its foundations. At one nod it was stretched out on the ground—the celebrated marvel of the noble philosophers overthrown by the hand of the soldier—and with it fell the one lurking there, not a demon or a god, but a kind of deceiver of souls, who had practiced his deceit for a very long time . . .

Eusebius regards this action as favorable to God and a manifestation of Christ's power on earth:

[N]ot in the sphere of fables was the righteous action of the Roman emperor which found favor with God. Manifestly through the miraculous power of the Savior Himself the temple there was destroyed to the roots so that not even a trace remained here of the former madness.[1]

The last inscription we have from Epidauros is dated 355 CE. It is dedicated to Asklepios of Aegae, grieving the destruction of his temple and raising a cry of protest against it.[2] The Asklepion at Aegae was destroyed in 331. At the same time, according to the ecclesiastical history written by Sozomenus, Constantine razed the temple of Aphrodite at Aphaca. To Sozomenus, a cleric writing two centuries later, Asklepios was not just a deceiver of souls (though that was evil enough), but a demon who appeared in the night.[3]

135

By the time of Constantine's actions against Asklepios and the other pagan gods, Christians had been attacking Asklepios's divine nature and his healing powers at least since Galen's time a century and a half earlier. Clement of Alexandria was thirty years younger than Galen. At about the time Galen was achieving success as a physician and witnessing the healing power of dreams, Clement wrote, "Aesculapius can do nothing against the affections of the soul." Scornfully, he declared that "birds defecate" on the statues of Aesculapius.[4]

What accounts for the massive shift in attitudes toward the gods during the Christianization of the Roman Empire? How and why was Asklepios transformed from a healer, savior, and "soul of the universe" to a "deceiver of souls" and a demon?

Here, in summary, is what seems to have happened: During the reign of Asklepios as the god of healing, the ancient matriarchy faded and was replaced by the Homeric-era patriarchy, either destroying chthonic gods or resurrecting them as Olympians. The heroic age passed into the classical. Reason awakened and replaced myth as the dominating form and organizer of consciousness. Reason and its servant, science, distanced the personal gods and altered the human relationship to them. Philosophers did not become godless, but rather continued the process of abstracting and distancing the gods until they became first principles and causes. This abstracting and unifying movement created the gateway for the entry of monotheism into the Greek world.

Meanwhile, Greek individuality displayed its dangers. The pride and powers of Athens and Sparta competed against each other, destroying much of the Greek world and its resources even as they created masterpieces of thought and art. Competition triumphed over unification, until Philip of Macedon and his son Alexander defeated the lower Greek city-states and unified the Greek and Near Eastern world under the banner of Hellenism. Alexander had a universalistic vision. He welcomed the deities, mores, and lifestyles of the Eastern world into his kingdom. New gods and goddesses, along with philosophers and merchants, entered his greater Hellenic world.

But unification was short-lived. The death of Alexander awakened competition and greed again, which split the empire between antagonistic rulers. Ongoing competition, conflict, and warfare opened the way for intercession from the huge, restless, and ruthless empire growing in Rome. With Jupiter the emperor god and Mars the savage war god leading the way, Rome became the new conqueror and built an empire that stretched from the western end of Europe all the way to the Middle East. Rome tolerated and even welcomed foreign gods, making them its own, as the Greeks had made some chthonic and Eastern gods into heroes, demigods, or Olympians.

Under the later Roman emperors, foreign gods, laws, lifestyles, and religions were crushed if they resisted their conquerors. When the conquerors were yielded to or welcomed, the invaded cultures were allowed to retain their own gods and laws and to practice self-governance under the greater confederation. Thus, many deities and philosophies found themselves at home, meeting and competing in the Roman world. Romans, Greeks, Jews, Christians, Persians, and Egyptians were found in the agorai of the cities, discussing, debating, arguing, preaching their beliefs.

The diversity and multiplicity of deities and philosophies at once served and undermined Rome. Early Roman religion had been a stiff, formal worship, filled with public ceremonies and duties. It helped shaped the Roman character to the virtues of practicality, worldliness, obedience to authority, discipline, and service to the state. But Roman religion lacked spirit and transcendence. It enabled its citizens to live effectively in this world, but did not teach them of another. It provided solace in that obedient Romans believed the gods were with them and favored them. But it did not lead followers into connection with a spiritual world or answer their questions about eternal matters.

Into this atmosphere came rational philosophies from Greece, mystery religions from Egypt, Persia, Greece, and Asia Minor, and new worldly philosophies such as Stoicism and Epicureanism. All of these fed the hungry Roman soul and enjoyed much influence and following.

In this same atmosphere, early Christianity grew. Aspects of both philosophy and the mystery religions favored the development of Christianity. In particular, Christianity built upon Neoplatonism. It was a relatively small step from the philosophy of the Prime Cause or the Unmoved Mover to a monotheistic belief in One God the Father. Christianity also repeated the motif of the death and rebirth of the semi-divine son found in the worship of Orpheus and Dionysos. It adopted the world-denying aspects of Orphism that declared a separation between world and spirit, with spirit being good and the material world, evil. And it benefited from the popularity of Mithra worship, a Persian import in which a hero god had a miraculous birth, defended the weak, and defeated death.

Christianity promised and provided aspects of solace and belief that its competitors did not. In particular, it promised personal immortality. In place of the earthly communion between gods and humans that mythology offered, Christianity promised an eternal home with the divine. It gave assurance that if humans were obedient, they would be loved personally by God. It offered forgiveness during a time replete with social and moral dilemmas. Rather than tolerating neighbors of different creeds, it encouraged practitioners to gain favor with heaven by weaning others away from their gods and converting them to the Christian one. And it offered a simple path, free of intellectualism and effort. As Paul said to the Korinthians, "Jews demand signs and Greeks seek wisdom."[5] Christianity required only prayer, faith, and surrender. The poor and oppressed found this new faith attractive and flocked to it, slowly at first, then in droves.

During the early years of Christianity, as long as they did not dissent or disturb Rome, the Empire tolerated the small numbers of Christians as they did other religionists. But over time, the numbers of Christians grew and paraded new and highly visible differences from their pagan neighbors. Christians would not worship or swear allegiance to the emperor. They would not swear or make offerings to the Roman gods. They talked of a Kingdom other than Rome to which they were loyal. They criticized aspects of Roman public life and separated themselves more and more from it. These practices amounted to religious resistance to Roman authority. To refuse to worship the gods or emperor? To refuse vows or sacrifices? To Rome, these were political threats.

Thus religious persecutions began. These were brutally conducted during the reigns of Nero, Domitian, and Diocletian. They occurred as well during Trajan's reign, while Rufus practiced Asklepian healing, and during the reign of Marcus Aurelius, while Galen practiced. During these oppressions, many early Christians accepted martyrdom as a holy act, inspiring others to follow a path that led to salvation in the face of suffering. And during these eras, Christianity developed its own intellectual and scholarly branch. Educated men, trained in Greek philosophy, created Christian doctrine refuting the teachings that had grown in the pagan cultures. From the educated and the simple, Christianity attacked the old gods and their ways.

From chthonic to heroic to Olympian to classical to Roman— Asklepios had survived all of these. For a millennium and a half, features of the Asklepian myth and identity had evolved with the times, as aspects of the changing culture were incorporated into his practice and worship. His healing practices moved from the mountains to the cities, from dark caves to light-drenched temples and sanctuaries. But he always remained the gentle god, the compassionate healer. Finally, Aesculapius was the popular and effective incarnation of the god in the Roman world. He was regarded as both healer and savior. He tended and protected both emperor and slave. But with the growth of Christianity, he met an adversary he could not overcome.

First, Christianity challenged the reigning conception of the material world and the soul's relationship to it. The Greeks had affirmed the beauty and value of this world. Life was lived here, now, and only once. The Greek underworld of Hades was a dreary place, full of the shades of the dead—not souls, but mere wisps who felt no joy and could not remember their earthly lives. By contrast, Christian believers were promised that the afterlife would be a place where the soul would experience eternal bliss, goodness, and satisfaction. Christianity offered a compensation for the difficulties of this life that paganism did not. But Christianity also painted this world as evil in a way that paganism never did.

Further, Christianity introduced beliefs into the culture that had been discarded by the classical enlightenment. Sokrates and Plato had banished the mythological demons of earlier eras. They demonstrated that the demons are within us, and that with self-knowledge, reason, discipline, and practice, the forces of chaos can be mastered. In medicine, Hippokrates humanized disease and its causes, teaching that illness was not punishment by the gods, but rather that imbalances in ourselves brought on illness. Galen and Rufus, centuries later, investigated both scientifically and religiously the contributions of an individual's psychology to the development of diseases and various human and divine means for restoring inner balance. Illness was of the soul. Both reason and the divine could guide us to its causes within and help us to regain equilibrium.

In Christianity's fallen world, however, demonology returned. Without rejecting humoral medicine, illnesses came to be regarded once again as the result of possession by evil spirits, particularly the devil. Thus Tertullian, a younger contemporary of Galen, affirmed that "psychic diseases are born from the corporeal matter" but insisted that "it is the Devil who acts on it and causes melancholy by agitating the black bile." Epilepsy, which Hippokrates had humanized, again became a divine malady. The devil, said Tertullian, "sending the vapours into the brain brings about epilepsy . . . he is the cause of vain images, he incites to hate and to the troubles of the soul."[6]

Christianity profoundly mistrusted the human passions, considering them forces easily tempted and won over by the devil. And it equally mistrusted human reason and discipline to overcome either the passions or the devil. Imbalanced, conflicted, or exaggerated passions were exactly the conditions under which the devil could act. Cassianus wrote:

> With man's assent . . . they cause an evil heart . . . which favors the devil's penetration into the soul . . . the mental disease tells us that the soul has become the devil's instrument . . . he acts on it as a toxic humour . . . as high fever.[7]

To these committed early Christians, the devil was the cause of evil. Evil lodged in the soul as sin and was the soul's disease. Evil sinfulness was the cause of all physical, mental, and spiritual illness. The only possible healing from such a condition was to fill oneself with Christ so that the devil could not penetrate. Or, if one had sinned and the soul was ill, the cure was penitence—being saved by Jesus. Essentially, demonic possession is the medical theory of the New Testament. This view was not prominent in either the Old Testament or in pre-Christian classical writings.[8] Accordingly, the pagan gods were themselves regarded as powerful demons, cunningly disguised as helpers.

This sin-based, demon-ridden medical philosophy defeated the sacred medicine of Asklepios. Observing the popularity of Asklepios in his roles as both savior and healer, the early church relentlessly attacked him and labored to replace his healing activities with their own. Gregory, speaking at the funeral of a physician during the fourth century, praised the man because "he did not need to be taught an oath by Hippokrates." The implication of this remark is that oath-taking in the name of the pagan god was fading away under the church's relentless attacks.[9]

Some healing aspects of Asklepios were demonized. The snake, which had been Asklepios's totem of connection to the earth powers as well as his companion in healing, was rendered evil. Tertullian regarded the snake as representing the corrupt aspects of the demonic body. This same earthbound creature that had been the source of beneficent healing now brought "trouble, anxiety, insomnia, spasms, false diseases."[10]

But the story of what happened to Asklepios in the early days of Christianity is not a simple case of a new faith crushing an old one. Important aspects of Asklepian healing were also incorporated into church healing. Clement declared that the pagan healing waters were dead. But the church used the purifying waters of the baptism font to cleanse people of their sinfulness. To further profit from Asklepios's popularity, up through at least the fourth century, the church used statues of the compassionate healing god, often centuries old, to represent Jesus.[11]

And while the church called Asklepios a demon, it still affirmed the healing powers of dreams. To utilize the dream's power to reveal and heal while simultaneously replacing Asklepian practice with its own, the church instituted dream incubation, often practiced in the chapels of various saints and martyrs.[12] One instance was the cult of St. Thecla. Thecla was a converted follower of St. Paul. She became the patron saint of her own incubation center. As had Asklepios, Thecla healed through epiphanies by appearing in the dreams of the ill who slept in her church.[13]

Thecla's cult was active in the mid-fifth century in Seleucia on the Turkish coast, not far from earlier incubation centers of Asklepios. Thus, sometimes, the church appropriated space that had been sacred to the pagan god and used it for similar purposes under the guidance of its own officers. In Rome, too, after Asklepios's temple on the Tiber island was gone, Christian monks built a monastery on the same site. Their particular ministry, of course, was nursing the sick.[14]

While Christianity adapted the techniques of using healing waters, dream incubations, and statues of the healing god to draw people away from Asklepios and toward Christ, it made a further declaration. As we have seen, physicians practicing at Asklepian centers had taught that prayer could be a beneficial adjunct to human, scientific healing methods. Now, however, to further denigrate the authority of both the scientific and religious branches of Asklepian medicine, some early church leaders declared that prayer itself could be sufficient to heal diseases—as long, of course, as the prayer was directed to Christ. According to Edelstein, this belief was a new development. Before Christian times, prayer alone had not been regarded as sufficient to heal.[15]

The church's war against Asklepios took centuries to complete. Asklepios was a most popular god in the Roman Empire. His popularity did not fade as easily as that of other pagan gods. The Emperor Julian, Constantine's nephew, resisted Christianity and gave Asklepios's followers hope, showing particular preference for the compassionate god,[16] drawing parallels between Christ and Asklepios,[17] and stressing that Asklepios encouraged care of both body and psyche.[18] While the worship of Christ gained in popularity with the masses, educated people, including poets, philosophers, and other intellectuals, continued to worship Asklepios, practice his ways, and compose poems and prayers to him.

One late story is told of the Platonic philosopher Proclus, who lived in Athens in the late fifth century CE. His neighbor's daughter, an only child, became very ill. Physicians were unable to cure her, and it seemed as though she would die. The father begged Proclus, known to be wise and pious, to pray for her. Proclus, who lived next door to the Asklepion, climbed to the sanctuary. Even though the Parthenon above was damaged, "the city still enjoyed the god's presence . . . and still held the temple of the savior unravaged." Proclus prayed "in the more ancient fashion." Immediately the girl's condition altered, her pain disappeared, and she regained her health.[19]

Asklepios appears to have had active temples into the sixth century, when paganism was finally eradicated from the Roman Empire. But he could not resist the Christian tide forever. Thus, almost two millennia after Asklepios first emerged from the mountains and caves of Trikka, his temples were torn down. Their pillars were used to build churches. His gentle-faced statues were pronounced to be images of Christ. His healing ways were either transformed into another ritual, performed under the guise of Christian saints and practices, or abandoned completely.

Shall we say that his healing waters finally dried up under the relentless heat of the Christian attack? Rather, it seems that one god image was destroyed, to be replaced by another, more acceptable to the dominant religious powers. The same power continued to heal, the health-giving waters continued to flow, but under a different name, with different imagery and sponsorship. The healer and savior put on a different mask, but the Asklepian healing tradition continued unabated. As Meier declared:

> Asklepios finally developed into a "Christian deity or saint"
> . . . revealed by the almost word-for-word similarity between the accounts of miraculous cures at Asklepian sanctuaries and those at Christian healing shrines during the Middle Ages and in the legends of the saints.[20]

In the inexplicable ambivalence of mythology, we come to yet another interpretation of the myth of Asklepios. With the hindsight of history, this story amounts almost to a prophecy. As we know, Asklepios raised a man from the dead and was then slain with a thunderbolt thrown by Zeus. Zeus is the mountain and sky god and father of all. He is the pagan equivalent of Jehovah, the mountain and sky god from the Middle East who evolved into the One God of Judeo-Christian monotheism. The pagan world did not believe in the corporeal defeat of death. It was not fitting for Asklepios to raise the dead. But as the pagan worldview transformed into the Christian, it would be the Father God Jehovah's half-human Son who would ascend to heaven and become God, just as his healing predecessor Asklepios had done. In the pagan myth, the sky father slew his grandson to protect the cosmic order, then allowed his resurrection as an Olympian to heal and serve the people. In the Christian myth, the Father allowed the Son to be slain by the people, then resurrected him in order that he might heal and serve.

144

The Greek world that had shimmered with passion and beauty was rendered corrupt and fallen. Triumph over death and this sinful world was reserved for the Christian Savior Son. The gentle and compassionate Asklepios, who did not rescue us from the world but restored us to our proper balance with it, was slain "by the hand of the soldier" and the thunderbolt of the Lord. The Lord's Christian Son may have taken the place of the pagan healer and savior, but his healing mysteries lived on.

luminous - full of or shedding light
- aka numinous

⊕ lumen / lumin - : light

movens - moving spirit or religious
emotion: mysterious or
awe-inspiring.

Rudolf Otto "explains numbers as a
non-rational / non-sensory
experience or feeling

# PART FOUR

# ASKLEPIAN HEALING TODAY

*Just about the majority of people get their knowledge of God through dreams.*

*—Tertullian*

*I am not interested in curing neurosis. My interest is in the numinous and I have to lead my patients to an experience of the numinous. (If you can have this experience you are freed from the curse of the illness.*

*—Carl Jung*

How does Carl Jung lead his
patients to the experience of the
numinous

Korinth: Couch for symposium or dream incubation

## Chapter Fifteen

# A Saint in the Mountains

## Krete, 2000

I t is early in the year 2000, fifteen hundred years since the destruction of the Asklepian tradition. I am leading a group of modern pilgrims to Krete. We have come to seek wisdom and inspiration from ancient sources as we celebrate the beginning of a new millennium. Some of us are psychological healers; others are seeking healing for themselves. We plan to visit the small and remote Asklepion of Lebena, its ruins tucked into the rough mountains along the southern coast of Krete.

As a base for our visit to Lebena and other sites on Krete's southern coast, we stay in a central mountain village about an hour north of the Asklepion by way of snaking mountain roads. From this spot, we hike on craggy trails to contemplate Minoan, classical, and Roman-era ruin sites. We visit several local churches and monasteries, some abandoned, some still active, that dot the windswept slopes. One small monastery, originally built around 1000 CE, is nestled in a deep gulch between rocky peaks. Some score of years before, the site had fallen into ruins. The stone church had crumbled, weeds and wildflowers sprouting through its walls to garland the rotting icons. The place had become a garbage dump and a refuge for wild goats.

However, today the site is in the process of being restored. An elderly, gray-haired woman greets us at the monastery's gateway. She is hunched and shrunken, missing a few teeth. Dressed in traditional black from head to toe, she is one of two women tending the sanctuary and its two resident Greek Orthodox priests. She serves us Greek coffee in cracked demitasse cups and chatters to us about the decades of work done by a small but dedicated group to reclaim the church from the goats and the winds.

We meet the priest. He is a large, middle-aged man with a full salt-and-pepper beard. His black cassock is faded and soiled, but his eyes are very dark and clear. They sparkle with a mysterious, enticing luster. This tiny monastery is dedicated to St. Nicholas. We have come here because one of our group, Jungian analyst and anthropologist Louise Mahdi, is researching the folk traditions behind the popular myth of St. Nicholas, the precursor of the modern Santa Claus.

The priest tells us in Greek that, shortly after his ordination, "I devoted myself to St. Nicholas because I saw so many miracles." As a young priest in the middle of the twentieth century, this man believed that cures sent by God were among the most urgent needs of the modern world. When he came to this church, he began the painstaking work of resetting its tumbled stones one by one. He picked up garbage, swept, weeded, planted, hammered, scraped, and painted. And he prayed. Soon local villagers and mountain peasants began attending services at the monastery.

Some came with special concerns. One local family, the priest tells us, had a young daughter with severe epilepsy. By age six, the girl was afflicted with seizures so severe that her family was terrified. In despair, the parents brought the girl to the priest and asked for his help. At his direction, on one particular evening, the parents laid their daughter under an olive tree that grew in the courtyard of the church and spent the night praying with the priest before an icon of St. Nicholas, while the daughter slept safely under the tree.

When dawn broke, the three went out into the small courtyard and found the girl sitting up and wearing a radiant smile. She told them that during the night an old bearded man had walked up to her, touched her head, and told her, "You are healed."

This child is now a grown woman. She has not had a seizure in twenty years.

The priest told us a similar story about a five-year-old boy from a nearby village who had edema and an undiagnosed blood disease. His parents had taken him to Athens to consult with medical specialists. The doctors told them that the boy's case was hopeless. "Take him home to die," they were told.

Instead, the parents brought the boy to this priest. He told them, "Stop all medications, and rely on your faith." On Good Friday, the parents laid the boy beneath the icon of St. Nicholas. The priest anointed the boy's wrists, hands, elbows, shoulders, knees, and several spots on his head. Then the priest and the parents prayed.

Six days later, the boy's edema began to shrink and fade. Now, a quarter-century later, the boy is a healthy, married official of a nearby town. He has never had a recurrence of his childhood disease.[1]

This priest is named Father Chariton, which means "Man of Joy." As he tells us this story and many others, his eyes radiate composure and confidence. He claims to know hundreds of such healing stories, many of which he witnessed personally or directed. He will not, however, tell us the story of the first such healing. "That must remain between me and God," he says.

I ask his opinion of the ancient Asklepian healings and their similarities to these miracle healings of St. Nicholas. At first he refers to the Hippokratic and pharmacological traditions, insisting that "the Asklepiads were only practical and rational." I mention cures through dreams, visions, and anointings that are similar to his and are recorded in Asklepian testimonies. Then he whispers with deep conviction, "It must happen all the time. God is everywhere."

No other priests I interviewed in this part of Krete would admit to presiding over miracle cures. Some quoted to me the church dogma that there could be no healing before Christian times because the pagan gods were false, even demonic. Healing and salvation, they declared, only entered the world with Jesus. Though he is quiet about it, Father Chariton's view goes far beyond that of most traditional Orthodox priests. In these remote Kretan mountains, near an archaic sanctuary of healing, Father Chariton is a Christian priest practicing in the tradition of Asklepios.

The stories Father Chariton told us demonstrate one contemporary form in which Asklepian practices still provide active and vital potentials for modern healing. Let us examine Father Chariton's healing ministry to see how it replicates the basic pattern and traits of the Asklepian medicine of antiquity.

This priest has devoted himself to a particular image of the divine as it manifests in a particular location. He feels a special calling or attraction to this image and its site. He believes our world is in urgent need of this image.

Moreover, Father Chariton is committed to a practice of religious medicine utilizing the power of his god image. He responded to a calling and then discovered his healing powers through experience. Now he mediates cures through his god image in his particular sanctuary. Over the years, he has become a familiar of this god image, such that, in some sense, it responds when he practices rituals in its name.

Father Chariton has labored for decades to rebuild and beautify his chosen sanctuary against the ravages of time and changing custom. He uses his sanctuary not just for the usual Christian devotions, but also for healing ceremonies conducted during the night while his patients lie in his version of an abaton—outside on the earth or in his candlelit church on an altar under an icon.

Like the Asklepian healers of antiquity, this priest differentiates between sacred and secular medicine. He supports the members of his community consulting scientific physicians. He does not tell them to reject modern medicine or its remedies except when medications and other treatments have proven ineffective, and hopelessness is the official prognosis. Only when the limits of secular medicine have been reached, does he advise people to "rely on faith" and attempt a cure by way of religious medicine. Though he is not a psychological healer himself, I surmised that Father Chariton also utilizes religious healing when there is a significant psychosomatic component to an illness.

Father Chariton's practice affirms what scholars of the healing traditions have noted. In Meier's words:

> [T]he incubation motif is eternal and ubiquitous . . . parallels to the healing miracles of Asklepios may be seen in the miraculous cures of the Church right down to the present day . . .[2]

Father Chariton would dispute that Asklepios is the source of his healing power. But he would agree with Galen and other priest-physicians in the Asklepian tradition that God is the ultimate doctor and that his patients "are being treated by the god."

## Chapter Sixteen

# MODERN DREAM HEALING

Most of us do not live in remote mountains, nor are we immersed in a culture of folk belief. How, we might well ask, are dream healing and religious medicine relevant to our lives in a modern urban and technological civilization?

To begin, we know that great numbers of people who are dissatisfied with scientific medicine are turning toward holistic healing practices. An article in the *Journal of the American Medical Association* reported in 1998 that "Americans made 425 million visits to alternative health care providers in 1990, a figure that exceeded the number of visits to allopathic primary care physicians during the same period." In 1993, the article continued, "34% of adults in the United States used at least one unconventional form of health care." In 1994, "more than 60% of physicians recommended alternative therapies to their patients at least once," and 47% of patients reported using them.[1]

Clearly, people are searching for alternatives to the standard medical model. These people are not seeking more technology, more medications, more specialization, more distance and detachment on the part of the health professionals. Rather, they are looking for something that is missing from contemporary mainstream medical practice.

We can begin to understand this trend by recognizing that many modern illnesses are caused and prolonged by stress or are in other ways psychosomatic. Both health care practitioners and patients are altering their behavior in reaction to this connection. For instance, after decades of successful practice, one cardiologist I know returned to medical school to become a psychiatrist. He told me, "I realized that only ten percent of my patients had any physiological heart disease, while ninety percent of all the heart complaints I treated were emotionally or psychologically based. I had to change my specialty to the mind in order to treat illnesses of the heart effectively."

Similarly, a combat veteran patient I was treating had entered psychotherapy for his psychological and physical complaints only after conventional medicine failed him. He told me, "My hospital treatment only offered me pain management by telling me to avoid discussing my combat experiences and giving me medication that numbed my symptoms. But managing pain and disguising my symptoms is what made me ill in the first place. I need healers to take me into my pain, not to manage or suppress it." These anecdotal reports are supported by research documenting that people reporting health problems with high psychosomatic components, especially anxiety, back problems, and chronic pain, are more likely to use alternative medicine.[2]

Scientific medicine has an array of medical weaponry created specifically to repress or alleviate the uncomfortable symptoms of our psychosomatic illnesses. However, it lacks successful strategies for treating the causes of stress-induced or other psychophysical complaints. Though we are bombarded with simple advice such as Hippokrates might have given—meditate, exercise, eat well, practice moderation, "smell the flowers"—little progress has been made in supporting our efforts to transform the modern lifestyle so as to reduce the incidence and severity of psychophysical ailments.

Perhaps medicine has failed because modern culture and modern medicine are experiencing the same spiritual crisis. As early as Hippokrates, medicine divorced itself from philosophy and religion, dedicating itself purely to the alleviation of suffering as a good in

156

itself. Questions of meaning, purpose, destiny, and mortality, and of our connection to self, community, nature, and cosmos, were left to spiritual specialists.

In this atmosphere, the traditions and practices of sacred medicine are of utmost relevance. Modern medical theory and practice, complicated and effective as it is in some particulars, occurs within a set of simple premises. These premises are as much expressions of the modern mindset as sacred medicine was expressive of its times. As summarized by physician and medical scholar Robert Wickiewicz, "the modern technological model" of medicine is

> firmly tied up with trends of modernity, particularly Cartesian dualism with a mind/body split and with the body considered a machine. Spiritual concerns, emotions, hopes and plans are all considered mind-stuff and irrelevant to treating disorders of the body-machine. Although individual physicians often deal with and appreciate psychosomatic conditions, these are peripheral to the ruling paradigm.

Wickiewicz stretches beyond the medical paradigm to expose the philosophical assumptions of contemporary practice:

> Francis Bacon taught that trying to figure out metaphysical riddles or discern the mind of God were vain pursuits and that the focus of the quest for knowledge should be "to relieve the human condition." This has been medicine's mission statement and herein lies the spiritual dilemma of modern medicine.[3]

Thus, though modern medicine with its studies and machines and medications focuses its considerable power on our suffering human condition, it does not struggle with questions of meaning. It does not try to unravel the slippery body/mind equation, because doing so necessitates spending a great deal of time with a single patient. This neglect continues even though people are attracted to alternative therapies "because they find in them an acknowledgment of the importance of treating illness within the larger context of spirituality and life meaning."[4] Instead, modern medicine stays within its comfort zone, striving primarily to preserve our physical life. It does not concern itself with meaning beyond the maintenance, repair, and restoration of the body as machine, the relief from pain and physical suffering, and the protection of the community against threats to public health.

Modern medicine is effective and convincing within these parameters and according to the present secular, utilitarian, economic, and mechanistic worldview.[5] Its ultimate philosophical goals seem to be the control of fate and the defeat of death. It tries to control fate by minimizing damage to the body so that patients can return to their conventional functioning as soon as possible. It tries to defeat death by prolonging life under all conditions, regardless of its quality.

Sacred medicine as modeled by the Asklepian tradition comes out of a very different mindset. It is rooted in a soul-based worldview in which human consciousness experienced itself as part of an all-encompassing cosmic order. There is no such thing as a mind/body split in sacred medicine. Mind and body are coequal, fully interdependent, and inter-expressive. The body is not a machine, but rather is the living carrier and container of soul on its journey through the world. The body is the material text of soul, the living matter on which soul inscribes its conditions as signs and symptoms. "Spiritual concerns, emotions, hopes and plans"—all the "mind-stuff"—are essential rather than peripheral to sacred medicine, because these functions are expressive of soul. There are, to be sure, disorders in the biological sphere, such as those caused by trauma, accident, and infection. Whereas ancient medicine was limited in its ability to respond to these conditions, modern scientific medicine is highly successful and has contributed enormously to the alleviation of suffering from them. But modern medicine is inherently incapable of recognizing or responding adequately to the concerns of a soul-centered worldview.

Moreover, medical experts recognize that all human afflictions have significant psychosomatic components. Many illnesses have their origins in the psyche. Others become fully developed over time, after the psyche has attempted without success to express its emotions, needs, imbalances, and disturbances through the body. Thus, psychosomatic conditions are central, not peripheral, to the repair and healing of the unified mind/body system.

As Hippokrates, Rufus, and Galen all taught, it is utterly necessary to include the whole person in the treatment of an illness or disorder. Healing, they believed, must strive to discern the metaphysical or symbolic riddle that each person's illness represents and to investigate the ways in which the individual's body/mind system has become imbalanced or misaligned in its inner logic and orderliness, its reflection of the cosmic order, or its connection to ultimate matters such as destiny, fate, meaning, community, and cosmos. When we treat bodies as machines to be repaired, when we ignore the complex psychospiritual lives that shape our health, when we attempt to make our aches and pains, signs and symptoms, disappear quickly through a medication "zap" rather than by listening to what they tell us of our complex inner condition of soul, we betray our uniqueness and our human dignity.

Sacred medicine understands that the needs and concerns of the soul are written into the operations of the flesh. It knows how to respond so that soul is heard, engaged, activated, restored. And it knows its human limits and when and how to engage transpersonal help.

Studying and practicing the principles of sacred medicine as modeled by Asklepios can give us a chance to recreate medicine so that it honors all that we are. Asklepian medicine in its full flowering during antiquity, or in its remnants in folk and religious cultures, is a sophisticated art and science that combines reason, faith, and experience. This combination can bring to birth more wisdom about the body and its connection with mind than we have yet achieved. And it can restore soul to its place of central importance in the healing process, thus attracting people back to medicine as a discipline in which they can believe and resolving health care's spiritual crisis.

But why should we modern people give any credence to the study of techniques attributed to an archaic pagan god? What dare we say about Asklepios as a living reality?

I am often asked if I believe in gods and goddesses, spirits and ancestors and their totem animals. Particularly, I am asked if I believe in Asklepios.

My favorite answer is, "It doesn't matter."

There are several reasons to say that "believing" in these old spiritual entities doesn't matter. The first is simple. It is exemplified by a story told by Joseph Campbell. Campbell was challenged by a Catholic priest for abandoning his religion of origin to study the powers in mythology.

"What happened to your faith?" the priest asked Campbell.

"Father," he answered, "I don't need faith. I have experience."[6]

Firsthand experience of transpersonal powers and events transcends questions of faith and belief. Through experience, we witness and we know. We have thus far heard much witness to ancient dream healings, enough to convince scientists like Rufus and Galen of the empirical effectiveness of the technique. We have visited with Father Chariton to witness modern healings he has conducted in his mountain sanctuary. Contemporary people who have had some kind of mystical or transpersonal experience are far more likely to be dissatisfied with traditional medicine and to seek alternative healing.[7] As I detail in the following chapters, I have witnessed and participated in a number of dream healings. Thus whether I "believe" in Asklepios or not, I have experienced the healing power of the god, just as did the physician-healers of antiquity.

The second reason belief doesn't matter is based on our psychological and spiritual makeup. Arguments about whether the gods are actually "out there" or whether they're projections of what goes on inside our heads are beside the point. The guidance and healing the gods provide are equally effective whether we attribute these

160

effects to universal or psychological potencies. The ancients taught that the gods do not ask much from us; just that we remember them. In modern terms, what is essential is that we study them, honor them, surrender to them in some form, and activate them in our imaginations so that they become living realities. We must come to feel, as one novelist writing on the Greek experience put it, that "A dream with a goddess [or god] in it is more real than a day without one."[8] We do not have to abandon our loyalties either to our mono-theistic religions of origin or to modern psychological thinking in order to awaken the gods in our lives, in order to enter the arena of living myth.

It is hard for us to maintain a relationship with the One God at all times. The gods bring God closer; they make God more personal and accessible. Every god image—including Christian saints, Eastern deities, and Greek mythological figures—is a specifically limited, directed, and purposeful aspect of God. Every god is a living set of images and patterns of energy and story—what Jungians call *archetypes*. When we admit the gods into our lives, we gain a powerful way to have a personal relationship with a particular aspect of the One.

We met Proclus as a late Greek philosopher living near the Athens Asklepion and praying in the old way, even as Christianity destroyed the old gods around him. He tells us succinctly the aspect of the One that Asklepios brings to us. In Proclus's words, Asklepios is that aspect of divinity "who causes everything to act according to nature ... who keeps the universe from falling sick or growing old, and the elements from relaxing their indestructible bonds."[9]

It is critical that we do not say that Asklepios "represents" or "symbolizes" these powers, but rather that he "is" them. Saying so is not idolatry. Rather, as Jungian psychologist James Hillman and Jung before him argued, in order for us to restore vitality to psychological life, to reclaim and heal our souls, we must not only *think*, but *experience* as well. In order to experience transpersonal energy, we must personify and imagine,[10] for we can only experience God through personification.[11] As Stephen Larsen explains, "a human affliction can be mythologized, brought to the realm of the gods. And the answer of the healing god can be humanized, rendered into a form relevant to the sufferer's personal predicament."[12] We do not worship Asklepios as a replacement or a substitute for the One. Rather, in our search for healing, we focus on Asklepios as a particular imaginal form through which the healing aspect of God came to the ancients and can come to us. We honor him as that aspect of divinity that causes things to act according to nature, that keeps the universe from sickness, and that holds the elements bonded in their spectacular and sustaining order.

How do images of Asklepios heal? Psychologically, we are all made of images. Imagination is a primary psychic function. According to Hillman, "the psyche's basic structure" is "an inscape of personified images."[13] Myths and dreams engender, dramatize, and organize the stories and patterns that constitute our psychic activity of imaging. In order to heal, we must have direct experience that radically alters the images in consciousness so as to change the flow of energy to body and soul evoked and directed by that imagery. Other mental functions, including thinking, conceptualizing, abstracting, even interpreting, give us control over and detachment from our flow of images and stories. But they also remove us from direct experience. Concepts can help us guide our lives; they can instruct, but they do not heal. Approaching Asklepios as an abstract concept, as a symbol or representative, is merely an intellectual exercise. Rather, as Hillman explains,

> healing required in ancient times being touched by the God in person, or in his snake or dog form. The cure was the god's presence in person, and healing did not require translation of images into concepts, dog into "instinct"....Asklepios and his healing appear simultaneously; the God is not a later conceptualization or allegory of the effect.[14]

As we have seen, the imagery, stories, and rituals associated with Asklepios overlapped, competed with, and were eventually taken over by those associated with Christ. When Christianity was young, as Hillman explains, Christ was imagined against the backdrop of Asklepios and several other gods, with whom he was either identified or in competition.[15] Over a period of centuries, the imagination of the culture changed. Christ, rather than Asklepios, became the god image of the healer and savior. After Christianity repressed Asklepios, the imagery of healing experiences came to the afflicted through the personification of Christ. Nonetheless, the healing principles and practices, the images and stories, derived from the same blueprint.

We experience God through a collection of images, stories, and associated feelings and sensations that occur in a particular form and pattern in order to infuse us with a focused dose of universal energy. Asklepios is one name for that aspect of the divine that keeps the universe natural, well, and in order. Through the image of Asklepios—or some other healing archetype, such as Father Chariton's St. Nicholas, or a goddess form, such as Kwan Yin, White Tara, or the Virgin Mary—*It* becomes *Thou.* Through Asklepios, we experience the divine as a living, imaginal being with whom we can relate personally. Once we say "Thou" to this complex we call a god, the deity and his or her associated stories and patterns start to show up in our waking and dreaming lives. We transcend the shackles of the conventional world and its secular, utilitarian imagery. We enter the realm of living myth through which dream healing is possible.

What must we do to evoke and invite a divine healing presence into our dreams?

In the Asklepian tradition, dreams were much more than psychological fantasies; they were miracles and epiphanies. These words, which elicit a "wow" response, refer to specific types of events. *Miracles* are events that seem to defy the laws of nature. *Epiphanies* are appearances by divine figures, personal visits from the gods.

In Asklepian dream healing, as we have seen, preparation and ritual were used to orchestrate a particular type of transpersonal dream experience during which epiphanies and miracles might occur. Through such dream visits, the laws of psychology, culture, and nature that seem to doom us to our prognosis might suddenly be broken or slowly but fundamentally altered.

Asklepian practice outlined the particular methodology through which such epiphanic dreams might be experienced. For example, this fragment from the Pergamum Asklepion of Galen's time leaves out the healing particulars. Instead, the fragment reads like a recipe from which we can extract the essential elements of the dream healing ritual:

> . . . let him enter into . . .
> . . . he will have ten days . . .
> . . . entering, after bathing . . .
> . . . to be set free, let him purify completely . . .
> . . . in a white chiton and with brimstone, and with laurel . . .
> . . . with fillets which let him purify completely . . .
> . . . let him go toward the god . . .
> . . . into the great incubation room, the incubant . . .
> . . . with pure white sacrificial victims garlanded with
> olive shoots . . .
> . . . neither seal-ring nor belt nor . . .
> . . . barefoot . . .[16]

From this ancient fragment, we can discern the elements of the dream healing ritual. We must leave ordinary time and space and enter into a retreat or sanctuary. We must spend some extended time there. We must not rush but rest and separate from everyday reality. We must cleanse and purify.

Seen in modern terms, purification might entail dietary changes, including fasting or restrictions; bathing and other forms of cleansing, such as sweats, saunas, or steam baths; dressing in simple or clean garments; abstaining from various activities, such as sex or reading, and engaging in others, such as walking, meditating, or observing silence; and other actions that free us from the distractions and stimuli of the everyday world. Gestalt psychologist Edward W. L. Smith argues that such complete body/mind practices (which Gestalt therapy seeks to invoke with or without the spiritual dimension) are essentially experiential and catalyze a here-and-now experience "under conditions of heightened awareness." These techniques bring about "concentration and presentification" that, when strong enough, lead to an altered state of consciousness. The effectiveness of the technique "is related to the degree of realness of the subjective experience ... the depth of the altered state of consciousness produced."[17]

The altered state of consciousness engendered by Asklepian purification and preparation rituals changes our body chemistry, disrupts our sense of time and space, and shifts our understanding of who we are and how the universe is organized. This shift allows us to approach the divine powers open, undefended, and vulnerable. In other words, purification entails surrendering our usual ego boundaries. During the ritual, these boundaries will be realigned into a new pattern that better serves our overall health and functioning.

After we have purified, rested, and separated fully from ordinary reality, we enter the abaton, a special place set aside for encounters with the transpersonal. We enter dressed as a supplicant, coming before the highest power barefoot, as God commanded Moses to be before the burning bush. We leave belts—those artificial supports that serve to "hold us together"—and signet rings—signs of our worldly identities—behind. We approach the god naked, stripped of the props of our worldly identities. Thus we enter the sanctuary trusting that the god or Logos, the higher power or greater order, knows who we really are and what we need and can offer us a larger, more complete identity.

Moreover, as in the sacrifice rituals of old, we show ourselves to be ready to experience the death of our old self that carries the disorderly and dysfunctional patterns that have manifested in disease. We offer up our old selves, our old ways of living and being, as sacrifices to the greater powers and show ourselves to be willing to undergo psychospiritual death. Then we sleep in the sanctuary and await the

*Abaton - a special place set aside for encounter with the transpersonal.*

dream in which a divine figure may come and show us how to heal ourselves or unfold our destinies.

I call such structured experiences "radical ritual." Radical ritual is a significant ordeal that breaks our old definitions and strains all aspects of our being. It requires us to enter an altered state of consciousness during which we flood ourselves with images, perceptions, feelings, and sensations that are of such impact and consequence that we are profoundly altered in our body/mind organization.

There are many forms of radical ritual. Vision quests, sweat lodges, spirit dancing, sacred chanting, prolonged meditation, pilgrimages to sacred sites, strenuous or dangerous excursions into the wilderness, or extreme athletic challenges can all constitute radical rituals. To be transformative, all such activities must be framed as purposeful and conscious attempts to evoke transpersonal energies, as attempts at conscious mythmaking. Dedicating such actions to a god image structures the ritual toward a transpersonal climax.

The result of such structured experience is often a vision or dream that includes an epiphany or personal encounter with the god. Such epiphanic events can either provoke immediate and radical changes in the body/mind system or point the way toward such changes. They do so by immersing the supplicant in a set of images and stories that reflect an archetypal pattern known for millennia to promote healing. Through the healing dream, reality can be altered, and we can be remade.

But how is it that dreams can function as conduits for holistic body/mind wisdom or for epiphanies?

 "Only when dreams are very highly valued can they exert great influence," Meier wrote.[18] Our first step is this: we must place much higher value on dreams and visions than the modern world commonly affords them as sources of wisdom and transpersonal energies that can benefit our body/mind system.

Dreams are living experiences of the soul. As such, they must be personified and encountered, rather than merely analyzed or interpreted. Analysis should support and guide dream experience, not substitute for it. When we awaken in the morning, we can benefit by asking ourselves, "What did I do in my dreams last night?" in addition to "What did that dream represent?" This step into greater valuation of our dreams brings us closer to the ancients and to many traditional peoples from around the world who regard the dream "as something that really happened" rather than merely "an imaginary experience."[19]

Considering dreams this way, as living experiences of the soul rather than as symbol systems to be interpreted, takes us far beyond the interpretation of dreams prevalent in the modern era. Freud's *Interpretation of Dreams* was a landmark that resurrected the serious consideration of dreams and set us again to the study of dreams as elaborate symbolic dramas to be interpreted and decoded. It is noteworthy that Freud mentions Asklepios only once in the book, in a footnote citing Asklepian practices to demonstrate that, contrary to the beliefs of Freud's own time, dreams can be both diagnostic and therapeutic.[20] Freud's breakthrough study resurrected the importance of dream work and our interest in it. It also set the standard for conducting dream work in the modern era. However, since Freud, dreams have primarily been symbolic objects of study to analyze and decode.

Following Freud, Jung recognized the transpersonal and collective dimensions of dreams. The analytic and humanistic psychology movements recognized that dreams can be predictive as well as regressive; that is, they can show us images of unrealized potential, as well as images of the repressed unconscious. But eras other than ours have noted far greater activity and potential in dreams than we permit, activity that includes not symbolized but living encounters with transpersonal powers such as occurred in Asklepian healing.

I am suggesting that we allow Asklepios to return to his position as High Priest of Healing Dreams. Asklepios is an archetype, a living god, and a vital set of energies and images that can be encountered in traditional or contemporary form. When Christianity banished him from dreams, it banished a particular form of divine encounter. It forbade the soul from achieving an imaginal psychodynamic enactment through experiential ritual of the presence of this particular power. Whenever a culture banishes a god image, in effect, it censors people from achieving certain kinds of awareness and having certain kinds of experiences.

An Asklepian dream is our soul's experience of an I-Thou encounter with a god, or, if you prefer, with a personified transpersonal image-energy field. Asklepios is the priest–healer personified; he is "the archetypal image of the physician's existence," as Kerényi called him.[21] He is the god who is the attending physician to our revealed souls, to whom we can speak when our conscious minds sleep. He is the god whose eternal job it is to visit us when we sleep in his guestroom so that we might have an imaginal experience of healing. Through the dream, our souls experience a god healing us. After the dream, our encounter is not a matter of faith or belief, but rather of experience. The god or his helpers touched or instructed us. Wisdom and intervention came from transpersonal sources to provide us with healing unavailable through scientific medicine.

I am certainly not the only contemporary healer who uses radical ritual to provoke significant healing shifts in my patients' chronic, resistant, or difficult life or health patterns. Many practitioners today offer vision quests, wilderness excursions, pilgrimages, extreme sports, prayer and meditation circles, and other modern versions of traditional rituals. Nor am I the only practitioner to use Asklepian dream healing. Other modern healers, transpersonal psychologists, and human potential teachers have utilized the Asklepian healing tradition in the consulting room and beyond.

Asklepios returned to the modern world unexpectedly and in a rush during the years immediately following World War II. The Edelsteins' collection and interpretation of Asklepian testimonies was first published in 1945 and significantly restored the study of Asklepios to the scholarly tradition. Carl Kerényi's scholarly and poetic interpretation of the archetype of the divine physician appeared shortly thereafter. Kerényi strove "to go back ... to the ancient world, to the immediately perceived realities of ancient existence."[22] His was an experiential and reconstructive effort. Finally, C. A. Meier examined the Asklepian tradition as the blueprint for the practice of psychotherapy, publishing his findings in book form in 1949. We can hypothesize that this reemergence of the healing god and his tradition in the modern era was an archetypal response—by the cosmos, the collective unconscious, the compassionate and loving powers of divinity?—to the universal pain and suffering of World War II and the Holocaust.

Fittingly, one of the most significant breakthroughs for Asklepian healing in modern clinical practice came through a dream. C. A. Meier, a disciple of Jung during the early years of the development of modern psychotherapy, was searching for the prototypes of psychotherapeutic practice in ancient religion. He reports that his first clue was reading that Galen called himself a "therapeut" of his "fatherly god Asklepios." His second clue was provided by a female patient who, at a critical time in her psychotherapy, had a dream that consisted entirely of the sentence "the best thing he created is Epidauros."[23]

Remember that in ancient practice, one person could sleep in the abaton as a proxy for another. Meier's patient's dream may have been sent not only for her, but for Meier and the entire psychological community as well. The patient's dream launched Meier on a search that led him to write a book on Asklepios, as we are told that Galen was similarly guided to write a book. Meier's work in turn influenced a generation of Jungian analysts, through whose study and practice (a form of incubation) Asklepios was helped to return to the modern world as a significant god image of the healer.

Human potentials teacher Jean Houston has been particularly dedicated to recreating the ritual of the Asklepion in modern times. She and colleague Gay Luce simultaneously experienced the healing power of Asklepios as a rush of unspeakable joy, familiarity, and calling during a joint visit to Epidauros in 1981. Shortly after that event, Houston and Luce created a modern version of communal and ritual dream incubation. Asklepian ritual became a cornerstone of Jean Houston's Mystery School, which has run continuously since 1984 and which has featured an annual Asklepian dream incubation ritual for participants ever since.[24]

Other therapists using myth and archetype report dreams of their patients that are recognizably Asklepian. These may come to dreamers spontaneously, through structured experiences such as guided imagery, or through incubation rituals. In discussing the appearance of inner guides through dreams, Stephen Larsen, who has visited Epidauros, slept in the sanctuary, and conducted Asklepions, reports the dream of one of his patients suffering from cancer and immuno-logical problems:

> I was lying in my own room and my friend said, "here is the doctor." The man was big and tall . . . had a smaller man with him. The big man kneeled down by me and put his hands on my shoulders, the smaller one by my feet. The people turned to black forms. I closed my eyes. I felt waves of healing power moving down my body. I remained lying there but felt myself getting well.[25]

Larsen comments that this dream represents a modern version of the appearance of Asklepios accompanied by his dwarf helper Telesphoros. The sleeper had not known of Asklepios before having the dream. Further, in archaic carvings of Asklepios, the healer is sometimes pictured as standing or sitting behind a reclining patient and laying his hands on the afflicted person's shoulders. Thus Asklepios and his helpers can come to us in our dreams today, even if we have never been exposed to his myth or tradition.

Thus we can see that there are many opportunities for practic-ing dream healing today, and many forms in which the healing god and his imagery and stories can appear. We will look at these possi-bilities in greater depth and detail as we explore specific cases of

Asklepian ritual and healing. For now, we recognize that the return of this god of healing to our contemporary world and his integration into the practice of modern holistic medicine can lead us to both general and specific applications. Later we will consider, in both theory and case studies, the focused practice of dream incubation for specific healing needs. And we will consider the broader psychological, medical, and cultural significance of restoring these practices and their associated roles and rituals.

Dream healing is a specific clinical intervention that works. Put simply, the healing aspects of divinity coalesce as a god, and that god comes to us as our doctor. An experience of this imagery occurs to us in a highly personal yet universal way. The personal that is dream and the universal that is myth[26] combine as one. We become actors in the mythic quest. The imagery we experience may serve as a remedy itself. Or it may deliver a prescription for a remedy for conditions that resist scientific intervention. Or it may offer clues to our soul malady for which we need guidance and interpretation. In any event, as dream students from Galen through Freud have recognized, dreams can be therapeutic; they can heal.

The healing power of Asklepian dreams is fueled in large part by the energy of myth. Myths, we must remember, are not just stories of the past, of magical times or of the folk imaginations of traditional cultures. Nor can myths be reduced to symbol systems that indicate existential realities or explain natural phenomena we cannot yet understand. Rather, myths comprise eternal images and archetypal patterns that are alive in the sense that they unfold symbolically in our lives. Myths are larger than our psychological lives. The ancients taught that when we neglect the gods, they abandon us; when we remember them, they return. In modern terms, myths and archetypes can awaken in and for us when we speak to and seek their powers as living god images and when we intentionally seek to immerse ourselves in their imagery and landscape.

Let us accompany some modern seekers as they travel to ancient Asklepian sites to seek dream healing.

## Chapter Seventeen

# THE SHIP OF DEATH AND LIFE

## GREECE, 1995

We are a dozen modern pilgrims traveling through Greece. Some are here to gather guidance and inspiration from the ancients, to learn more about the deities and their myths so that they might incorporate them into their own lives and work. Some are here to drink in the beauty and bask in the friendliness, food, and Mediterranean warmth. A few seek healing from specific life-threatening or life-diminishing conditions.

Dave, one of the travelers, is a good-natured, upbeat, husky man of about forty, with thinning blond hair and laughing eyes. He is suffering from hemochromatosis, a rare genetic blood disorder that prevents his body from assimilating or releasing iron. He has explained that though most people do not absorb much iron through the gastrointestinal tract, people with hemochromatosis do. The overabundance of iron is deposited in the liver, heart, kidneys, and other organs. Typically, someone with this disorder accumulates significant levels of iron in the liver and eventually dies of cirrhosis. The treatment for this condition is to be bled regularly of iron-rich blood. The body then draws off some of its stored iron as it manufactures more blood. However, bloodletting is only a delaying tactic. At the time of his journey to Greece, Dave's iron count and deposits are chronically high, and he is exhausted from the ordeal of having a pint of blood drawn each week. Dave's life is clearly at risk, and there is no known medical cure for his condition.

Another traveler, Shirley, is a psychotherapist and avid photographer in her early fifties with a thick crop of short gray hair and a warm smile. She has come on this journey without a particular healing agenda. But the night before we leave, Shirley has a significant dream. In the dream, a golden mask is being placed over her face. She knows that if the mask covers her face, she will fuse forever with the rigid sheet of golden metal. She runs and runs to escape this fate. In recounting the dream as we prepare to leave, she speculates that it indicates that she is seeking to rid herself of artifice so that she can birth a more authentic self.

Our first stop is Athens. We wander the winding streets of Plaka, the oldest part of the city. We climb the smooth marble stairs of the Akropolis and stand before Athena's temple. We visit Sokrates' jail cell and read aloud his *Apology*, the words echoing back to us from the dank cave. We walk beneath Hadrian's Arch and visit the towering columns of the temple of Zeus.

From Athens, we travel through dust and sunlight to ancient Korinth. We drink Greek coffee, tea, and lemonade beneath the old tree in the square and chat with villagers. At the ancient site, we explore the agora, marvel at the spot where St. Paul preached, and stroke the broad columns of Apollo's temple. In the museum, we view mosaics and statuary from Greek and Roman times. During our visit to the museum, we notice that Dave has disappeared.

Some of us hike, others taxi up the steep road that leads from the lower ruins to the mountain fortress of Akrokorinth. No one has seen Dave. I hike with several others along the road that winds around the face of the mountain and then snakes through the fortress. At a fork in the path, the group hiking with me takes the path leading toward the summit. The other path leads to castle walls that stand stark sentinels against the blue Aegean sky.

At the summit, a single white marble block in a rectangular

foundation marks the site of the ancient temple of Aphrodite. I take in the circular view of the distant gulf and the rolling countryside patchworked with orchards and villages. Looking back toward the castle walls on the path I did not follow, I see a tiny figure silhouetted against the pastel sky. It is Dave. Standing on the high walls of a crumbling watchtower, he gazes into distances only he can see. Next to him, miniscule against this expanse of land, gulf, and sky, is a black dog.

Later Dave tells us that he left the group while we were in the museum to climb and pray alone. At the base of the steep ascent, a dog appeared from the underbrush. It nuzzled up to him and attached itself to him, following him up the difficult climb and onto the crumbling heights of the castle wall. The dog remained with him during his meditations and then followed him back down the mountain, until he found our group again back in the village. Then, as if Dave no longer needed a guide or companion, the dog walked away. Dave remarks that he feels that the dog is special and that he is sure he is being beckoned by it to approach the god.

We spend the night in the seaside town of Nauplion. As a strong wind whips across the sea and rain slashes against our windows, Dave and I both develop high fevers, as if our bodies are being purged. We take hot baths and spend the next day resting while the others visit nearby Mycenaean sites.

That night, before we leave for Epidauros, Shirley has an unusually vivid dream. She sees a magnificent golden eagle coming toward her from the east, its eyes, beak, wings, and talons sharp and clear. It seems to be a sign of future good fortune. Suddenly a giant black bear rears up in the west. The bear swallows the eagle whole, feathers floating down from its mouth. Shirley wakes horrified, as if the bear has consumed her hope.

When Dave awakens, his fever has passed. The birds are chirping; the church bells ringing. He feels drenched in beauty and splendor. Our group meets, and he reports this dream:

I was with Liz [another traveler]. Liz was in a wedding dress, happy, smiling, and beautiful. There was another man with her. We were preparing for her wedding. I was the minister. I felt happy and sad because I love her . . .

I then saw myself in the sleeping chamber cocoons for healing, and I became possessed. My attendants asked if I needed help and if I was OK. My body was jolting, my voice had deepened, my head even spun around at one point. They fetched Ed, who asked if I was OK. I said, "Yes, of course! Leave me please!"

A heart came towards me. Once it reached me I noticed it was the head of a snake. It swallowed me whole. Once I was in it, it grew venomous fangs yet did not hurt me. It was like a protection rather than a threat, but I was afraid. I had a knife with me. The snake allowed me to cut myself out and be freed if I wished. So I cut open the belly and got out of the snake. Once I realized that I was allowed to get out, I went back in, and the snake healed itself around me.

I started to shrink in size. I was shaking and jolting about within the snake. I was changing physically, on the cellular level. When I was finished, I was birthed by the snake, squeezed out of its belly hole. I was completely different, a new man standing barefoot, young, and handsome.

Dave tells us that he is sure that his dream has come from the god. The group wonders if he has not already achieved his epiphany, but Dave does not feel finished with his incubation because nothing has changed in his medical condition. Since Dave feels himself to be in the midst of a sustained process, we resolve not to disturb it with interpretations.

Shirley has also shared her dream. The group wonders whether Shirley's journey toward the east, symbol of new beginnings, must pass through the west, the direction from which the bear came, and whether the bear indicates a coming time of devouring darkness. Unsure earlier about the spiritual purpose for her journey, Shirley now feels called by her dream to quest further.

A few hours later we are in Epidauros. We sit in the great theater, a few of the group standing center stage to recite or sing to the rest of us sitting in the high tiers. We visit the museum and contemplate the great statue of Asklepios holding his staff, his eyes gazing down on us with compassion. We explore the ruins, imagining together what this sanctuary must have been like when it was full of supplicants seeking healing. Finally, we gather in the bright sunlight at low marble foundation stones deep in the sanctuary grounds. These are the remains of the temple of Asklepios.

Since awakening from their beckoning dreams, Shirley and Dave have been fasting. In turn, each stands and faces our group. Shirley takes off her hat and stands with her back to the entryway of the ancient temple. She offers a prayer for herself, a psychotherapist, on behalf of all healers that we may be true to our calling and faithful in service to the good of others. Then she addresses Asklepios but struggles with her words. A former nun, she finds it difficult to pray to divinity in pagan form. Her rationality rebels—this is all a myth! But, in the end, she requests the gift of healing, calling on the god to be healed herself and to be a conduit of healing for others.

Next Dave stands in the portico of Asklepios's temple. He gives thanks for his snake dream of the previous night and prays for his children, one of whom is handicapped. He prays for the planet and its inhabitants. His face and eyes are radiant, and his gaze is far away, as though he is still in the snake's belly. Finally, he prays for himself, not to be saved from death, but to be visited in any way the god sees fit.

In the late afternoon, we drive through the steep mountains to the village of Galatas, where we will board a small ferry to take us across a narrow strait of azure waters to the tiny island of Poros[1] where we will spend the night. *Poros* means "passage." The island is named for this narrow passageway that separates it from the Peloponnesian mainland. As we churn through the glistening waters, I look at Dave and Shirley, who gaze intently at the harbor village on the opposite shore. In ancient times, Demosthenes had fled to Poros.

Famous for practicing oratory by filling his mouth with marbles, Demosthenes roused Athens to rebel against Macedonian supremacy. He was pursued here, and rather than be taken captive, he committed suicide on the steps of Poseidon's sanctuary atop the island's central plateau. Here Demosthenes made the passage from life to death.

I had visited Poros several times. It seemed an appropriate place to recreate the abaton and to quest for the god's healing. For the abaton, too, is a passageway between worlds—between the mundane and the sacred, the ordinary and the mythic, the living and the eternal. I pray that extraordinary dreams churn through the void between our waking and dreaming selves, between the god and those who seek him.

We arrive at our small quayside hotel named for the sea winds. The balcony of the room we choose to be our sanctuary looks out over the shining waters toward Galatas and the distant mountains. We set out candles and incense. Some volunteer to sit up in shifts in support of the dreamers, like priests and priestesses in attendance through the night. The attendants will meditate, respond if needed, and provide a grounding in ordinary reality for the dream questers.

A blanket of darkness spreads over Poros. Dreamers and supporters gather. Shirley declares that she wishes to be healed from fear. Dave thanks Asklepios for his snake dream and declares that the goal of his search is to be released from fear of the consequences of his illness, whether this be disablement or death. He is careful not to ask for a particular outcome.

The attendants wrap the two dreamers ceremonially in sheets and blankets. As she is being encased, Shirley panics for a moment; then as she later reports, she reminds herself that she is in safe hands and allows herself to relax. Later she says, "that act alone was my first healing." In her account of the night, Shirley tells us that she is concerned, at first, that she will not be able to sleep. She has a headache from fasting that intensifies as she begins to drift off.

A series of dreams begin, quickly. She sees vibrant colors. She reports that she feels herself rise out of herself to watch herself dream her dreams. She sees herself running away from someone. She believes it is her mother, the embodiment of her fear. When one dream ends, she hears a voice say, "Just wait. There will be another." In the next dream, she is still fleeing. Her wrappings are like a shroud, and she cannot flee. She is being carried by an unseen being. She wonders if she is carrying herself.

In the middle of the night, Shirley awakens. Her headache is piercing, and she finds the confinement of her blanket cocoon frustrating and terrifying. Seeing Dave in his wraps, she decides she can endure. As watchers come and go in the night, she feels loved, tended, and soothed. But even in sleep, her headache persists. She wrestles with her resolve to remain in her cocoon. One voice commands her to finish the ritual. Another says that confinement is her source of fear. She panics, dozes. Then she remembers that traditionally, when the dream is finished, the dreamer is released from the abaton chamber. She listens. No voice declares that another dream is coming. She knows her dreams are over. She whispers that she is finished and asks for help. A watcher named John unwraps her and soothes her throbbing head.

As Shirley gazes up into John's gentle eyes, she tells us later, his face changes. She sees her brother Tommy who died years before. Her eyes fill with tears. Tommy's eyes look down on her. His voice wishes her well. She hears the spirit of her brother say, "Live fully."

Dave's experience is quite different. He tells us later that he finds it very difficult to sleep. He, too, struggles in his wrappings. Then he remembers that his quest is about accepting his own death. Though he thinks of himself as a spiritual person, he realizes that when the time comes to leave this life, he will find it hard to let go. As he drifts toward sleep, Dave is flooded with a sense of his unworthiness. "What right do I have to be called here to be healed?" he asks himself.

As the night deepens, Dave surrenders to feeling vulnerable and helpless. He is keenly aware of all of his bodily sensations, as if he can feel every cell. Sharp pains stab through his liver, kidneys, and testicles. These pains are accompanied by surges of energy. From this point, he reports, he does not sleep much. But when he does, he dreams. In one dream, he sees a man named Tom with whom he has been friends from age twelve until about two years ago, when the two had an irreconcilable business dispute. In the dream, Dave and Tom are close friends again. They build a small home together and go on with their friendship as if nothing had ever happened. After the dream, Dave has a hard time sleeping. He spends the rest of the night in discomfort and internal struggle.

Early light filters into the chamber. Supporters arrive for the morning shift. Shirley's friend Marty sits by her head. Shirley feels comforted and dozes into a final vision. She sees the bear that had swallowed the eagle. It opens its mouth and releases the eagle, which flies free again.

After breakfast, the group travels up the long, winding road that climbs to Poros's central plateau. My fever having returned during the night, I am exhausted and so remain in bed while my wife and partner Kate Dahlstedt guides the group. At the highest point on the island, in a setting dotted with wind-bent pines, are the ruins of the sanctuary of the sea god Poseidon. Group members sit on scattered marble columns beneath the fragrant pines and listen as the dreamers share their incubation experiences.

Dave tells the group that he experienced the night as a fierce wrestling match with death—in many ways, a descent into Hades. Unlike the welcoming comfort of his snake dream, he felt himself to be abandoned by God and by Asklepios, haunted instead by the shades of his own expectations and fears. He explains that he has always found it hard to let go of anger, such as his anger at his friend Tom, who had showed up in his dream. In response to a question from Kate, he begins to formulate a tentative connection between the iron molecules that are poisoning his body and the negative feelings and judgments that are poisoning his spirit. In different ways, he realizes, he has been holding on to both.

He expresses the wish to cleanse himself of his tendency to

cling to the pain of the past in a way that prevents him from getting on with life. Everything around us is always changing, he tells us. "But when we cling, we cannot change, either to die or to be reborn." He does not claim to have resolved this struggle, but as he breathes deeply of the pine-scented air, with the bright Greek sun on his face, he is clearly braced up by the new understanding that has come in the night.

Shirley listens closely as Dave tells his story. As she describes her dreams, she tells us that she runs from life because she is fearful. She has surrounded herself with false beliefs—like the mask in her first dream—so that she does not have to live authentically. But now she feels that joy is with her, that there is nothing she must escape and no one else she needs to become. Somehow, her incubation has brought her to herself.

She reaches into her pocket and takes out the Alcoholics Anonymous medallion she received on completing eight years of sobriety. She tells the group about seeing her brother Tommy in John's face. She holds the medallion up so that sunlight glints off its metal surface. This time without hesitation, Shirley offers a prayer of thanksgiving to Asklepios who gave her the gift of her brother's visit, and to Poseidon whose island this is and who is our host. Then she buries her medallion beneath an old column in honor of her brother.

Many of the traditional components of Asklepian healing are evident in Dave and Shirley's experiences. Dave's need—an incurable and life-threatening condition that could not be addressed by scientific medicine—fits the ancient formula perfectly. In Shirley's case, a beckoning dream indicates the themes of her search—a flight from fear and a quest for authenticity. The group's journey to Epidauros fulfills another traditional pattern. Though we did not travel to Asklepios's temple on foot or by donkey, the time, money, and effort expended by each modern pilgrim entailed sacrifice and expressed the depth and sincerity of our intentions.

The dog that accompanies Dave during his visit to Korinth is another ancient element. Dave had left the group because he felt alone in his illness. The dog appears as a companion to let him know that he is not alone and to beckon him further along his path. The dog, of course, is one of Asklepios's known totem animals, a representative of the god in four-legged form.

Both Dave and Shirley are visited by significant dreams during their journeys. The flattened golden mask in Shirley's dream is similar to the hammered gold death-mask of Agamemnon displayed in the Athens archeological museum. This symbol had appeared to Shirley on the night before the group left for Greece, several days before our visit to the Athens museum, as if an image from myth and legend had emerged spontaneously from her unconscious to announce the agenda for her journey.

Shirley's later dream of the eagle and the bear seems at first to have arisen from the symbolism of the Native American medicine wheel, with which Shirley was familiar. The eagle, which stands for awareness and rebirth, is swallowed by the bear, who arrives at dusk to plunge her into the underworld of chaos. In the Greek tradition, however, the eagle is a totem of Zeus, the masculine deity of power and control. The bear belongs to Artemis, the wild feminine principle of nature, maidenhood, and freedom. In the dream, the feminine bear swallows the controlling masculine eagle. In its Greek form, Shirley's dream was telling her to surrender her reason and to give primacy to the instinctual and the feminine. Her final vision, in which the eagle is released, symbolizes a new balance between these two sides of her nature.

Dave's dream work unfolds in three phases. In his first dream, he experiences the divine marriage, Jung's *coniunctio*, a union of opposites, at which he officiates. An ex-brother of the church, Dave reclaims in the dream his role of minister and, at the same time, ministers to the reunion of his alienated inner masculine and feminine principles. This theme appears again in his dream of reuniting with Tom, his alienated best friend. Jung observed that two classes of imagery are inherent in rebirth symbolism: the union of opposites and the descent into the darkness of the cave, the baptismal waters, or the womb.[2] Both kinds of imagery are present in Dave's dream work.

The second phase of Dave's dream shows him actively engaging in his incubation while being attended by traveling companions as his modern priests. A supplicant before the god, he responds with irritation at human intervention and surrenders to the incubation process. It is as if his soul is crying out, "Get out of the way! I'm ready to be alone in the dark and seek the god!"

Finally, Dave is visited by the god in snake form. The head of the snake appears as a heart, as if the god were coming to Dave in love so that he need not fear it. Dave is then devoured. With the snake god's permission, he delivers himself from within its belly by Caesarian section. The god seems to be telling him, "you cannot hurt me, and your rebirth is truly under your control. I need your consent to help you heal." When he realizes he is not trapped, Dave reenters Asklepios's healing snake and feels himself being recreated on a cellular level. Finally, he emerges through a "belly hole," reborn.

Shirley's encounter with her brother's spirit seen in John's face demonstrates the Asklepian principle that a healing epiphany might come through a dream in the abaton or through a vision while awake but *in extremis.* Her brother's spirit gives her blessing and permission to live fully, releasing Shirley from chronic grief and survivor's guilt so that she can embrace her own life.

Dave's abaton experience seems to take him down into the dark, back into the belly of the snake to complete his incubation process. It is as if Dave's soul, because of his fear and his anger at his imperfect, disordered state of health, had refused to inhabit his body fully. Through wrestling with his dread of personal death, Dave finally comes to accept his body, his disease, and his life circumstances. When he agrees to live the life he has been given, the god-power works on him on a cellular level, sending pains and energy surges through his iron-storing organs. This process triggers a healing realization for Dave: that he needs to learn new ways to release the toxins he is holding and to let go physically, emotionally, and spiritually.

Though their stories and needs were quite different, both seekers wrestled with questions of life and death. Each experienced in modern form the key elements of an Asklepian healing:

- a call to relinquish the old self through radical ritual

- a sense of having reached the limits of scientific healing and a desire to seek further healing through nonrational means

- the willingness to sacrifice and surrender

- beckoning dreams that announce that dreamer and cosmos are aligned

- visits from animal representatives of divine powers

- a descent into the underworld where dream work occurs

- the sense of grappling with hidden forces revealed through the descent

- the realignment of the body/mind into a new depth organization

- the rebirth of a new unified, integrated, and aligned self

- immersion in a community that supports the unfolding of radical ritual

It is significant that Shirley and Dave each felt that the death of the old self and the birth of the new were their primary achievements. Whatever the particulars of any individual's healing journey, death and rebirth may be the eternal and exclusive theme of Asklepian healing.

Plutarch[3] once wrote a beautiful letter of consolation to his wife on the occasion of the death of their daughter, which occurred while he was traveling. In speaking of his daughter's life, he counseled his wife "not [to] call a blessing a great affliction because it was short" and "always [to] speak well of Deity." He reminds his wife that they are both initiates of the Mysteries and thus know from experience that the soul is immortal.

Keeping the inner eye fixed on the eternal life of the soul, accepting what fortune sends us, refusing to measure the blessings of our lives against our own wishes, and accepting death—these are the realizations that come to all initiates into the Mysteries. Mircea Eliade teaches that *another*—a totally different person—emerges from the ordeal of initiation.[4] The initiation experience, Meier concurs, signals the birth of a new person, who through participation in the Mysteries has encountered and therefore "knows god."[5]

How did their healing initiations change Shirley and Dave? What new people did they become?

Soon after her return from Greece, Shirley saved her childhood home from sale and destruction and moved into it. She experienced the wounds of her childhood as being healed. She consciously fostered more joyful memories, as Plutarch had advised his wife to do. She added to the original house, creating space just for herself. She left agency work and began a private practice. In all these efforts, she was amazed at her lack of fear and her ability to move forward without resistance. Now she reports experiencing ongoing peace and joy and seeks to live a more deeply and actively spiritual life.

From all signs, Dave experienced a full Asklepian healing. Though his iron levels are still tested regularly, they have never returned to the dangerous peak he experienced prior to his dream questing. Now Dave gives a single pint of blood every three months to monitor his health. Scientific physicians are baffled by the transformation in his condition; such radical improvement is not generally seen in patients with hemochromatosis. It is not that Dave is cured and no longer has the disease. Rather, it appears that Dave has experienced a profound body/mind realignment. His system no longer "holds on" to iron—or to emotional poisons, for that matter. Rather, Dave accepts and works with his disease condition.

As a footnote to Dave's healing, it is interesting to recall that Jung, in his exhaustive study of alchemy, reported that medieval alchemists named iron along with other substances as the *prima materia,* the "primal matter" that is the focus of the alchemist's transformational art. Jung redefined primal matter in psychological terms as that unknown substance upon which we each project our psychic content. According to Jung, the alchemists could not name only one substance as prime matter, because each individual projects differently.[6] The target of any person's projection alters according to his or her need for a particular holistic symbol.

Thus at the deepest level, Dave has altered his relationship to iron as his *prima materia*, his unique life-giving or life-denying substance. In his new integration and wholeness, his body/mind is able to assimilate or expel iron and other poisons so as to maintain a more appropriate state of balance.

After we returned to the States and were continuing our healing work, Dave shared the finale of his dream-vision. After he was swallowed and rebirthed by the snake, Dave told me,

> I was a new man with a ship and a destination. I had my strength back. Healing had been gifted to me. It was then my charge to go and offer the same. My destination was the world, to sail the seas, to bring this wisdom and knowledge to all people.
>
> The ship was large, made to hold many people and provide a sanctuary—a school, a place of worship, and a haven. It was and is a sacred ship yet a practical one. It was durable and big enough to cross the oceans and be thrown about. There were many sacred objects aboard, like Poseidon's scepter. Aphrodite, Athena—all the gods and goddesses were there. Pan played his flute.
>
> The ship held healing sanctuaries, psychotherapy, massage, love, sacred prostitution, the sacred texts of all religions. There were holy men, medicine people, herbalists, and nutritionists. There were many animals aboard, spirit healers and guides. There was regression therapy, dream healing, handicapped ramps, even a plank to go over the edge with life rafts and life jackets. We had wood and stones for sweat lodges. We had sacred blankets to cover the lodge.

Wherever we went we had the capacity to learn from that culture and their holy people and accept them as part of God's way of communicating to us. We understood the new practice and incorporated it into the ship's offerings. All cultures and lands as well as all planets were represented.

There were warriors of all kinds aboard with armor and weapons—not for fighting but for wisdom and knowledge. We honored the dead, the murdered, the slaughtered. We made memorials not to forget, and we added to them as we traveled.

My sacred objects were on board. Among them was a medicine pipe. It gave me its light, guidance, and wisdom. It spoke to me in my heart. Wrapped around the stem was a snake.

The ship had endless rooms to allow for the needs of many. It grew and shrunk as needed. It was as if the ship were alive. It was a way station for all dimensions and all universes.

So much knowledge and wisdom is shared here. Blessed are all those who come. They shall find what they seek!

I listened to Dave's vision in awe. Then I asked, "Have you ever been to Rome or seen a picture of the Asklepion in the Tiber River?" He had not. I took out a picture of the Tiber island Asklepion, carved like a ship of stone, commemorating Asklepios's voyage to Rome to rid it of plague. The sanctuary was a ship meant symbolically to sail the seas and bring healing to all in need. Dave looked at the picture, awestruck. It was the ship of his vision.

D. H. Lawrence once gazed at a small boat recovered from an Egyptian pyramid tomb. He named it "The Ship of Death," for it was meant to carry the soul of the deceased across the great and terrifying void between our world and the world of spirit. Lawrence warned us to be prepared to embrace our many deaths:

And it is time to go, to bid farewell
to one's own self, and find an exit
from the fallen self.

With an affirmation of death's inevitability and a vision of the soul's
rebirth, Lawrence wrote words that could apply equally to any vessel
of soul, in ancient Egypt, as the form of a Roman Asklepion, or in
the dream vision of a modern supplicant:

Build then the ship of death, for you must take
the longest journey, to oblivion.
And die the death, the long and painful death
that lies between the old self and the new.[7]

Indeed, Dave's soul had sailed upon the ship of death and life.

## Chapter Eighteen

# "WHAT DREAM THE GOD HAS SENT"

## PERGAMUM, 1998

On this journey, several among my travelers are seeking healing. Among the group is Zoë, a Greek-American woman in her mid-fifties with short gray hair and a generous nature. Zoë was diagnosed with breast cancer during the year prior to our trip. She had surgery earlier in the year and finished her radiation and chemotherapy just before leaving for Greece. During her cancer treatment, she resumed psychotherapy with me. She has studied the Asklepian tradition and prayed to the Greek gods that are part of her ethnic heritage, seeking clues to the psychospiritual dimensions of her illness.

Zoë is an avid dreamer who often awakens feeling like she has "been through the mill," though she can rarely remember the details of her dreams. However, during her first psychotherapy, long before her diagnosis of breast cancer, Zoë reported this dream:

> I am in a house I lived in when I was younger. I am in bed with my sister's husband John, who is making sexual overtures. He then turns into another John. He looks like both President Bush and my boyfriend of my teenage years. I am startled and fall off the bed. I look under the bed and see a very sick dog. My sister comes charging down the

hallway, angry about John. Two beautiful deer appear, who stop my sister, then bound down the stairs and outside.

Various spiritual traditions and psychological schools teach that dreams can be premonitory. Zoë dreamed the possibilities of love that were before her—illicit as with her brother-in-law, cold and detached as with George Bush, or passionate and satisfying as with her first love. None of these choices seemed possible in her current life. In confusion and despair, she looked under the bed to discover what was going on "beneath the surface" of her love confusion. There, years before she discovered that she had cancer, she saw an image of the canine companion and guide of Asklepios, seriously ill. Her sister, representing conventional morality, was angry with Zoë's search for love. But two deer protected her and showed her a way to escape.

When Zoë was diagnosed with breast cancer in October 1997, her oncologist told her that from the size of the tumor, she may have been growing it for years. She underwent surgery almost immediately. The underworld experiences of her brush with death awakened complex and vivid dreams that she is able to remember in detail. A few weeks after surgery, Zoë dreamed:

> I am in Troy, New York, where I had lived as a child. I walk down Excelsior Ave. An announcer is describing the homes I pass as I walk. Some are Victorian. I come to an open field. A huge bell, like the Liberty Bell, rings out a frightening sound. I am scared to death. Then in front of a Victorian home, a sliding bell comes right at me, scaring me even more. A woman walks up to me and says how strange it is to have bells in our neighborhood. Then my first love John embraces me and holds me tight. I face him and tell him to take care of his health.

As a result of her cancer surgery, frightening alarm bells were ringing for Zoë. She realized that her attitude toward her disease would significantly determine its outcome.

In mid-December, Zoë dreamed:

> I am with my parents, washing dishes like a dutiful daughter. My mother criticizes me for not doing them well enough. I am angry. My father lies quietly on the couch, uninvolved. I grab a dishtowel off the floor near my father. Under the towel is the head of a dead wolf-like dog. I wipe my hands and go to put the towel back on the dog. The dog comes viciously to life, shows its canine teeth, then bites me hard on the leg. I grab the head and forcefully pull it off me. Then I throw it against a door where it smashes open. I command my father to pick up the head and get rid of it.

Zoë tried in conventional ways to attain satisfying love. She tried to "wash her hands" of her problems, then to "replace the towel" to cover them up. But she could not. The canine guide of Asklepios returned, decapitated and vicious. The cancer that had been cowering under the bed in her first dream was now savagely attacking her. Zoë discovered her own anger, ripped the illness from her body, and smashed it.

In January, Zoë dreamed:

> I am holding an infant boy in my arms who has been semi-decapitated. The boy is screaming and crying. I turn to the gods and scream at them for causing this tragedy. I damn them for it, cursing the gods without fear of retribution. Then I find and replace the head and face of the infant, pressing it back onto the remaining face as if it were clay, then remolding and fixing it. The child comes to life and smiles as if to say, "Thank you. You did it."

Again, a psychic wound appeared as a damaged head. This time, Zoë tended and repaired the wounded head and was not attacked by it. She was angry at the gods who sent these disfiguring and life-threatening wounds. But like a creator goddess, Zoë shaped new life out of

191

clay, the primal substance of mortal life. The wounded child came to life and was grateful. The powers over life and death were no longer outside of Zoë but within.

Zoë decided to travel with me to Greece to seek further healing from her cancer. She wants to understand the inner meaning of cancer as a disease of love that she grew and for which she is responsible.

Also with us is Bloom, a tall, sensitive psychology professor and poet approaching age sixty. During the year leading up to our trip, Bloom had been saturated with death. His eighty-five-year-old mother died of Alzheimer's, his sixty-one-year-old brother died of pancreatic cancer, and he discovered the body of a brilliant but troubled undergraduate from his university who had worked closely with his wife and him. She was dead by suicide at age twenty-three. Bloom is looking, in his own words, for "healing from death."

Though his own health is not obviously at risk, Bloom, like Zoë, is saturated in the imagery, feelings, and energy of death. He feels as if he has been in a war zone. Too much loss, too fast, has left him feeling vulnerable and depressed. As his brother lay dying, Bloom received an urgent call to come to the hospital. He and his family took a ferry from their home to his brother's community. He described the crossing: "It was a grim, gray night with a fog-shrouded mist enveloping the ferry and angry, dark foam-crowned waves tossing the boat. I felt I was in the company of Charon crossing the River Styx into Hades." He arrived at the hospital just seven minutes after his brother died.

Bloom helped arrange his brother's funeral and read a poem he composed for the occasion. Afterwards I reminded Bloom, "We living must visit the land of the dead. Your ferry crossing was not your brother's soul leaving forever with Charon. It was you entering the underworld, like Odysseus's descent to visit the shades in the *Odyssey*."[1]

"Yes," Bloom affirmed. "Odysseus first meets the shade of one of his men who asks for a proper burial."

"You have made the crossing with your brother. He must remain in Hades, and you must return to the land of the living. Like the ancients, you have honored him with a poem at his funeral. You have given him a good crossing to the other world."

Nevertheless, Bloom grieved.

Eight months later, his student committed suicide. The young woman did not report for work one morning. Concerned, Bloom went to her apartment, climbed onto her roof, and peered through a window. There on the floor, motionless, with a bag over her head, was the gifted and beautiful young woman Bloom and his wife had befriended in an attempt to help her overcome her abusive past. Her death was like losing a daughter.

"I feel like Job," Bloom cried. "My faith is sorely tested. Death is at my elbow, and each blow is more severe, more tragic."

"My soul screams with yours in rebellion and pain to hear of the loss of one so fine and dear," I told Bloom. I reminded him of the words of Alexis Zorba, the Dionysian character we both love, immortalized by writer Nikos Kazantzakis as *Zorba the Greek*. When a beautiful Kretan village widow is cruelly murdered, Zorba, who has tried to defend the woman, has the following conversation with his friend:

> "Why do the young die? Why does anybody die? Tell me?" Zorba demanded.
> "I don't know."
> "Then what's the use of all your damned books? If they don't tell you that, what the hell do they tell you?"
> "They tell me about the agony of men who can't answer questions like yours."
> "I spit on your books," Zorba answered.[2]

"Yes," Bloom responded. "I may have to spit on their books. But is there a dance like Zorba's to honor life?"

"Yes," I said. "Death is at your elbow. We must look death in the face and learn to love and dance and cry and celebrate anyway—especially because death is there, and this is all we have."

He read me a lament he had composed that expressed anger at the dead student's parents: "My temple was desecrated in life / and now in death."

"How desecrated?" I asked.

"Her parents have cremated her body and plan no funeral."

The ancient Greeks were intimate with this theme. So I invited Bloom to a performance of Euripedes' play *Hecuba*.

Hekabe, the Trojan queen, has lost a husband, grandson, and most of her children during the defeat of Troy by the Greeks. Now, just after the war, Hekabe watches as her daughter Polyxenia is murdered as a sacrifice on the tomb of Achilles:

> O grief! What can I say?
> What are the words for loss?
> O bitterness of age,
> slavery not to be borne,
> unendurable pain!
> To whom can I turn?
> Childless and homeless . . .
> What god in heaven,
> what power below
> will help me now? . . .
> Why should I live? How live in the light
> when its goodness is gone,
> when all I have is grief?[3]

Hekabe then discovers that her last surviving son, Polydorus, who was sent for safety to a friend, has been murdered for the money she had given to support him in refuge, his body tossed into the sea. We watch this great woman sink from nobility into despair, rage, and finally savagery as extreme suffering wracks her:

> O my son, my son,
> now the awful dirge begins,
> the fiend, the fury,

singing, wailing in me now,
shrieking madness! . . .
No, not freedom.
Revenge. Only give me my revenge
and I'll gladly stay a slave for the rest of my life.[4]


After the performance, Bloom declared, "It's all there—betrayal, anger, and revenge. It's eternal. I want to run my student's father over with a truck."

Will Bloom, too, descend into savagery?

"We must break the compulsive repetition of violence," Bloom told me. He quoted Yeats to underscore his conviction. "We must 'cast out remorse' so that 'we are blest by everything.'" Suffering, he told me again and again, is not itself the cause of our anger. Rather, "our grief or our own cravings easily turn to anger, if we are not careful."

"Though she is dead," I told Bloom, "your student will not leave you. She will be your lifelong friend. Your wound and your healing will embrace in pain and love."


Shortly after these events, Zoë, Bloom, and several others embark with me for Greece. Visiting Epidauros, we explore the theater, fountains, dormitories, temples to various deities. Bloom chooses a quiet corner of the sanctuary and perches on an ancient wall under a tree. He closes his eyes, concentrates on his grief and loss, and meditates. A strange vision floods his mind. He sees billowy cloud-like foam that bubbles up until it covers everything. Then cleansing water starts to dissolve the foam. The water flows and spreads until all the foam is washed away. Bloom watches for a long time, feeling that the world and all it contains is being cleansed for him.

Bloom opens his eyes and looks around at the gray stones, the fallen white columns, the green trees, the brilliant blue Greek sky. The entire world is as in his vision—clear and sharp. He feels cleansed and refreshed, as if he has bathed in the ancient fountains of purifying waters that ran for supplicants in every Asklepion.

When he rejoins our group, he learns that the spot where he had this vision is the site of the ancient temple of Asklepios.

We fly to Istanbul, tour the city's wonders, and then travel down the western coast of Turkey. We pass Gallipoli, where the war dead sleep in soil soaked with their suffering. We visit Troy. I stand atop the ruined walls and recite the hero-warrior Hektor's farewell to his beloved wife and child. In Troy's amphitheater, we recite the laments of women wounded by the ravages of war, penned by Homer and Euripedes, as true and moving today as they were more than two millennia ago.

After a few more days' travel, we arrive at Pergamum, the healing center of Galen and Aristides. We spend the first day exploring the bazaar of modern Bergama. Tomorrow is a day I have planned for some time. We will visit the mountaintop ancient city in the morning, the Asklepion in the afternoon, and engage in a dream incubation in our hotel at night. Of the twelve people in the group, only three, Zoë and two other women, express the desire to dream quest. I will join them. Bloom demurs because he doubts he will dream and is afraid of disturbing the others. We plan a schedule that allows the four of us to dream quest in two-hour shifts. Three will sleep at a time, while one stays awake to attend the other questers.

We four are fasting the next day as the group climbs the akropolis. One of the questers, a woman named Lucy, sits with me on the old palace walls at the edge of the cliff. We watch an eagle riding the wind currents that we take as a good omen. Halfway down the mountain, we climb through ruins amidst dandelion, plantain, and wild oregano that perfumes the air with its sweet bite. We are seeking the ancient temple of Demeter. A two-columned propylon is the entrance to the temple, one of the oldest at Pergamum. We descend the grand staircase and sit in front of the long rectangular stone floor surrounded by low walls and column bases. Here the ancient mysteries of Demeter and Persephone were enacted.

Persephone was the daughter of Demeter who was abducted by the death god Hades and brought into his underworld domain. Demeter's grieving caused all growth on earth to cease. To preserve life, Zeus ordered Persephone's return. Since she had eaten a pomegranate seed in Hades, she would spend a third of the year below as Queen of the Underworld, while wintry winds blew on earth. Her return heralded the spring.

At this temple and other sanctuaries to Demeter—most notably, Eleusis—the ancient world practiced complex mystery rituals during which participants reenacted the myth. Initiates experienced a symbolic descent to the land of the dead and a springtime rebirth.

Sitting on the steps of the sanctuary, we retell Persephone's tale, giving it a matriarchal twist. In this version, the daughter of the earth mother is not abducted. Rather, she willingly leaves her possessive mother to descend to Hades as a necessary and chosen initiation into the dark mysteries of womanhood. We eat pomegranate seeds to honor the descent and the search for rebirth, proclaiming our willingness to enter the darkness where spiritual death and rebirth take place.

Later, we visit the Asklepion at the far end of Bergama. We pause near the fountain of healing waters so praised by Aristides, Galen's patient and Asklepios's devotee. Zoë stretches out her hand, cups the bright clear liquid, and bends to sip as though she were bowing to the god. Later Zoë tells me, "I prayed to be rid of this disease that threatens my life. Those waters tasted indescribably sweet and pure. I felt moved to my core, as if I were in a holy place performing an act of particular spiritual power. When I drank, I felt even more curative powers than I do during communion."

We gather in the old temple of Asklepios. Squinting in the sunlight, I retell the myth of Asklepios and describe his ancient practices. I take out a bottle of wine and fill an etched copper goblet bought in Istanbul for this purpose. I pour libations to the god of healing, asking for his blessings and guidance through dreams, visits, or experiences for any seeking him. Each quester takes the cup and says a prayer. Several other travelers who will not quest pour thanksgiving offerings for their journeys as well.

We sit in a circle on the temple floor. Bloom tells of a powerful dream that awakened him the previous night:

> I drive through a street that resembles the white-tiled corridor of a hospital. The driver is an unfamiliar dark figure. Behind us is a faculty colleague riding a motorbike. This faculty member wounded me deeply a few years earlier. I remember saying "he didn't have a soul."
>
> Suddenly, I notice the motorbike slide out of control, sending this professor sprawling across the pavement. I tell the driver to stop so we can help. He says someone behind us will come to the rescue. I scream, "This is a colleague. We've got to stop and help!"
>
> We stop. As I approach the body, I am overwhelmed with powerful feelings of distress. I cry out, "No more death! We need help! Is there a doctor?" Then I notice a vague white form over my colleague's body. I hear the voice of the doctor respond, "He'll be all right. It looks a lot worse than it is."

Bloom told us that he awakened with a jolt. He had been sleeping in a position that aggravated his stiff neck. As he straightened his head, the bones in his neck cracked loudly. Then, as in his vision of water clearing away the foam, all of his pain flowed out of him. He was free of pain, fear, and grief. Moved to his core, he felt lightened, liberated, and blessed. After telling his story, Bloom pours a generous libation to thank Asklepios, the archetypal doctor, for bringing him a healing dream.

Back in town, the four questers find the Turkish bath house. We are served sweet apple tea as we await our turn in the steam room. Wrapped in towels, we lie on the smooth marble slab in the center of a circular room. A Turkish masseur makes the circuit of our group, soaping each of us down and massaging every joint and muscle. Each of us smiles as we listen to our companion's sighs under the strong, skilled hands. As the steam surrounds us, we feel cleansed and purified.

It is growing dark when we return to the hotel. Zoë's room, with three single beds, will be our incubation chamber. We create an altar with personal tokens and light a candle. Zoë, who will be the first watcher, helps wrap each of us in a cocoon of sheets and blankets.

I do not remember dreams from that night of sleep. But my experience while awake and supporting the other dreamers through the long Turkish night, just up the street from Galen's ancient sanctuary, was one of the most profound of my life. I describe it later in the book.

When the morning is full, we awaken, stretch, and wash the sleepiness from our faces. We spread a picnic breakfast of Turkish bread, cheese, figs, dates, and oranges and share our stories of the night.

"I hoped for a dream," Zoë says, "but I've already been having healing dreams during my cancer treatment. Last night, I felt deeply cared for and looked after like a child. I slept peacefully and woke up feeling comforted and bonded to you all in a way that could not have happened without this ceremony."

The next day, we leave Pergamum and visit Ephesus. From there, we cross by ferry to the mountainous Greek island of Chios. On this island, birthplace of Homer, Zoë has a middle of the night attack of severe heart palpitations. We take her to the local hospital. By morning, her heart stabilizes, and she is judged to be out of danger. Throughout this ordeal, she tells us, she feels utterly safe, as she did during the dream incubation ceremony. She is beginning to understand that though she had grown an illness in her breast, her gland of love and mothering, her real malady lies in her heart. If she seeks and receives the love she needs, her heart can be stable, strong, and healthy.

What healing did Asklepios send to the seekers on this journey?

Zoë's healing really began with her first round of psychotherapy, before her cancer. Raised in the Greek Orthodox tradition by immigrant parents, Zoë began studying ancient Greek mythology, history, and philosophy when she started to work with me. These studies helped broaden her Greek identity to include its cultural treasures, which provided her with imagery and stories through which she could express and interpret her soul's journey.

Zoë's dream work reveals how deeply these studies penetrated her consciousness. The sick and decapitated dogs in Zoë's dreams are both symbols of her illness and Asklepios's guides. One is ill; the other wounded unto death and vicious. James Hillman states that what is wounded, sick, or dying appears in dreams in order to lead the dreamer into Hades. Such images do not mean that the dreamer is dying; rather, they guide the dreamer on an underworld descent so that change can take place.[5] In Zoë's personal mythology, the dog of Asklepios has become Cerberus, guardian of the underworld. Just as Zoë needs to pull the biting dog off her leg herself, she needs to find the personal power to take the illness from her body and transform the love that has become vicious into friendship and aid.

In her dreams, Zoë hears voices telling her to meet conventional expectations. Her sister is angry about finding her in bed with her brother-in-law, her mother wants the dishes washed correctly, and a strange woman asks why there are bells in their neighborhood. None of these figures support or understand her personal search for love. Even her father is indifferent. John, her first love, turns up repeatedly as a symbol of idealized love. But a powerful symbol of liberation appears in the form of two deer that block her angry sister's path. In Greek mythology, deer are totems of Artemis, the wild and free spirit of a woman who is independent and close to nature. Zoë must find such a free spirit in herself so that she can courageously "bound out the front door."

In her first post-cancer dream, Zoë is in Troy, at once the city of her childhood and the Troy of myth, to which Paris and Helen have fled in love and lust, provoking the Trojan War. Zoë is on Excelsior Street, again the place of her childhood and a name from myth that stands for the Greek ideals of excellence and victory. Her cancer is the bell ringing a wake up call or rushing at her to shock her into action. The bells may also toll her death knell. But they are also "Liberty Bells" that urge Zoë to proclaim rebellion.

In her final dream, a head wound occurs again, this time to a human infant rather than to a dog. The cancer/wound has become humanized but is still profoundly threatening. In discussing this dream, Zoë reveals that her son had sustained a head injury as an infant, and doctors feared the boy might be brain damaged. Zoë and her husband responded responsibly, and their son recovered fully. Now Zoë's dream reveals that her inner wound is to her head—her values, attitudes, beliefs, and thoughts—as well as to her breast—her capacity for nurturing. Both must be healed. Just as she tended her injured son, so she needs to tend that part of herself that is young, undeveloped, and wounded.

Demeter, the archetype of the earth mother, is a powerful figure to Zoë. Her dream replays part of Demeter's story. Mourning for her abducted daughter, Demeter comes in disguise to Eleusis. She is welcomed and hired as midwife for Demophon, the infant son of King Celeus and his wife Metaneira. The goddess wishes to gift the child in her charge with immortality, so she holds the boy in the fire. She is surprised in the act by a terrified Metaneira. Angry at being interrupted, the goddess throws the boy on the ground and reveals her true identity. Themes and events from this story are enacted in the Eleusinian Mysteries.

In her dream, Zoë is Demeter, the mother goddess responsible for saving the decapitated child. The child is at once her own son and her wounded inner child. In the dream, she takes on the power to mold new life from clay and to nurture all wounded children, including herself. Though she cannot promise her child-self immortality, she can bring the child to life, repair its wound, and acknowledge herself for having done so.

During the incubation ceremony, Zoë did not dream. But she did experience two other aspects of the ritual as profoundly healing.

The first was drinking from Asklepios's fountain in the sanctuary at Pergamum. In this water, Zoë tasted the living presence of the healing god. She felt as though she were taking communion and experienced a moment of intense religious feeling. Zoë's "disease of love" was the ache in her soul to feel blessed and loved. Drinking the god's water, she did so.

Zoë's second important experience during the incubation ritual was her experience of communion with other seekers. In her first dream, she was shown the way to liberation by a pair of Artemis's deer. Zoë yearned for and needed companions. The communal ritual brought a depth of bonding to Zoë, so much so that she experienced being cared for like a child, comforted and accompanied in her illness.

Finally on Chios, returning from Turkey to Greece as Zoë's mother had done decades earlier, Zoë experienced a crisis with her heart. Medical doctors took care of her compassionately and generously. Since the services of Greece's socialized medicine are available even to visitors, Zoë was not charged for the medical services she received. Symbolically, Zoë's ethnic homeland took care of her heart and treated her as one of its own. Zoë left Greece knowing that her illness was a wound of love and that the power of healing dwells in her heart.

Like Dave, Bloom had been working on his healing for months prior to our journey. And like Dave, his epiphanic dream came on the night before our visit to the Asklepion and the incubation ceremony.

Considered in traditional Asklepian terms, we can map Bloom's journey over time. As a poet and psychologist, Bloom knew that the ancient mythological ways offer maps for our souls. He wrote and recited laments for his brother and his student. He honored their souls' crossing, not passively by sitting while another officiated, but actively and consciously through celebrating the dead.

He attended a Greek tragedy that mirrored his own, and his

student's story came back to him. He felt his rage and grief to the utmost. Euripedes' play provided both catharsis and insight. Bloom knew that his student's sacrifice and his own rage was of the ages. He saw it mirrored and could affirm his own wish to murder in revenge.

With this preparation in poetry, ritual, and drama, Bloom left for Greece and Turkey consciously calling for an Asklepian healing.

Healing events arrived unexpectedly. Unaware that he was sitting at Asklepios's temple at Epidauros, Bloom had a vision of foam that clouded and waters that cleansed his soul. At Pergamum, Bloom had an Asklepian dream in which he saw an accident endangering a man he considered an enemy—a man without a soul. In that dream underworld, Bloom could have chosen revenge, letting his enemy die. But from his depths Bloom cried out, "No more death! We need help. Is there a doctor?"

This was the cry of a soul who had seen too much death and destruction and who refused to add to its toll. This was the cry of a soul to the archetypal physician, the healing power of God. This was the cry asking God to tend all mortals tainted with death.

In the dream, Bloom was being driven by a dark figure—Charon or Hades. But when Bloom cried out against death, out of the shadows, a vague white form appeared and a voice offered comfort for the immediate danger and for our eternal condition: "He'll be all right. It looks a lot worse than it is."

In that moment, Bloom knew that he would be all right. The deaths he had experienced would not kill his soul, for death was a part of the eternal cycle. Death, Bloom had been told, looks a lot worse than it is.

The god of healing does not answer each person in the same way. To some, he brings dream epiphanies in which the sleeper encounters the god or his representative. Others see visions or hear voices. Still others feel the emotions and energies associated with the deity.

Most of the ancient testimonies of Asklepian healing refer to incubations. But among them we also discover that the god appeared not only at night in his abaton but during the day, outside of his temple, on the road, and in the homes of his friends.[6] An epiphany through a dream, a vision while awake, a startling encounter in nature, a long and intense dream series, or immersion in the divine presence and in the peace and community available in the sanctuary—all these are tools with which the god practices his healing art on our behalf.

On the evening of our last night in Turkey, we sit in the basement restaurant of an old mill in a small Turkish village. Outside goats bray and cocks bid the sun farewell. Inside, we sit in soft candlelight. We raise our glasses to toast the gifts of Turkey.

Bloom stands up at his place at our dinner table. His tall frame reaches nearly to the low overhead beams. He asks to recite for us. We look up at the professor whose eyes flash with an open and joyous light. He has composed a short poem about his Asklepian dream and its meaning.

> And yet, amidst the pain
> I dream
> an Asklepian story
> of the devil's fall
> and my mercy
> in healing his wounds.
> There, and only there
> in those depths
> of soul
> are the twisted
> bones repaired.

## Chapter Nineteen

# SOKRATES ON KRETE

## LEBENA, 2000

I have already described my visit with Father Chariton, the Greek Orthodox priest devoted to St. Nicholas, who conducts his Asklepian healing ministry in a remote mountain monastery in Krete. But we have come to Krete primarily to visit Lebena, an important southern sanctuary of Asklepios.

The drive toward Lebena is spectacular—pine forests, mountain vistas, scattered villages of white-washed houses and rambling olive orchards. We stop at several important ruin sites, some dating from Krete's glorious Minoan past, others from Roman times. After crossing the mountain range that clasps Krete's southern shoreline, we arrive at Lebena.

Perched on an earthen slope, Lebena was active as a healing center beginning in the third century BCE. Some older buildings pre-date Asklepios by two centuries and were dedicated to Apollo.[1] By the Roman era, Asklepios was identified at this site with Zeus-Serapis and given the epithet *Iatros*, meaning "doctor" or "healer." He was also called *Teitanos* from the Asklepion of Titanes and *Lebenaios* from his power at this sanctuary.[2]

The shrine at Lebena was so popular that all of Krete and many Libyans from across the sea flocked to it. It has a fine small bay where small rock promontories break the surf. One of these outcroppings is said to resemble a lion. We are told by the third-century CE philosopher Philostratus that this lion-shaped rock gave Lebena its name. This creature frozen in the cliffs, he says, was once a lion yoked in harness to Mother Rhea.[3] I remind the group that Asklepian healing goes back to early earth goddess origins. Just as Asklepios's dream incubations once occurred in caves that were the earth's womb, and his daughters were originally identified with the earth mother's breasts, so here his lion totem once pulled the great goddess's chariot.

Climbing near this supine stone lion, we enter the sacred precinct. In this remote place, there is not even a gatekeeper. A villager will arrive at dusk to lock it for the night. Now we have it all to ourselves.

We wander in the bright sunlight among the foundations, walls, and fountains. One member of the group gasps in delight. The rest of us gather quickly to marvel at the remains of a mosaic floor. Carefully arranged colored tiles create the portrait of a galloping white horse. Instead of hindquarters, the creature has a long curved tail like a serpent. It is surrounded on all sides by cresting waves. This horse-serpent seems to be a melding of Poseidon's usual totem, the wild horse, and the snake of Asklepios. The image of this beast galloping through the waves might have been meant to curry the sea god's favor on this rugged coast open to his winds and storms.

Toward the lower end of the sanctuary, arched aqueducts tunnel back into the hillside to channel waters from underground hot springs famous for their curative powers. People seeking healing bathed in these waters in two reservoirs near the shore. These baths were in use from the fourth century BCE until about twenty years ago when, a local man tells me, the waters were rerouted toward another village.

An Asklepian miracle from the first century CE is recorded regarding these wells. Sosus of Gortys and his son Soarchus both served as sacristans at this sanctuary. During each of their tenures, the healing springs failed. Soarchus left an inscription that praises Asklepios for appearing to his father twice—in a dream while his father was asleep and as a sacred snake while he was awake—calling him into the temple. Soarchus declares that he was guided in the same way. Through their dreams and the waking guidance of the holy snakes, father and son were instructed how to refill the springs with running water.[4]

I stare into the aqueduct tunnels, damp from ground water but otherwise empty now. I inhale deeply to smell the tinge of old vapors and wonder how the healing waters might flow again.

In the midst of our wandering, photographing, and contemplating, one of the group members asks to speak with me privately. Jennifer is traveling with her husband Bob, a corporate lawyer. Jennifer tells me that Bob has a rare form of leukemia. She asks if we can do a ceremony for him here.

Before this journey, none of the travelers had made a specific request for healing. Though we are paying attention to our dreams as we travel, I had not planned an incubation ceremony. I know, however, that being in sacred surroundings often spurs people to acknowledge a spiritual need and that asking for divine help is an important early step in the healing process.

According to the testimonies, incubations did occur at this sanctuary. In the second century BCE, when Demandrus from nearby Gortys developed sciatica, Asklepios beckoned him to Lebena. While sleeping, Demandrus dreamed that the god operated on him. He was healed. Phalaris of Lebena, at age fifty, wished to be a father. Asklepios beckoned him to send his wife to incubate in the temple. In the abaton, she saw the god put a cupping instrument on her belly; then she was ordered to leave quickly. Shortly thereafter she became pregnant.[5]

I ask Jennifer whether her husband joins her supplication. She tells me that she asked his permission before speaking with me. Though he is skeptical, they both wish to pray to the healing god and receive whatever benefits might come.

I gather the group in the sanctuary building that is most intact. Three of its stone walls are set into the hillside and crowned with wildflowers. Between them stand two upright marble columns and the bases of several others. I invite Jennifer and Bob to explain their request. They describe their battle against Bob's illness. Jennifer, in tears, says that Bob is fighting for his life and that she lives with the fear of losing him.

Sitting between the columns of Asklepios's temple, I retell the god's myth and history. I invite everyone who wishes to participate to join in calling on the god's healing powers on Bob's behalf. Everyone is willing.

Bob is invited to lie on the ground between the two standing pillars of the temple, with his head pointing toward the sea so that, as the horse mosaic hints, he can receive blessings from both Asklepios and Poseidon. The rest of us sit in a circle around him. I implore Asklepios for the gift of healing. We put our hands on Bob's head, chest, stomach, thighs, hands, and feet. I call on the universe to send its healing powers through us and invite each group member to become a channel for the energy. Bob closes his eyes and relaxes deeply.

Elizabeth, a sensitive red-haired woman in the group, has been particularly interested in visiting this sanctuary because for months prior to our journey, she has experienced intense dreams. Many of these include vivid encounters with animals, especially wolves and birds. Shortly before leaving on the trip, Elizabeth had this dream:

> I am lying in bed and there is a conversation going on between a wolf and an eagle. Then the eagle speaks to me. I roll over and see the eagle lying next to my bedside. He is the size of a person. I look at his head. His feathers are white as snow. Then I look at his black feathers. I wonder why he is lying face down. When I awake, the image is so crisp and clear that I feel it wasn't a dream but that I actually saw the eagle.

Elizabeth told me that she felt that the eagle had appeared to her for some special but unknown purpose. Now in Lebena, Elizabeth's hands are on Bob's stomach. As she touches Bob's belly and prays for his healing, she calls on both the spirit of Asklepios and the spirit of the eagle. She is confident and comfortable. Suddenly her breathing becomes deep and rasping. Her eyes flutter as if she is in dream sleep. She starts to shake. As she tells us later, she feels as if her human mind is leaving so that she might become a vessel for powers beyond the ordinary. Her last thought is concern that others in the group might be frightened by what they are about to see. Then she has no more thoughts.

Elizabeth's hands become rigid. Her fingers twist like talons. Her facial features tighten and scrunch. She looks like she has a beak. She is breathing quickly, snorting. Her talons scratch and claw at Bob's stomach, as if to tear out the hidden illness. Her neck muscles become taut. She lets out a high-pitched eagle's scream. She claws and caws.

Though Bob lies calmly beneath her, a few other travelers are confused. Suddenly, the eagle seems to leave Elizabeth. She is trembling. Her head aches, and her stomach and back hurt. She and Bob cry together. The group gathers around them, offering hugs and support.

Bob stands slowly. He is moved but unsure what to think. Elizabeth feels exhausted and frightened. She is finding it difficult to walk and has to be supported by other group members.

We descend into the village. We sit in a taverna sipping wild herb and honey tea, while Elizabeth naps in the van. The nearby sea rolls and sighs.

Before the journey to Krete, Bob tells me, he has not slept well. He often has disturbing dreams and is tired when he awakens. After the ceremony in the sanctuary, Bob's sleep is flooded with a different kind of dreams. He dreams vividly every night, sometimes three or four times. In the morning, he reports the dreams, and some of us gather to discuss them. Just as Bob was the center of our circle in the healing sanctuary, his dream activity brings us together as a community as we travel.

Soon, a theme and a key to interpreting Bob's dream experiences begins to emerge. Ancient sculpture depicts the philosopher Sokrates gazing outward with a fierce glance, his eyes sharp and clear like an eagle's, his brow furrowed in urgency and contemplation. Bob's dreams seem to be an examination of his personal and professional life as if under the fearless and challenging gaze of the spirit of Sokrates.

On his last day in prison, Sokrates prepared for his execution by discussing the immortality of the soul with his close friends and disciples. During these final conversations, Sokrates reported a dream that he had had all through his life. The message of the dream was that Sokrates should "make music and work at it." Sokrates had always interpreted this dream as encouraging him to go on with his philosophy, "the greatest kind of music." However, in prison in the last month of his life, he decided to follow the dream more literally and began to compose poems.[6]

Sokrates' life was dedicated to a few fundamental principles that he presented to the citizens of Athens during his trial. First, he strove to know and to perfect himself. "[T]alking about virtue and looking into myself and others is the greatest good," he said, adding, "the unexamined life is no life for a man." He also strove to do what was good for his soul and his city and to inspire others to do the same: "I tried to make each of you care more about becoming better and wiser, than about what he can get, and to care more about the state itself than for its possessions." Finally, he strove to fulfill the service that his god asked of him even if it meant sacrificing his life: "When the god has given me a station, as I believe, with orders to spend my life examining myself and others, am I to run away through fear of death or anything else?"[7]

In contrast to these lofty ideals, Bob tells us that he often feels that his corporate law practice is characterized by compromise and manipulation. He sees his task as ensuring that his clients comply adequately with the letter of the law or with interpretations of the letter that will stand up under legal scrutiny. He finds that corporate morality is relative at best. For many of his clients, profits take precedence over laws and regulations, community agendas and responsibilities. Though Bob does what he can to steer corporations toward responsible behavior, he often settles for guiding them toward doing the least harm while conforming to basic standards of legality and fairness. Often Bob feels that he works in a moral quagmire and that doing so is depleting his energy, enthusiasm, and idealism.

How different is this approach from Sokrates' view of the law! When his friend Krito encouraged him to escape prison and save his life, Sokrates answered:

> Suppose, while we were getting ready to clear out, the Laws of the Commonwealth were to come to us and ask this question: "What is this, Sokrates, that you are planning to do? Are you doing what you can to destroy us? How can the state go on at all if legal judgments are to be flouted by private persons?[8]

Sokrates expressed his gratitude to the spirit of Athenian laws, under which he had been raised and which made his life and work possible. He acknowledged his responsibility to uphold these laws even if they were applied wrongly, even if they cost him his life.

Bob's soul seems to be on trial in his dreams. Sometimes he sees himself in negotiations with clients or conducting trials. Sometimes he relives moral dilemmas he actually faced in the court or boardroom, or faces new dilemmas. Sometimes he fights for strict adherence to a law; other times, the laws and its application are twisted out of all recognition. Sometimes he sees himself being chased or in danger, and he must fight or flee for his safety. Other times he sees himself struggling to keep out of prison. Bob's state of mind varies with the contents of his dream work. Sometimes he feels compromised and sad; other times, redeemed and proud.

Every night, it is as if the spirit of Sokrates is questioning, examining, and challenging Bob, as the moral philosopher did so often in his dialogues with the citizens of Athens. "What about this case,

Bob?" a dream might ask. "Or this law? Or this situation? Or the community good versus your client's profits?" Ultimately, Bob feels challenged to ask, "Who was I once? What did I believe? Why did I choose to serve the law? Who have I become? How do I wish to serve?"

Bob has borrowed my traveling volume of Plato's *Dialogues*. Often, he spends the afternoon sitting on his balcony and poring over Sokrates' words while the rest of us hike or visit some village or ancient site. Though he hasn't read philosophy since his undergraduate days three decades earlier, he recalls how much he had loved it and how he had planned to apply its ideals to the search for justice, before the realities of the corporate world distracted him from this noble pursuit.

Throughout this process, Bob talks openly with our group and energetically with Jennifer. She is beginning to accept that she cannot know if he will survive his leukemia. But hearing him give voice to long suppressed moral dilemmas helps her to feel closer to him. Jennifer experiences her husband as more self-aware and expressive. While she still hopes that his leukemia will heal, she sees inner and interpersonal healing occur as we travel. Bob is clearly changing. In connecting to our group in uncharacteristic and nurturing ways, he is coming to know himself and his inner conflicts in a new way.

As for Elizabeth, it takes her a long time to recover from what seems to be a shamanic shapeshifting experience. She feels physically, mentally, and spiritually drained. Yet Elizabeth also feels free to make deep friendships within our group and to bask in the sun and sea, flowers and mountains, villages and people of Greece. As she recovers and integrates her experience, she is also feeding her soul.

One day late in the trip, Bob rejoins our group after spending the afternoon studying Sokrates. His face is relaxed and beaming. He tells us that after having read for a while, he took a nap—his first sleep in years without a bad dream—and awoke at peace and refreshed. He expresses the hope that he has found his way back to inner peace, contentment, and moral harmony. Jennifer smiles to hear it.

Months after Lebena, Bob was still dreaming. He and Jennifer often talked about the dreams and marveled at Bob's new access to his unconscious, his growing powers of self-expression, and his awareness of his moral struggle. These conversations were an aspect of a new and mutually satisfying marital intimacy.

Elizabeth's dreaming quieted for a time after the trip. For months afterwards, she told me, she wished for a simple, cloistered life "in a barren structure with only a bed on the floor and a wise old crone to care for me so I could do nothing but go into a deep sleep." Elizabeth sometimes visualized such scenes as she fell asleep. She imagined her bed as a pool of water in which she floats and stares up at the stars. She told me that often during prayer or meditation, she felt a deep "grief and longing for Spirit. I no longer want to be in this world. I pray for an out-of-body experience where I can fly off with the eagle."

Why the eagle, I wondered? In Greek mythology, the eagle is a messenger and totem of Zeus, the sky god and arbiter of order and justice. Elizabeth was raised Catholic. Zeus is God the Father, the king of heaven who evolved into the One God of the Judeo-Christian tradition. In various North American traditions, which Elizabeth also studied, the eagle—the strongest and highest flying bird—represents the Sacred Mystery, the divine spirit in nature. Thus, through her encounter with the eagle, Elizabeth experienced intimacy with God as represented in all the traditions she honors.

As a result of her experience, Elizabeth felt more urgently that she must live a spiritual life. She spent more time praying and meditating in front of her home altar. As she described her experience in Lebena, "My world expanded to an infinite universe for those moments." Though her interpenetration with the spirit of the eagle remained a mystery she could not explain, she carried it with honor and awe. She told me, "I, too, had a healing, and this is not a mystery."

Before Lebena, Elizabeth had never thought of herself as a healer, but when she returned home, she began to explore that possibility. She had become keenly aware of the brokenness we all carry. Like

213

Bob, she seemed to be hearing Sokrates' challenge to live a life of morality and service, whatever the price. "Sometimes I worry that I will not walk the path that God wants for me and that I keep hitting up against the same brick wall," she told me. Yet, months after returning home, Elizabeth reported this dream:

> I am running down a path. At the end of the path I see a small house with the sun right at the rooftop. I know that God is there and that I have a direct line to God. As I run down the path, I yell to God to help me. I hear God say, "Your head is through the wall."

Elizabeth felt answered. Through her dreams and her eagle vision at Lebena, she had begun to penetrate the wall between herself and spirit. Though she experienced significant personal losses after returning from Greece, she was comforted by a sense of strength, peace, self-love, and trust in the universe that she had not previously known. As she put it, she was transforming "from a daughter of my parents to a daughter of the universe."

In ancient Greek thought, as we have noted, healing means becoming whole. Wholeness requires that we repair what is broken or damaged in the soul as well as in the body. Repairing soul damage may mean restoring a connection to nature, community, or divinity, finding a new sense of purpose and destiny, or harmonizing our being with the Logos, the inner and cosmic order.

From the archetypal perspective, physical symptoms express what is broken in the soul. The ways we are false, misaligned, or disconnected within ourselves are our primary wounds. These misalignments might include a disordered moral sense, such that our values are twisted out of life-affirming and supporting perspective. All soul wounds make our bodies vulnerable to disease processes. Diseases that are psychosomatic in origin can often be healed if we attend to the disharmonies in our souls. Even diseases that manifest primarily in the body may have roots in imbalances in our psychospiritual lives.

Sometimes, as in Bob's case, the body may be too far along in a disease process or too damaged to restore. But even if the body cannot be healed, what is broken in the soul can be repaired. Even as a disease takes its course, we can be guided toward our destiny or challenged to be true to our inner natures. This "healing" can occur whether or not the body recovers. It can even occur as the body moves toward death. As Marcus Aurelius told us, the restoration of physical health is only the secondary goal of medicine, one that we may or may not achieve. The primary goal is that our illness guides us to restore the well-being and integrity of our souls and to unfold our destinies.

Thus Bob's Asklepian healing was successful, whether or not he became free of leukemia. As a result of his encounter with the god, his personal, professional, and spiritual wounds were exposed, treated, and healed. He realigned his values such that he felt morally true and in integrity with his inner Logos and with the cosmos. His wife Jennifer's healing was to have a depth of intimacy restored to her marriage. Elizabeth's healing was a profound spiritual encounter that motivated her to seek ways to deepen her connection with the divine and to serve others.

Sokrates chose to die rather than forsake his soul, his mission, or his god. To know himself, to live a virtuous and examined life, to do what is good for his soul and his community, and to fulfill whatever service his god required—these comprised Sokrates' recipe for a good and healthy life. Our challenge, in Sokrates' words, is "to make the vision of what is true and divine the soul's only food."[9] In their encounters with the god of healing, Bob, Jennifer, and Elizabeth each met this challenge and found an appropriate way to nourish and heal the soul.

## Chapter Twenty

# THE SNAKE RETURNS

How is it that Asklepios, arguably the most popular and widely worshipped of the pagan gods, the one who outlasted all others, has all but disappeared from Western consciousness? Though his healing tradition led directly to the development of Western medicine, few physicians know of him. Though his attendants were the first psychotherapists, few psychologists use his techniques. Though we are fascinated by dreams, and bookshelves are loaded with manuals on interpretation, few dream experts mention or study his tradition. And in compilations of mythology, his myth and history are given short shrift.

We have already suggested one explanation for this curious omission. Because Asklepios was so popular, other religions, notably Christianity, saw him as a threat and actively suppressed him. Yet the reasons for Asklepios's disappearance may go deeper. As we have seen, Asklepian healing requires active cooperation and inner change. A person seeking healing has to be willing to examine every aspect of the body/mind, including potentially painful psychological material. Most particularly, the supplicant has to be willing to examine the content of dreams and to consider that this material may contain, in fact, divine revelation.

Here, perhaps, is the crux of the issue. In our hyper rational and secular world, most of us believe that the age of revelation is over.

The gods, we agree, no longer speak directly to mortals. Though divine revelations occurred earlier and have been recorded in the sacred texts, we do not expect that we are going to hear voices, wrestle with angels, or see the fire that does not consume. Most of us are content to know God through studying the texts of revelations past.

Asklepios, who works through epiphanies or dream visits, defies such censorship. If divinity no longer reveals itself to us directly and personally, then Asklepian healing cannot work. If, on the other hand, Asklepios can still heal through dreams and other appearances, then revelation is an ongoing phenomenon and we, as did our ancestors, can still approach the god directly and benefit from his healing ministrations.

In what ways, we might ask, might such Asklepian revelations occur today? Must we travel to Greece or work with a particular guide in order to seek and achieve an Asklepian healing? As we have seen, pilgrimage to sacred sites where the archetype of Asklepios has traditionally surfaced and engaging in healing work with the help of an experienced practitioner can be profoundly useful. But ultimately the gods wish only to be remembered and respected. It is entirely possible to evoke the archetype of Asklepios on your own.

Asklepios may surface spontaneously through his imagery or story. He may visit unbidden or by grace. Or you may decide to seek him. You may have a series of dreams or unusual experiences that replicate his imagery, story, mythology, or rituals. Equally, you may have an urgent need or ailment and declare yourself to be a supplicant on a search for healing. You may purposefully structure a sequence of experiences that evoke his imagery, story, or ritual and that serve you in your own search for healing and wholeness.

Asklepian experiences can occur anywhere in both spontaneous and deliberate ways. Let's begin our exploration of the ways we might benefit personally from Asklepian healing in our ordinary lives, without the help of a special guide, by looking at four spontaneous appearances of a key aspect of the Asklepian archetype today.

Barbara is a therapist. A decade ago, just after turning fifty, she suddenly and inexplicably developed an attraction to snakes and snake imagery. Her fascination began when she was walking through the woods and stumbled across a large section of a fallen tree. With difficulty she dragged it home and placed it beside the path to her psychotherapy office door. Only after putting the piece of wood in place did she realize that it was shaped like a serpent, even to neck striations, a protruding head, and eye sockets. Barbara put white garden stones in the eye sockets. Now the snake greets every patient coming to her office.

Shortly thereafter, Barbara bought two coffee mugs that entranced her because their handles were shaped like entwined serpents with their heads resting on the rim. She also bought an expensive serpent pin that she hardly wears but is glad to own. Later, Barbara felt compelled to purchase a molded dragon with frightening features. She placed it in the garden near her office door and believes it frightened away at least one new patient. Wondering why she would want to own this intimidating creature, she felt the snake answer, "You are angry and can't escape it." After that, she moved the dragon to a more distant spot in her garden and bought a baby dragon, which she displayed prominently.

Another significant purchase was a pair of gold earrings that soon became her favorites—graceful golden serpents entwined in a circle. Shortly after Barbara bought the earrings, a patient of hers reported a dream in which she experienced a snake biting her. The patient felt surprise but no pain.

After this dream, for the first time in her therapy and after much resistance, the patient focused on her troubled marriage. It had been a long marriage, its unhappiness becoming overt after all the children left home. The patient wanted to save her marriage and was struggling with how to cope with its lack of passion and her husband's controlling ways. Simultaneously, she began to confront her own need for control.

Barbara asked, "Were you bitten by a surge of wisdom you are only now discovering?"

Mike is a middle-aged psychotherapist living in the Southwest. He uses sweat lodges and vision quests for his own and his patients' healing needs. Suddenly and for no reason he could discern, for several months prior to a vision quest of his own, he encountered many poisonous snakes.

During a wilderness quest in the mountains of Colorado, Mike had the following vision:

> I become a snake in a stream. I attack a large toad and bite him. The release of poison feels like an ejaculation. I stare into the toad's eyes as life fades and my spirit enters the toad's body. This begins a series of encounters with and deaths of numerous animals. Each one ends when I look into the eyes as my own spirit moves from one body to the next. Each time I feel my own power growing and myself transforming. My vision ends in a Sacred Meadow of Creation where life is continuously ending and beginning.

Donna, a real estate agent in the Southwest, decided to change careers in mid-life, so she entered graduate school to study transpersonal psychology. At about the same time, after decades of living alone, she began a live-in relationship with a man.

At the same time as these changes, Donna discovered that a snake was living under the cement slab on which her house is built. At first she was frightened, then curious as to how the snake could live there. The slab was thick. She did not believe the snake could burrow deeply enough to be safe. Moreover, her home was in an urban inner city where there was almost no wildlife.

Donna tried to befriend the snake, leaving it saucers of water and milk and worrying about its well-being if she did not see if for a few days. In this way, the snake made its way into Donna's daily routine.

Gina, a middle-aged secretary, was raped. Afterwards, as part of her healing, she acquired a dog as a companion and protector.

One day during a difficult time in her healing process, Gina stepped into the back yard of her inner city home with her dog. As she stood on the stairs, she noticed a three-foot-long snake lying on the ground in front of her. She had never seen any snakes in her yard or neighborhood in twenty years of living there.

Her dog walked down the stairs and stepped over the snake as if it were not there. The snake did not move, but Gina felt it watching her. The dog walked back and forth over the snake several times, neither creature disturbed by the other. Gina felt the snake continue to stare at her until she broke the connection. She intuited that the snake had come to guide and reassure her. It was as if the snake were telling her, "Be still like me. Let yourself rest from your ordeal. Hibernate, like I do, in deep places away from the world."

Of course, we cannot say that all snakes encountered in dreams or in nature mean that Asklepios the healer is coming to us. Just as we should not limit snake imagery to its Freudian phallic meaning, we should not freeze it in an Asklepian interpretation either. However, in psychospiritual and earth-based healing traditions, when an animal or other symbol recurs in attention-grabbing ways, the archetype it represents may be attempting to make its resurgence in us.

Snake encounters like the ones above may beckon us toward an encounter with the healer archetype. They may call or challenge us to seek healing from natural or psychospiritual sources. And since the healer archetype often comes to supplicants in snake form, such appearances may themselves constitute a healing, if we are willing to embrace and examine them as significant events on our inner journeys.

Snakes are among the most ancient and universal symbols. From biblical times to the modern era, snakes have been regarded as powerful symbols of transformation and transcendence. The snake that appeared to Eve in the Garden of Eden has been tainted in Judeo-Christian thought with an unfortunate association with sin. As a messenger of evil or the devil, the snake was blamed for Eve's disobedience to God's commands. However, if we set this bias aside, we find that in many mythological systems, the snake is regarded as the messenger of earth healing and represents the "close to the ground" powers of instinct, the potential that we can "shed our old skin" and be remade, as well as the more usual sexual connotations. Looking at Eve's encounter in this light, we see that the snake brought Eve consciousness of her sexuality, femininity, instinctuality, and independence. Through her encounter, Eve was transformed from a dependent child to a self-aware and mature woman.

Snake worship and snake religious and healing practices were common in Near Eastern and matriarchal religions as long as five thousand years ago. Healing rituals using serpents were practiced in Egypt and Mesopotamia. The Canaanite fertility cult used snakes to help awaken the healing powers of the Mother Goddess. On Minoan Krete, the snake was the symbol of the Mother Goddess, whose cult statues show her holding two snakes aloft, while other snakes twine around her arms and breasts. Minoan priestesses wore, carried, danced, and conducted rituals with snakes. The oldest statues of Athena show her wearing a snake-fringed peplos. The identification of the snake with the goddess may derive from their mutual association with the transformational energies of fertility and the chthonic realm of death and rebirth.

Early Judaism pronounced negative judgments against the totems and practices of other religions, in part to differentiate the new religion from its competitors. Thus, early Judaism made the snake a messenger of evil rather than a symbol of the Divine Mother or of the healing powers of the earth. The remythologizing of the snake as an instrument of evil was designed to wean people away from worship of the goddess and turn their eyes upward toward the Old Testament sky god.

However, later in the Old Testament, the snake makes an appearance as a healing symbol. During their time of wandering in the desert, the Israelites became restless, angry with God and Moses, and particularly weary of eating the manna provided by God, remembering their better diet in Egypt. In response to their complaints, "The Lord sent fiery serpents among the people. They bit the people and many of the Israelites died."

The people then realized that they had "sinned by speaking against the Lord." They begged Moses to intercede on their behalf. Moses implored God's help and was answered with this command: "Make thee a fiery serpent, and set it upon a pole; and it shall come to pass that every one that is bitten, when he sees it shall live."

Obediently, Moses built what was, in fact, a large caduceus: "And Moses made a copper serpent and mounted it on a standard; and when anyone was bitten by a serpent he would look at the copper serpent and recover."[1] The copper serpent was venerated for many centuries, until King Hezekiah destroyed it in order to stamp out the idolatry of worshiping a totem instead of the One God.

In this biblical tale, we see some principles of Asklepian medicine. The Israelites were punished with the serpent plague for complaining too much about their lot in the desert. Their irritable and ungrateful attitude brought about their sickness. As we have seen, Asklepios sometimes commanded supplicants to correct their attitudes or negative character traits before he would heal them. Thus, in this ancient story, we see the origins of psychosomatic illness in negative or hostile attitudes toward life and its challenges.

The Judaic tradition stresses that this incident influenced the Israelites to look up at the snake on the pole rather than down at the earth.[2] The Mishnah says that the totem itself was not the cause of the healing. Only when the Israelites raised their eyes skyward toward God and subordinated their individual wills to divine will were they healed.[3] Though this interpretation seems to undercut the healing power of Asklepios's snake, in fact, it affirms an aspect of the Asklepian tradition. According to the tradition, our illnesses are remedies sent by divinity to help us shape our destinies. By looking skyward, the Israelites were further healed of the slave mentality they had been sent to the desert to correct and prepared to assume the destiny of settling the Promised Land.

In contrast to its primarily negative connotations in the Judeo-Christian tradition, in many Native American medicine traditions, the snake is among the most venerated animals. Because it lives in the earth's body and thus knows earth's moods, needs, and ways, the snake is considered sacred to Mother Earth. Moreover, snake medicine has important shamanic uses. In some cultures, shamans purposely allow themselves to be bitten by snakes in order to enter the spirit world or use the venom of poisonous snakes to induce visions. Among some southwestern American traditions, a medicine person who is bitten by a rattlesnake and survives is considered to be a most powerful shaman.

Snake dreams also have a venerable history. Around the end of the second century CE, Artemidorus, who was born at Ephesus, traveled extensively to collect, study, and interpret dreams. In this early dream book, snakes are a symbol of the monarch or ruler because of their power and a symbol of time because of their length and their ability to shed their skin and renew themselves. Artemidorus also says that snakes often guard treasures; thus they represent wealth and possessions.[4]

The scholar Macrobius, writing around 400 CE, gives numerous reasons why the snake accompanies Asklepios and Hygieia.[5] He says that the snake shedding its skin symbolizes our body "shedding the skin of infirmity" and restoring its vigor. Further, as serpents have sharp vision and are ever watchful, they see the unfolding of our destinies, just as Asklepios and his divine father Apollo offer a divinatory look into our future. Thus, just as snakes keenly examine all that is before them, Asklepios, the divine doctor, thoroughly examines our condition, sees our ills, and knows how to heal them.

In modern psychology, snakes have also often been recognized as transformational symbols. When Jung decided to resign his chair as professor of psychology in 1949, he called his disciple C. A. Meier to meet with him at his summer home on Lake Zurich. As the two men were discussing possible candidates for Jung's chair, a water snake came out of the lake and crawled between Meier's legs. Jung said to

Meier, "Well, it looks as though psyche has made the decision for us." Meier became Jung's successor.[6]

In Jungian interpretation, snakes are a common symbol of transcendence[7]—the emergence from darkness into light. In psychological terms, transcendence implies particularly the movement from the unconscious into consciousness. When the snake is present in a patient's dream work, earth powers—in particular, instinct, the body, sensuality, sexuality, the feminine, the mystical, the irrational—are coming forward into the light of conscious awareness.

Moreover, according to archetypal analyst James Hillman, "the snake is perhaps the most ancient and universal carrier of the genius spirit, the figure of a protective guardian, the 'genius' itself."[8] Here Hillman uses *genius* in its original sense of "guardian spirit" or "tutelary deity." In other words, when the snake is present, your genius may be returning to you, bringing you awareness of your own fate, guidance toward fulfilling your destiny, or help in accepting your fortune. A snake apparition may be attempting, as it did for Eve, to break you out of a state of childishness or dependency and move you toward mature selfhood, consciousness, and creativity.

With the history of Asklepian healing as our background, and ancient and modern interpretations of snake imagery in mind, we can reflect on the guidance found in contemporary appearances of the healer archetype and his snakes.

Barbara experienced her surge of interest in snake imagery during the decade following her fiftieth birthday. The arrival of the snake coincided with her leaving a stifling marriage and developing confidence and expertise in her position as a senior psychotherapist and a wise older woman. Initially baffled by her fascination with snakes, Barbara began an in-depth dialogue about its meaning with her adult daughter. These conversations led to new intimacy between mother and daughter, to Barbara's first exploration of goddess religions, and to Barbara's adoption of the caduceus as a meaningful symbol for her healing practice as a psychotherapist.

For Barbara, then, the coming of the snake represented her shedding her old roles and her rebirth into a new life stage and professional status, as well as new access to the wisdom of the feminine, both in its traditional forms and through intimacy with her daughter. This personal experience helped Barbara see that her patient's dream of a snakebite symbolized the release of a flood of latent inner wisdom. Given her similar experience, Barbara was now amply prepared to guide her patient in its creative use.

Mike's encounters with poisonous snakes before his vision quest and his vision of transforming into a snake represented a profound initiation into the mysteries of life and death. Mike had initially been frightened by his encounters with snakes and saw them as threatening him with danger or death. But his vision showed him that though an individual animal or human being might die, death is not an ending, but rather a doorway into a series of endless transformations into different life forms. This realization was the lesson of the Eleusinian Mysteries, an understanding that brought peace of mind to many thousands of ancient people.

Further, Mike experienced the power of death to release spirit from body so that spirit may return to the Creator. He learned that the snake is not merely a carrier of death, but a vehicle for an individual's transcendent return to the source of life. After this vision, Mike knew that the soul does not die. So, we recall, Plutarch reminded his wife in comforting her after the death of their young daughter.

During a most transformative period in Donna's life, a snake appeared in her urban neighborhood and took up residence under her house.

In ancient times, house snakes were common in the Mediterranean region. People often kept snakes in their homes, fed them, and consulted them regularly. The behavior of the house snake—whether it ate food offerings, whether and when it hid or appeared, whether its skin was smooth or shedding, whether its behavior was friendly or distant—were interpreted as signs indicating favor or disfavor, harmony or disharmony, with the gods and with one's unfolding destiny.

Donna unconsciously and spontaneously practiced this ancient tradition when the snake appeared. It quickly became her house snake. She looked forward to seeing it and feeding it, and she worried about its well-being if it did not appear. The snake signaled Donna's transitions as she shed the skin of her old profession, became a student of transpersonal wisdom, and began a new intimate partnership. Further, the snake propelled Donna toward a daily relationship with nature, even though she lived in an urban setting. For Donna, the snake carried the message that she should continue moving from the darkness of the unconscious into the transcendence of a new and richer life.

Gina, who had been raped in her own home, also met the snake in an unfamiliar urban setting. Because of her trauma, Gina felt unsafe and wanted to flee her home and the world. But the peaceful encounter between Asklepios's two principal totems, the snake and the dog, gave Gina the message that she could work with the rape as a transformational experience rather than merely a destructive one and that healing forces were coalescing in her service.

The message to Gina, like the realization of Dorothy returning from Oz, was that she could find what she needed, including spiritual help, "in her own backyard." Speaking through her inner wisdom, the snake seemed to be advising her to take a sabbatical from the pressures of the world—to hibernate for a period of time—as an aid in her recovery. Receiving this guidance confirmed to Gina that she still had a vital connection to her inner sources of wisdom, a realization that broke the hold of a severe depression.

In these contemporary examples we see how the presence of snakes in dreams, recurring imagery, or unusual encounters in nature may signal our access to the healing wisdom of Asklepios. When we dream about or encounter a snake, it is as if we have slept in the abaton. As a result of this incubation, something that was latent, dormant, or hidden in our lives announces that it is about to reveal itself to us. Specifically, snakes may indicate any of the following:

- the awakening of earth powers

- unconscious material becoming conscious

- new levels of individuation

- new life stages

- restoration of our connections to the earth

- the call to heal illness in body or psyche

- the call to destiny or creativity

- the call to new forms of power or wealth

- the development of keener vision through altered states of consciousness and/or deepened insight

- entrance into a transformational process during which we must undergo an inner cycle of death and rebirth

- the approach or presence of transpersonal aid in our quest for healing

Snake dreams and encounters should not be considered coincidental. They occur with much greater frequency in people deeply engaged in a transformational processes. C. A. Meier's student and biographer, Jungian analyst Thomas Lavin, reports that his patients who are engaged in a deep healing process through archetypal analysis often report as many as ten snake dreams a month.[9]

The lessons of the snake are these: We must stop clinging to old forms or "skins." Life unfolds in an endless process of transformation. Death and rebirth constitute the eternal cycle of which we are each a part. There is an immortality of spirit beyond our personal lives. The mysteries of self and life that are invisible to us will surface at their proper times, often with transpersonal assistance. These are essential principles of ancient Asklepian medicine and are built into its practice.

We could, in a fashion similar to our exploration of snake imagery, examine each of Asklepios's attributes for examples of contemporary manifestation. For instance, the dog, the cock, the staff, the doctor, the female or dwarf attendants, sleeping on couches and in chambers, underground descents—all of these symbols might appear in people's imagery, dreams, and experiences today.

We know that dreams often replicate particular myths as our psyches pass through universal spiritual or developmental ordeals. Dreams also draw on imagery or scenes from myths in idiosyncratic ways to express deep issues faced by the dreamer. Since the myth, archetype, and practices of Asklepios are now largely unknown, its symbols might easily go unrecognized or appear in fragmentary ways.

However, now that you have taken an imaginal pilgrimage in the Asklepian tradition, you are familiar with Asklepian imagery. You can watch for and recognize its appearance in your dreams and experiences and contemplate the meaning of the archetype as it appears in your own life. By doing so, you gain access to the personal help of a powerful healing ally.

## Chapter Twenty-One

# ASKLEPIOS MAKES HOUSE CALLS

Nothing can guarantee a miracle. Nothing stops us, however, from seeking one. Using the treasures we have gathered from the Asklepian tradition, we can seek personal healing that goes beyond the practice of medicine as applied technology and supports the goal of restoring the universal ordering principles of health, wholeness, and harmony to our bodies and souls.

Most of the ancient testimonies record Asklepian cures that took place in the god's sanctuaries, places of particular healing power. However, it was said that Asklepios also visited his friends at their homes. Earlier we heard the story of the successful appeal to the god made by Athenian philosopher Proclus on behalf of his neighbor's ailing daughter. Proclus was also the recipient of a house call from Asklepios. Here is how it happened:

Proclus's father had suffered from arthritis. Knowing that arthritis is an inherited disease, Proclus feared that he, too, would develop the infirmity as he passed into his middle years. The attacks of foot pain that he suffered seemed to be evidence that he was indeed becoming arthritic. During one such attack, the philosopher put an absorbent compress on his afflicted foot and rested on his couch. Suddenly a sparrow landed beside him, grabbed the bandage in its beak, and pulled it off. Since the sparrow was one of Asklepios's sacred animals, Proclus felt hopeful at this sign.

231

Still Proclus was fearful. He prayed to the god for relief, begging Asklepios to speak to him clearly. One day he fell asleep after his prayers. In his sleep, he saw someone arrive from Epidauros, bend over his legs, and kiss them.

Proclus lived to a healthy old age. He ceased to fear arthritis and never developed the condition.[1]

What can we learn from Proclus's experience? What must we do to invite Asklepios to pay a house call on us?

Pioneering hospice psychiatrist Michael Murphy has listed four essential stages of an Asklepian healing quest that he uses as a model for personal and communal healing and retreats.[2] According to Murphy, the stages are these:

- The quest: acknowledging that we cannot heal ourselves sets us off on a search or an actual journey

- Fellow pilgrims: undertaking our quest with other supplicants supports our personal healing process and connects us to a community of people who share our concerns

- Preparation: engaging in special activities, such as cleansing, attending theatrical and musical performances, and seeking guides, helps us leave the ordinary world behind

- The dream: entering some form of abaton and sleeping there with intent or engaging in meditation or some other practice leads to a dream or vision that heals us or teaches us how to heal ourselves

To stage an Asklepian healing for yourself, follow these four stages in ways that are comfortable and appropriate for you. Here are some suggestions.

The first step of an Asklepian quest is that you recognize your urgent need for healing, acknowledge and name whatever is diseased in your life, and accept that this condition is a cause of disequilibrium in your soul. It is also important that you have explored conventional methods of restoring health and found that these cannot resolve your problem. In other words, as a preliminary to Askelpian healing, you should consult a physician and make sure that you have availed yourself of the best conventional diagnosis and treatment. Asklepian healing, you recall, was practiced in ancient times alongside and in addition to scientific healing methods. No one should construe that dream healing is a substitute for regular medical treatment. Rather, it is best used as a support and supplement for conventional therapies, as a way of addressing the psychosomatic roots and hidden causes of ailments, and as a way of treating conditions that are deemed chronic or incurable by conventional methods.

Questing also means leaving the familiar behind and traveling to unknown territory. A trip to Epidauros or another of Asklepios's traditional sanctuaries is certainly an attractive option, but you can also travel to the ocean, the mountains, or the desert—any place where you can withdraw from the normal stresses of your life and devote quiet and private time to your search for healing. Acknowledge that whatever trip you are taking is a healing quest and that, by breaking with routine and taking the time to get quiet and listen, you are seeking divine support and answers. It is also possible to begin a quest by entering psychotherapy and using the therapist as guide. Or you can set up an altar at home and spend a weekend or other period of time engaging in prayer and meditation, reading and reflecting on myths or other stories of healing, and calling on your own god image of the healer for guidance and help.

The second step, gathering fellow pilgrims, helps you avoid feelings of isolation or despair as you engage in an active quest for healing. You can find companions by traveling with others, by confiding your urgent healing need to friends or family members, by finding or creating a support group for people with like needs, by seeking the help of a psychotherapist or a spiritual guide, and by reading stories of others' quests and pilgrimages or the literature of questing from around the world. In all these ways, you become a pilgrim, as were those who traveled to Canterbury, Lourdes, or Epidauros before you. When you identify yourself as one traveling in the company of other pilgrims in search of healing and spiritual re-birth, your self-identity changes from someone who is content with the status quo to someone who is in search of transformation.

The third step, preparation, can also take many forms. Suppli-cants who traveled to Epidauros in ancient times spent days or weeks preparing to sleep in the abaton. They did not enter the incubation chamber until they were beckoned. Acknowledge to yourself and to your companions that you are in preparation for incubation and pa-tiently await a beckoning call or dream. During this period, engage in activities that help you purify, cleanse, and purge those aspects of your lifestyle that burden, oppress, or sicken you. In Epidauros, sup-plicants exercised in the open air, adopted healthy diets, and received hydrotherapy and massage therapy. They also attended theatrical and musical performances and rested from the ordinary world and its demands while they waited to be beckoned. You can do the same.

Preparation is designed to help you enter an altered and more nourishing reality and to declare to the cosmos that you are request-ing a sacred encounter. Though you might find it uncomfortable to fast, consider dedicating a day of fasting as a willing sacrifice to your god image. You may find it troublesome to exercise. However, exer-cise may be more meaningful if you imagine that you are strengthening yourself for an encounter with the god. You may not want to attend a particular tragic play. But you may be more willing if you remind yourself that the sorrow you see on stage is mirroring what is in your heart and, like a balm, draws your pain outwards so that your wounds can be cleansed. You may feel too busy to take hot baths with candle-light and music. Try imagining that you are at Epidauros, your bath a special therapy taking place in a temple created for healing. The fuller and more conscious your preparation time, the more you attune your body and soul toward the equilibrium necessary for healing.

During preparation, your faith and trust may be tested. Beck-oning may not come quickly, and you may be required to practice patient waiting. During the period while you are questing but have not yet been answered, you may find yourself feeling emotionally out-of-control, frightened, or needy. You may waver and waffle, want to quit, run, or hide. Comfort yourself with the knowledge that preparation is a necessary step in the healing process. Let your preparation be a gift to your god image that demonstrates that you are sincere in seeking a personal message or encounter.

When you deem that the time has come to seek the dream, enter some form of the abaton. Joseph Campbell suggests taking daily time for withdrawal from the world to nurture one's soul with art, music, reading, writing, silence, meditation, or whatever gives you bliss. Such sacred time can function like an incubation chamber, especially when you journal or record the insights that come during your periods of rest and reflection. Another approach to incubation is to practice the Sabbath, giving yourself one day each week to withdraw from worldly concerns or pressures in order to refresh the soul. You might also use a trip to an art museum as an incubation experience. Hold your healing need in mind as you reflect on the images in paintings or sculpture and see what messages or insights emerge. Since entering the abaton means reentering Mother Earth's womb, being active in nature by taking walks or sitting or lying on the earth can also be a form of incubating. Shamanic teacher William Taegel asks his students to sit under a tree for twenty minutes each day for up to a year and do nothing but watch.

But the abaton is not only an external place in which you seek a dream or vision. The abaton is also the tomb and the womb, the place of death and rebirth. Thus it is important that you regard whatever activity you are using as a means of incubation in soulful terms. As analyst Thomas Lavin explains:

> The abaton must ultimately become an inner Holy of Holies. Once we realize that the abaton is within us and learn how to enter inner sacred space, then the planet becomes our Asklepion. Since the required journey is an internal pilgrimage, Kos is every night our head is on the pillow. When we realize that the entire world is our Asklepion, we overcome greed and possessiveness because

the tradition does not belong to Greece or Japan, Christianity or paganism any more. The modern priest is aware of the inclusiveness of the process. It is not Freudian, Jungian or any one form, but all.[3]

Sometimes, incubation comes upon you unbidden. You may feel blue and unmotivated and not feel like going to work or even getting out of bed at all. You may even feel as if you can no longer function in conventional ways. If such symptoms persist, you might assume that you are depressed and seek medication or other intervention from a therapist or physician to restore normal functioning as quickly as possible. However, depression may also be a form of incubation. The soul may be at rest, unwilling to cooperate any longer in a life that irritates, disturbs, hurts, or is untrue to your destiny. Depression may be the manifestation of the soul's sojourn in the underworld. Your goal should be to support your questing soul in its incubation, seek out what it needs, give it time. If you do not support incubation, the soul may force it upon you in disturbing or distorted forms.

The last step in the questing process is the dream. As you have seen, healing dreams may present themselves in several ways. You may experience a "big dream"—full of apparent symbols, its import clear and life transforming. Or a healing dream may come piecemeal over a period of time, dream fragments or images that add up to a complete message. Images in the dream may come in traditional and recognizable Asklepian form. But they may also appear in forms personal to you. You may not even recognize the healer or understand the message that the dream carries.

When you are actively engaged in a process of dream healing, it is important that you regard whatever dreams or images come as precious gifts from the god. Upon awakening, linger with your dream images. Recall and record all you can. Save and savor them, reflect and associate to all images, compare them, read them as chapters in the tale of your healing odyssey, pray, request further dreams. Treat your dreams as gateways between the otherworld through which your soul travels while you sleep and your everyday reality.

In the *Odyssey*, Odysseus traveled to the underworld to visit the shades in order to receive instructions for finding his way home after the Trojan War. He approached the underworld by going to the end of the ocean, where there was an opening and meeting place between the worlds of life and death, body and soul, matter and spirit. All of us know this place. We have all been there. Rather than flee in terror we must, like Odysseus, offer sacrifice, allow all images that press upon us to surface, recognize them, and receive their wisdom and instructions. In response, we offer prayers of thanksgiving for the messages the god has sent and do our best to put the advice we receive into practice.

As an example of a modern Asklepian healing, I'd like to tell a personal story. Although the details of my ailment and its cure may be considered somewhat embarrassing, I share them to demonstrate that the method of Asklepian dream questing does work, with wonderful and health-giving results.

Close relatives on both sides of my family have suffered from chronic digestive disorders. It is no surprise that I learned to cope with stress in a similar manner. By the time I was in my mid-twenties, I was diagnosed with irritable bowel syndrome, a chronic psychosomatic stress disorder. There is no known medical cure. Millions of people tolerate and manage this unpleasant condition their entire lives.

I tried numerous forms of conventional and alternative treatments to heal my disorder. Over many years I tried dietary regulation, digestive aids, nutritional supplements, psychotherapy, acupuncture, massage, reiki, hydrotherapy, guided imagery, meditation, relaxation techniques, and affirmations. I was able to modify and somewhat lessen the symptoms, but not cure the condition. I had lived with my condition for a quarter of a century, and I expected to have to manage it for the rest of my life.

I teach an adult workshop on ancient Greece. As part of our work, we had been reviewing the Epidaurian testimonies, subjecting them to psychological, scientific, and medical scrutiny. I returned from class one evening rather frustrated. My students had been reviewing the testimonies of Asklepian cures as would modern scientists, as some of them are. When they read accounts of dream surgeries, relief from long pregnancies, or the restoration of eyesight to the blind, they dismissed them as exaggerations, fantasies, or distortions designed to make believers out of gullible and superstitious people. Despite hundreds of testimonies, many of my students were convinced that Asklepian cures were scientifically impossible and thus could not have happened. Moreover, they were certain, such cures could not happen for us. Such belief, of course, precludes any possibility of healing. Where we say the gods cannot be, there they do not go.

With Epidaurian testimonies and modern despair crowding my mind, I fell asleep. That night, I had the following dream:

> I am lying in my bedroom in the dark. A gray-haired, gray-bearded doctor, one of my Greek studies students and a friend, walks into my room and right up to me, until he is standing next to the bed, just as doctors once did when making house calls. He is holding an enema bag. He tells me that he had heard me praying to him for a long time to heal my digestive ailment. He says that in order to heal it, I should take an enema of lemon juice and vinegar. I see the doctor beside me and myself stretched out on my bed as if I am outside my body watching. The entire scene is suffused with light. Everything else is in darkness.

I awoke with the dream as clear in my mind as if it had occurred in daylight. I was fascinated and baffled. Could lemon juice and vinegar possibly be the cure for a condition that was psychically determined and deeply embedded in my functioning since childhood?

That day I consulted with the physician friend who had repre-

238

sented Asklepios in my dream. He had never heard of such a treatment but saw no potential danger. In fact, he insisted that I test it. In the evening, I placed a small statue of Asklepios on the bathroom counter, lit incense and a candle, and did what the god suggested.

That night, I experienced a satisfying and mellow glow of comfort. I felt as Aristides had described after taking his remedies at Pergamum, "a certain inexplicable contentment" not of human origin. Over the next several weeks, my condition improved dramatically. Symptoms ameliorated and my general mood became significantly lighter and happier. I felt as if I had been given the chance to decide freely not to allow stress to impact my digestive system. I made such a choice, talking to my body and thanking Asklepios for the opportunity.

My experience convinced me beyond a doubt that the Asklepian healings I had been reading about and conducting for years were genuine. My case followed the classic model in many respects: I had asked for help from Asklepios for a condition that medical science could not cure. I had journeyed with fellow seekers to sites where Asklepian healings had happened, read accounts and testimonies of such cures, engaged in purification practices such as altering my diet, receiving body work, hydrotherapy, and massage. I believe that the discussion I had with my students about the accuracy of the accounts of Asklepian cures was my beckoning call. In my mind, I was being challenged to prove that what I had been teaching about Asklepios was true. As I lay down to sleep that night in my darkened bedroom, I was clearly ready for the god to appear.

My dream follows many aspects of the ancient formula my students and I had been discussing. Asklepios appeared in the guise of bearded and wise elder man. He gave me instructions and a particular remedy for my condition, one that seemed at the time paradoxical or nonsensical. As we have seen, Asklepian cures often included humor or irony. I consulted a physician to make sure that what I was about to attempt would neither harm me nor exacerbate my condition. And, certainly as important as any of these, I believed.

I believed that Asklepios had really appeared, and I believed that what he told me to do would help.

And so, of course, it did.

In the time since these events, I have thought much about my experience and sought to understand the soul message implicit in my illness and its cure. Once when discussing my ailment and likening the intestinal tract to a "sewer system" for which the god had prescribed an acid wash, I slipped and said that the "acid was for my suicide." My eyes flooded with tears, as I realized that I had been holding death energy in my abdomen—a self-defeating and death-dealing tendency to respond to stress with irritation. The acid wash prescribed by the god was a perfect homeopathic remedy—acid to burn off irritability—that restored equilibrium to my soul as well as to my body.

Since my cure, I find that I respond to stress with patience, acceptance, and tolerance, rather than with irritation, resentment, or neediness. I avoid entering into stressful situations, or if I do enter them, I do not embody them. As a result, I am a happier and more relaxed person.

Asklepios is that loving aspect of God whose task it is to minister to us in our suffering. When we call on this power, we may have, through a dream or vision, the imaginal experience of the god coming to heal us or instruct us what we must do to heal ourselves. The touch of the god heals in ways that defy rational explanation. By definition, such events are miracles. In this manner, Proclus was healed of arthritis, and my digestive ailment is no more.

Call upon Asklepios, or whatever image of the healing god is most appropriate for you, and you, too, may find healing.

## Chapter Twenty-Two

# THE FUTURE OF ASKLEPIAN MEDICINE

I magine great changes in the ways we practice medicine and therapy, changes so profound that they resolve the crisis of confidence that is undermining practitioners and patients and lead to miracles in healing as well. Imagine further that these changes derive not from the latest medical technology, but hearken back to the origins of Western medicine and draw on complex holistic principles that honor the link between mind and body and work to heal the whole person, not just relieve symptoms or control pain.

In particular, imagine a hospital that is truly a sanctuary from the modern world and its stresses: A place where beauty, quiet, quality food, massages, healing baths, meditation, and strolls through beautiful surroundings are routinely available. A place where music and theater are performed. A place where patients who practice within a specific spiritual tradition are encouraged to surround themselves with its images, music, and rituals. A place where patients are so rested and nurtured that they relax their defenses, loosen their ego boundaries, and become amenable to spiritual as well as scientific healing.

In this hospital, patients who wish to dream quest as part of their healing process are given the opportunity to do so. They are offered guidance and support, a safe and sacred environment where dream incubation takes place, and the opportunity to discuss their dreams with a trained professional who helps them to understand and interpret a dream's symbolism and message.

A hospital such as we are imagining is not an illness repair factory but a medico-spiritual sanctuary. Physicians who practice there are trained in the art of healing the soul as well as repairing the body. They understand that illness expresses the soul's condition and acknowledge that the sacred is everywhere and that encouraging patients to be in relationship with the sacred furthers their healing. They understand as well that the use of radical ritual as an adjunct to conventional healing positively impacts the outcome of a treatment procedure and are skilled in creating and conducting them.

As we near the end of our journey together, let's remind our-selves of these and other principles underlying Asklepian medicine and explore ways they might be integrated into our healing practices so that a hospital like the one we are imagining might come to be.

Asklepian medicine, as we recall, had two branches, the scien-tific and the sacred. Each branch had a different purpose. Rightly understood, these two can coexist, cooperate with, and complement one another today, even as they did in ancient times.

Scientific medicine can do wonders, especially in response to trauma and other emergencies and in the control and healing of infectious diseases. It is also highly successful at relieving pain and in helping to manage chronic conditions. However, scientific medicine is limited in its ability to treat the psychosomatic conditions that account for so much modern illness. All too often, patients who pre-sent subclinical symptomatology get lost in a labyrinth of tests and specialists and find very little help for what ails them. For illnesses caused by stress, for instance, the endless merry-go-round of trying one medication after another seldom leads to relief. In these cases, it would be better for patients to admit that they have a condition for which there is no scientific cure. Then they could surrender to soul work.

Long ago Plutarch affirmed the need for both sacred and scientific medicine and lucidly presented their strengths. In this regard, he related the story of a one-horned ram brought from the country to Perikles, ruler of Athens. The diviner Lampon examined the ram and said that it indicated that though there were two competing parties in Athens, leadership would eventually fall to Perikles. But the natural philosopher Anaxagoras cut open the skull and showed how distorted anatomical structures caused the root of the horn to grow incorrectly. The people cheered Anaxagoras. But later, the party opposing Perikles met disaster, and Lampon was considered wise. Plutarch comments:

> Yet there was, I think, no reason why both the natural philosopher and the diviner should not have been right, the one discovering the cause of the phenomenon, the other its meaning. It was the business of one to find out why the thing happened and how it came about, and the other to tell for what purpose it happened and what it betokened. Those who say that when the cause of a sign is found, the sign is disposed of do not realize that they are denying the value not only of heavenly signs but also of human signs . . . Each of these, besides being caused and prepared, is made as a sign of something.[1]

As this ancient tale illustrates, finding the cause of a phenomenon and explaining its meaning are two equally important functions. As applied to the two branches of medicine, Plutarch is saying that the job of scientific medicine is to find out why and how a condition came about and how to treat it. The job of sacred medicine is to tell for what purpose a condition has occurred and what it means. In other words, the task of sacred medicine is to unfold and reveal the larger matrix of which a particular illness is a part.

We might argue that understanding the purpose and meaning of an illness is rightly the job of the psychiatrist, psychologist, or minister, and that patients can seek such insight if they choose. However, sacred medicine holds that responding to an illness scientifically without understanding its meaning can be dangerous or destructive. Illnesses are inherently, as Plutarch reminds us, signs of something. When we disguise or suppress symptoms, or when we treat a physical condition without attending to its meaning and message, we deny the value of the sign. Functional health may be restored, but nothing has changed, nothing has been learned, no growth has been occasioned, no rebirth has occurred. Moreover, a sign suppressed or treated without deeper understanding often resurfaces as another sign, even as another catastrophe or illness.

In our culture, Anaxagoras is clearly the winner. Once we think we understand the cause of an illness, we are concerned only with how to fix it. However, when we approach health issues in this materialist way, our connection to the web of life is severed, and we feel ourselves to be alone in the universe. Our suffering, then, is without meaning, when it might be seen as a sign pointing us toward wisdom and transformation.

Asklepian medicine teaches us that we must learn to perceive and admit the limits of who we are as human beings and what we can and cannot do. We must affirm that illness and death are inevitable processes of life. When we are helpless, we must admit it. This admission does not mean that we fall into doing nothing. Nor does it mean that we rationalize suffering as inevitable and predetermined. Rather, we are responsible and proactive, but in new ways.

Once scientific medicine has reached its limits, we allow sacred medicine to take over. Once the physician as technician can no longer serve, we consult the physician as priest or guide. Reaching our human limits, we stand before the unknown and yet quest further. Rather than sending our chronic or hopeless cases home to suffer or die, we send them to the sanctuary, where the ways and means of seeking for deeper understanding—even, for healing—are practiced, as they have been for millennia.

Changes as profound as these require nothing less than a shift in the way we look at ourselves and our world, a shift that takes us out of our usual mechanistic, materialistic, and existential worldview and into mythic consciousness. A purely scientific mindset cannot explain the ancient or modern cures we have examined in this book. Nor can reducing them to results of the power of suggestion or the placebo effect. In mythic consciousness, inexplicable cures can and do occur through dreams and visions, because such images are understood to transmit archetypal energy and divine wisdom. According to the mythic worldview, miracles of healing are possible because we inhabit

- an ordered universe whose order is reflected in us

- a personal universe that can communicate with us

- a symbolic universe in which events are also metaphors for the soul's condition

- a poetic universe that offers us the imagery we need to express our inner lives and to achieve connection to otherwise inaccessible universal forces

- an interrelated web of life in which events and their signs are related to and expressive of the whole

Of course, we cannot return to the simpler days in which science was subordinate to spirit. Rather we must find a way to honor reason and science as well as myth and to widen the scope of healing practice so that imagination, creative expression, and spirituality are regarded as equally potent medical tools. In order for Asklepian medicine to work, we need to accept that what we call gods and goddesses, guides, helping spirits, and totem animals exist as imaginal realities. We need to believe that they are concerned with us and can be evoked through prayer, practice, and ritual—that they answer when we call out to them. As moderns, we reenter the mythic view consciously and with rationality, but also with a great and renewed respect for the powers of the imagination to promote health and healing.

245

In order for the imagination to aid in our healing, we need a set of images that can inspire us and serve as metaphors for the soul-healing lessons brought to us in dreams and visions.

In the Asklepian tradition, healing images—the boy, old man, dog, snake, female, and dwarf attendants—were everywhere present in healing sanctuaries, in various artistic forms. Supplicants were receptive to these images because they had been given time to contemplate the artistic forms and to read and hear the testimonies of others in which these images appeared. When they entered the abaton, they felt honored to enter the holy of holies, the god's consulting room. While they awaited a dream, their psyches were spinning and tumbling with the imagery of the healing tradition. When they slept, it was with the hope and expectation that this imagery would present itself to them and that it would work, thus mobilizing healing potentials in their own psyches.

Our contemporary practice of medicine rarely provides such nurturing images as the ancients created; nor is our cultural creation of imagery shaped toward healing and wholeness. In traditional cultures, according to Joseph Campbell, individuals were ushered through socially maintained rites by means of which they had significant experiences. This was once the case with Asklepian medicine. In our era, however, Campbell observes, we have reversed the order. Now each individual has an idiosyncratic experience and then seeks the signs through which to communicate it. If the experience or its expression is significant enough, it may become the culture's myth. Thus Campbell calls ours an era of "creative mythology."[2]

In our day, we come from diverse ethnic backgrounds and highly individualized lives, legacies, and imaginal histories. This atmosphere provides great freedom for individual creative expression. As a result of this individuality, however, ritual behavior has lost its integrity and significance, dream imagery varies greatly between dreamers, and visionary experiences are often disbelieved or pathologized. Though archetypes are universal, it is harder for us to recognize them because we do not carry mythological caches of imagery in common. Thus today's dreamers are often unable to recognize the mythical motifs in their own dreams. Perhaps Asklepios and his helpers appear in dreams more often than is recognized, but we do not notice because we have never been taught their characteristic imagery, patterns, and story.

In contrast to the paucity of our modern archetypal imaginations, Asklepian medicine

- restores the primacy of the imagination to the processes of healing

- recognizes that our souls use our bodies for their images and metaphors

- surrounds patients with imagery rich in potential for healing and inner exploration

- repotentiates those sets of images and practices recognized in other ages and cultures as effective for healing and discovers such imagery of its own

In particular, evoking Asklepios or another god image of healing is effective in awakening energies that are of transpersonal origin. Jean Houston explains that imagining or identifying with a healing archetype moves us away from our dis-ease and toward that universal creative energy whose purpose is healing. We move out of identification with our personal and localized illness and into a relationship in which archetypal forces greater than our illness can come to us to touch, teach, heal, and provide meaning.[3]

In addition to healing imagery, rites of transformation—what we have called radical ritual—have been all but lost in our culture. Many of our contemporary medical practices, such as surgery, radiation, chemotherapy, and medications are designed to stimulate radical changes. However, guided by a philosophy of restoration, we continue to believe we are preserving the same person through these procedures, simply giving the individual a replacement part or improved chemistry. When we remove or replace a piece of the body, however, or introduce chemicals that alter cerebral functioning, we are, in effect, creating a new person. Many of our scientific healing practices, seen rightly, are actually rituals of death and rebirth.

Many patients who survive major surgery understand this truth. In transplant surgeries particularly, patients may experience that they are carrying another person's feelings or soul or that they have not adequately attended to the soul of the donor.[4] In our current culture of healing, such transformations generally go unrecognized, unguided, and unattended. As a result, patients often experience confusion, grief, depression, despair, and sometimes the physiological or psychological rejection of the health benefit the procedure was designed to achieve.

Asklepian medicine, by way of contrast, teaches that we *are* different people after illness and healing. Like Asklepios's snake, we have shed our old skin. Moreover, Asklepian medicine itself aims at significant transformations of the body/mind system—not through surgery or drugs, but through dream quests and other applications of radical ritual. We have seen much evidence in the cases discussed in this book that the imagery that presents to supplicants during dream questing alters their psychic structures and patterns. Often, mind/body organization is transformed such that the mind can immediately or over time learn to direct and manage the body's functioning differently, even at the cellular level.

However, unlike the unsupported transformations of scientific medical procedures, patients in Asklepian sanctuaries are not allowed just to lie back and be treated. They are not helpless recipients of their physicians' expertise. Rather, they participate in what Kerényi called "a religion of the patient." Asklepian patients are expected to do the primary work of their own healing. The physician's role is to support and guide them through this process. As a result of this shift in responsibility, the mind/body transformations that Asklepian patients experience "belong" to the patients, not to their doctors. Thus the benefits are more easily integrated into patients' lives.

Because radical ritual is the heart of Asklepian medicine, it is particularly effective in dealing with psychosomatic ailments. Ritual operates simultaneously on body, mind, and spirit. Cures are successful because the imaginal experiences or practical remedies suggested through ritual dreams have the power to rearrange, reorient, or reintegrate the structures and patterns of patients' psychosomatic functioning.

In our culture, psychosomatic conditions are generally seen as troublesome excuses for not functioning. "It's only in your mind" is the diagnosis; "get over it" the prescription. However, Asklepian medicine recognizes that psyche guides body and that the relationship between body and mind is infinitely complex. Asklepian medicine returns respectability to psychosomatic conditions, honors the primacy of mind and its influence over the body, and offers strategies for addressing all of our ailments.

In the ideal medical future we are imagining, identifying psychosomatic conditions and treating them with Asklepian healing would constitute an entire branch of medicine, helpful to millions of sufferers. Asklepian physicians would recognize psychosomatic conditions as effective ways for the body/mind to communicate. They would accept that psychosomatics is a language and strive to understand its messages.

Not only is the body/mind connection honored in Asklepian medicine, but the body/soul connection as well. Asklepian healers understand that the body is the soul's poem. Image, metaphor, and symbol, including the symbolic actions that manifest as psychosomatic symptoms, constitute the soul's language. For the soul, dream images are not analogies, not "symbolic of" something. Rather, the soul experiences "as if" as an imaginal reality.

To our imaginal function, it really does rain cats and dogs, our love really is a rose, and our heart really breaks. Reason stands by imagination's side, reminding us that what soaks us is only a heavy downpour, the one we love is a human being not a flower, and the

249

pain we feel in the middle of our chest is sadness. Reason grounds us in the physical world, but we need imagination to invigorate our exchanges with it. When we sleep or are otherwise in an altered state, reason rests, while imagination is freed. The dreams and visions that arise during imagination's primacy are the soul's experiences during its withdrawal from the physical world.

In normal consciousness, we can contact neither the gods nor the soul directly. As the philosopher Heraklitos said, "The god whose oracle is at Delfi neither speaks nor conceals, but gives signs." Divinity and soul are observed through events, including physiological events, that are their signs. And signs require interpretation, intervention, and action.

The ancients might say that Apollo sent a plague upon a city because of the bloodguilt of its rulers. We moderns counter that this explanation is superstition because of ancient people's inability to explain the plague scientifically. However, we easily observe in our modern world how corrupt rulers encourage a corrupt citizenry, causing many forms of modern plague to descend on people. The ancients gave Lampon the diviner's answer: what something means. We moderns give Anaxagoras the natural philosopher's answer: how something came about.

In a holistic system, both kinds of answers are necessary. A modern Asklepian physician might say, "You developed breast cancer (or a heart attack) because of these physiological causes. Your condition can be treated by the following methods. Now let us examine together how and why your soul chose this particular target in your body. Here are some ways I can help you find out what this illness means and what you might do to restore harmony to your life. Through these methods, you may discover what your illness expresses about your soul's condition regarding love, morality, connection to self and others, nature, divinity, purpose, meaning, fulfillment, destiny, money, power, sexuality, and history."

Illness read as physiological dysfunction expresses merely materialist concerns. Illness read as a metaphor for the soul expresses

ultimate concerns and guides the transformations that bring wholeness. In an ideal Asklepian future, Lampon as well as Anaxagoras will
be at the bedside.

Unfortunately, this balance between cause and meaning is seldom achieved in medical practice, even when the patient is conscious
of the importance of both physiology and soul. Steven B. Katz, poet
and professor of rhetoric, wrote the following poem after a hospital
stay for an acute illness:

Out of Hospital

Sick, stripped to the bone, relieved
     of all functions, he now begins again
to put on the body's habits
     one by one, like clothes
forgotten, hanging in a closet.

He touches the floor that seems to shift,
     rising to his feet that fall,
floating him out the door. He is leaving
     the room that was his world—

the quiet light of flowers, cards initialed
     like memories on the wall.
He takes a shower down the hall,
     Skin hectic, wet, and hot—

The ritual of initiation
     before daily life is undertaken.
The flesh rinsed of pain.
     He dresses, assumes the human role again,
Prepares to reenter in a new-born globe. [5]

When he presented this poem to a medical journal for publication, Katz was challenged to express himself literally rather than
metaphorically. "Does the floor really rise to his feet?" he was asked.
"Isn't it the other way around?" A medical-minded editor mandated

that Katz exchange key words in the last two lines, so that the published version reads: "He . . . assumes the human globe again, / prepares to reenter in a new-born role."

This response is emblematic of the contemporary medical mind's inability to hear metaphor or respond to the soul dimensions of illness. Physicians are comfortable with the concept that recovery from illness is a resumption of the "human globe" of the body and that a patient's post-illness roles will be reborn. But they are not able to accept the poet's more soulful expression that during illness he has forsaken the "human role"—become, in a sense, other than human. Nor can they accept the poet's psychospiritual interpretation of disease, consistent with mythic consciousness, that the self dies and is reborn during illness and that both self and world are transformed as a result.

In the editing of Katz's poem, we observe a vivid example of what he calls "the rootedness of the grounded modern medical mind." This rootedness leads to two significant dilemmas regarding the symbolic language of disease. First, physicians are unaware of the degree to which their labors are ruled by cultural metaphors. Katz writes,

> So successful has the "medicine is a war against disease" metaphor been that we can hardly conceive medicine in any other way. Within the narrative that this metaphor gives rise to in our culture, medical doctors have been elevated to the status of scientific war heroes who possess or are granted a high degree of credibility and power . . . For in the scenario of the doctor as warrior, the patient's body can become a battlefield . . . [A] patient can and often does become merely the "scene" of the medical "act," rather than an "agent" who has the power to participate in decisions concerning his or her own life—or death.[6]

Second, and of utmost importance to the future of Asklepian medicine, the groundedness of physicians in the concrete makes them unable to hear metaphor. If they cannot hear metaphor, they cannot interpret psychosomatic conditions. If they cannot interpret psychosomatic conditions, they cannot hear the language of the soul and how it inscribes the body. If they cannot hear the language of the soul, they are unable to practice sacred medicine.

Scores of my patients entered psychotherapy in despair after failing to find relief for their psychosomatic conditions within the medical community. Their doctors failed to recognize that these patients' bodies were expressing their souls' complaints. The grounded medical mind responds to dis-ease only when it is a clinically established illness presenting significantly distorted physical symptomology. All too often, patients are devastated by the message, "Come back when you are really ill."

Rather than telling a patient "nothing is wrong" when headaches, stomach distress, heart pains, dizziness, back pain, or a myriad of other symptoms fail to respond to conventional treatment, an Asklepian physician would turn attention to the patient's soul. Skilled in metaphor and imagery, the Asklepian doctor would understand such symptoms as expressions of the soul through the body and treat the symptoms by examining what they reveal about the soul's disharmony.

The root meaning of the word *therapy* is "to serve or attend." Asklepian physicians turn their attention to a patient's soul by serving or attending them in relationship. Asklepian medicine is conversational and personal. It takes time to listen and elicit all the concerns, associations, and connections that exist between a complaint and the person who experiences it. Hippokrates left us complex case studies demonstrating how particular lives manifest particular diseases. Rufus taught that we must attend the whole person through conversation. Edelstein stressed that Asklepios's great healing power was the attentive gentleness of his presence.

Rather than a quick fix, Asklepian medicine tends the whole person, taking all the time that is needed to comprehend what the soul is trying to say through its distress. Equally important, Asklepian medicine stresses that in helpless or hopeless cases, healing must take place through direct encounters between the patient and the healing powers of divinity. It understands that the most important therapeutic relationship is between the individual and the god. The task of sacred medicine is to nurture this relationship.

In a profound sense, the goal of Asklepian medicine is friendship. Plato's ideal physician Eryximachos stated that Asklepios knew "how to plant friendship and accord" in hostile and competing elements.[7] Asklepian medicine restores friendship on every level—between competing elements in our bodies, between body and soul, patient and attendant, individual and community, individual and cosmos and, ultimately, each individual and the god.

Another relationship fostered by Asklepian medicine is the connection between a patient and the place where healing occurs. In ancient practice, the appearance of Asklepios or another deity was often linked to a specific location. Earth-based traditions recognize power spots where the earth manifests energies favorable to a particular deity. Seekers, for example, went to great trouble and expense to make the pilgrimage to Delfi to receive Apollo's oracle or to seek healing in one of Asklepios's many sanctuaries.

Plutarch tells us that sometimes people or cultures changed such that seekers could no longer receive the deity's messages; other times, the earth itself changed so that its powers were no longer conducive to the deity speaking from a particular place.[8] Thus both earth and human factors are important in making Asklepian healing available. In modern Greece, hospitals and churches are sometimes built on the sites of ancient Asklepieia. The hospital at Voula, south of Athens, for example, is built on the site of an ancient Asklepion. In both ancient and modern times, healing centers on this site have specialized in the treatment of bone disease.[9] Jean Houston tells the story of falling ill while traveling to Krete as a young woman. A group of concerned traditional old women took her to the Church of St. George, a patron of healing on the island, where she was prayed over by the priest. The church was built over an ancient Asklepion.[10]

Asklepian medicine recognizes that beauty is food for the soul. Thus, beautiful natural settings, treatment rooms, bedrooms, and other surroundings are regarded as therapy for weary and troubled souls. Immersion in beauty helps patients affirm the goodness of the world and reinvigorates their desire to remain part of it.

Perhaps the most important consideration of place is what we allow to happen there. When C. A. Meier first applied Asklepian principles to the practice of psychotherapy, he translated incubation into modern terms. Incubation for him was "a means by which conditions were created in which healing dreams could happen." In the Asklepian future we are imagining, hospitals and clinics could themselves be places like Asklepieia, "where attention could be given and space made for the autonomous healing factor in the psyche." In his clinical psychiatric work, Meier took his patients' dreams and psychotic fantasies seriously, as if they had resulted from an incubation process.[11]

Our hospitals, too, could be places in which the psyche is taught, supported, encouraged, and protected as it descends into the collective unconscious to seek radical resuscitation and reconstruction.

What symbol should we use to represent the new Asklepian medicine we are imagining?

The shoulder-high staff entwined with a single snake became the recognized emblem of medicine after Asklepios's arrival in Rome. Though the god was eventually overthrown and demonized, his staff remained medicine's emblem for many centuries. Another snake-wrapped staff, this one entwined with two snakes, is the traditional symbol of Hermes, god of communication and commerce, travelers and thieves, and guide of souls to the underworld. It is believed that a printer's error in the sixteenth century, substituting Hermes' staff for that of Asklepios on the cover of various medical texts, shifted the symbol of medicine from its traditional form. This error was compounded in the nineteenth century when the Public Health Service, the Marine Hospital Service, and the Army Medical Corps of the United States all adopted the two-snake caduceus as their symbol.[12] Murphy interprets this substitution as "the serendipitous selection of a more kindly totem [that] seems like the yearning for the guidance and wisdom of Hermes by a medical system that is coldly Apollonian."[13]

We have explored many interpretations of both symbols. The dual snakes symbolize life and death, male and female, sexuality and fertility, body and soul, secular and sacred medicines. The single snake symbolizes the life force moving up the spine, the totemic healing animal of the god, reconciliation with nature and its helpers, recognition that birth and death are a single process, the healing of the body/mind split, and the healing power of rebirth through the shedding of old skin. A case could be made for either symbol to represent Asklepian medicine.

However, though Asklepian medicine clearly needs Hermes' help to communicate and to guide the souls of seekers through the underworld, healing is not Hermes' province. Perhaps if we take back the single-snake staff as the symbol of healing, we will become more fearless in facing our destinies and in reconciling the splits between body and mind and between science and the sacred. Asklepian medicine transcends duality. In it, the two branches of medicine become one great and compassionate human achievement. In it we are led to find the eternally still, peaceful, birthless and deathless place within. In Asklepian medicine, each of us is the staff carried by the god, who sends his one great serpent from the depths of the earth to kiss and heal us.

Sacred medicine teaches that disease and destiny are inextricably linked. In fact, disease may lead us to our destiny, as it did for Galen's patient Aristides. Without the experience of a particular disease, we may not discover what we need to know about ourselves or even be the right people to fulfill our destiny. Here, then, is another meaning of the caduceus: disease and destiny are two serpents twining around the central wand that is our soul.

Marcus Aurelius, philosopher and emperor of Rome, was a devotee of Asklepios. As we learned, Aurelius received remedies for his ailments through dream visits from the god. In his *Meditations,* he urges us to accept the role of disease in shaping our lives and to use the wisdom of Asklepian medicine to realign our characters, goals, and values with concerns that serve not just our health but the unfolding of our life's purpose and that of the universe itself:

> Just as we understand when we are told that Aesculapius prescribed for this man horseback exercise or bathing in cold water or going without shoes; so we must understand it when we are told that nature prescribed for this man sickness or mutilation or loss or something else of the kind. For in the first case prescribed means something like this: he prescribed this treatment for this man as a thing adapted to restore health; in the second case it means that which happens to each man is fixed for him in a manner suitable to his destiny.

Thus, for Aurelius, the restoration of health is not itself the goal. Rather, it is a tool we can use for living a good life and for being of service to our ultimate purpose. Beyond our pleasures and comforts are the reasons why we are here, the meaning we give our lives, the genius we express. Aurelius's great wisdom is suggesting that everything that happens to us, including illness, misfortune, trauma, and loss, must be seen as part of a great web of connection and matrix of meaning that helps us evolve toward fulfilling our purposes in living.[14] For him, the "germ" in a disease, crisis, or catastrophe may be the "genius" waiting to be discovered and tended. Aurelius continues:

> [T]hings are suitable to us . . . when they fit together into a given whole. For in everything there is one fitness. And as the universe is made up of all bodies to be the body it is, so out of all existing causes fate is made up to be the

cause it is . . . Let us then accept our destiny, as well as the prescriptions of Aesculapius . . .

We humans are not wise enough to see all the interconnections that exist. But we can perceive that all beings and all things are inextricably interwoven. Our lives evolve as they do out of a great tapestry of universal life. Our diseases are not random or accidental, but rather expressions of the whole as it impinges on our bodies and souls. We may not like what happens to us. We may sometimes suffer greatly. But sacred medicine helps us accept whatever happens as the inevitable unfolding of our destinies. If we regard our illness as the prescription of Asklepios, we heal our outrage at life's unfairness and align ourselves with the web of forces of which we are a part. As Aurelius says,

> So accept everything which happens, even though it seems disagreeable, because it leads to the health of the universe and to the prosperity and felicity of Zeus. For he would not have brought on any man what he has brought, if it were not useful for the whole . . . For two reasons then you should be content with whatever happens to you; first, because it was done for you and prescribed for you and had some reference to you from the beginning, and the most ancient causes spun it with your destiny; secondly because even that which happens separately to each individual is to the power which administers the universe a cause for felicity and perfection, nay even of its own continuance.[15]

It is most difficult for us to accept and find meaning in our cancer or heart attack, abuse or rape or survival of war, debt or divorce or drug addiction. It is most challenging to accept that we had to suffer in just this way because of our place in the web of unfolding events and forces. And it is especially difficult to see that our suffering leads to the health of the universe. Our greatest healing may occur when we seek the ways in which this might be so. Thus, war survivors can be our best witnesses against violence. Cancer survivors are the best guides for those newly afflicted. Rape and abuse survivors have taught us invaluable lessons about the damage done to the soul by trauma.

Asklepian medicine teaches us to accept our trials and sufferings as the workings of the universe in our individual lives. And it teaches us that though this medicine may be difficult to swallow, our illnesses and traumas are the remedies sent by Asklepios "who keeps the universe from falling sick or growing old" so that we may serve its unfolding by playing the very part we were destined to play.

Lay your head on your pillow as if you were in Epidauros, Kos, or Pergamum. Imagine yourself before the tall statue of the god of healing in his sanctuary. Stare into his gentle and compassionate eyes. Feel whatever dis-ease is yours and allow your quest for its healing to stir deep in your own soul. Imagine that the wonders of Asklepian healing are fully available to you, right here and right now, and begin to hear what the divine physician wishes you to know.

# Part Five

# Benediction

*Let us then accept our destiny, as well as the prescriptions of Asklepios.*

—Marcus Aurelius

*And thus are you welcomed, Master. By this song I beseech you.*

—Homeric Hymn to Asklepios

Asklepios with Hygeia behind heals a patient by laying on his hands, Piraeus Museum.

## Chapter Twenty-Three

# THE BLESSING OF ASKLEPIOS

## PERGAMUM, 1998

I t is deep night in Bergama, Turkey. Silence presses against the windows of the hotel room. Down the road, the sanctuary of Asklepios stands in stillness. The healing fountain gurgles in the darkness. Hydrotherapy and sleeping chambers yawn beneath the earth. The columns of the temples and the sacred way point upwards toward the diamond-belted sky.

Zoë first, then Lynette have stayed awake in support of the other dream questers in the small room that we have turned into a modern-day abaton. Her nightwatch finished, Lynette gently wakes me, then slips quickly between the covers of her bed. I help to co-coon her in blankets. She drifts immediately into sleep in search of dreams. Zoë and Lucy are wrapped and sleeping in the beds next to hers.

I have not had a dream I can recall during my four hours of sleep. No epiphany. No miracle. But that is not my concern now. I will pray and meditate for my questers, asking the healing powers of Asklepios to visit them in their dreams. I turn from the beds and tiptoe across the room to the chair reserved for the watcher next to a small round table on which a single candle burns as our vigil light.

Suddenly, I stop in my tracks. I stare at the candle. It is tall,

263

square on the bottom, and tapering to a pyramid. I blink my eyes and rub them. I look around the room to make sure I am fully awake. Yes, there are Zoë, Lynette, and Lucy all peacefully sleeping. There is the door, the bathroom. There are the windows through which I can make out the shadows of the silent Turkish street. I am awake and everything is as it ordinarily is.

I turn back to the candle and look again at its yellow fire, staring in disbelief, confusion, and wonder. I walk slowly around the table. What I am seeing is the same from every angle. I shake my head, blink. Again and again I check to make sure I am awake, to see if my eyes are watery or otherwise fooling me, if what I am seeing is just a trick of light. But no matter where I look, what angle I try, the vision is the same.

From the base of the candle flame and proceeding upwards is a radiant halo. The circle of light is thick, round, and green, perhaps the size of a basketball. It is opaque. No matter where I stand, I cannot see through it to the other side of the room. It does not flicker or sputter but glows with a constant intensity. After a while, the green color fades on the circumference of the ball. Then a thin line of orange fire surrounds and defines the circle. For the next hour, the ball of light burns in full splendor, accompanying me as I sit and watch through the Pergamum night in search of Asklepios.

*Halo* in Greek is φωτοστέφανος, *photostefanos*, "crown of light." A *stefani* is one of the central symbols of a Greek Orthodox wedding. It is the crown Greeks don when they marry, symbolizing the couple's union with God's blessing.[1] And just down the road from where I am sitting, the Apostle John had told the Church of Smyrna, "keep faithful, and I will give you the crown of life for your prize."[2]

I should have fallen to the floor in awe and thanksgiving. I should have collapsed in tears and trembling. But I just sat there, all night, watching. Indeed, the ball of light looked similar to halos painted behind the heads of the holy in religious iconography. But this was neither ancient Greece nor Byzantium. It was the very end of the twentieth century, and I was not a mystic. Yet here, in this humble town, just down the road from Galen's medical center, Aristides' refuge, and Asklepios's own healing sanctuary, an ordinary candle flame became a shining globe. Here, while watching over four modern seekers practicing a nearly forgotten tradition of sacred healing, the Presence of Light—Asklepios himself—had shone forth in all his divine brilliance.

What was Asklepios telling me?

Perhaps he was reminding me who he was: A princely hero who became a god. An archaic god of the earth who studied with the horsepeople. The son of the golden god and a mortal woman who walked the earth as a healer, gathering disciples, teaching and touching with utmost compassion, establishing sanctuaries for the afflicted wherever he went.

Perhaps he was telling me that after long wandering, he overstepped his mortal limits and raised the dead. That at that moment when he seemed to promise human beings the possibility of immortality, his grandfather, the ruler of heaven and protector of cosmic justice, slew him with a thunderbolt. That he was then brought up to live with the gods. And that now, he has all eternity to spend visiting those who suffer, bringing them healing or the means of healing through his dreams and visions.

Perhaps Asklepios was teaching me as well that he comes to seekers wearing different faces, that he has been called in various times by various names. That after his tradition crumbled, his spirit entered a new god image. That in this new guise, he continued to walk the earth in compassion, touching the afflicted in body and the poor in spirit, performing miracle healings. And that when he died to this world for spreading teachings mortals could not yet understand, he was resurrected into the eternal. And that those who seek him in this guise continue to believe that he brings visions and healing blessings.

These things and more Asklepios teaches me. He teaches me that we must do all we can to heal the world through our tenderness, mercy, generosity, friendship, reconciliation, and wisdom. Through him I hear the promise that the universe is generous and compassionate, that prayers for healing will be answered. He teaches me that healing can make us whole and that every illness or ordeal can make us wiser and lead us toward fulfilling our destiny.

He reminds me that we must not forget to be grateful and that we must thank the gods for all of their gifts. He teaches me that death, too, can be a healing. As Sokrates said, with his final breath, "Krito, we owe a cock to Asklepios. Don't forget."

In the course of this book, we have listened to the tales of many healings from the ancient and the modern world. We have heard many cocks give their final cries as they were sacrificed to Asklepios in thanksgiving for the healing that was received.

Now, let us give thanks as well. For in small ways, we have participated in the rebirth of the Asklepian tradition with its promise of healing for our own ills and for the ills of our entire system of medical care. And we have learned that, if we seek his blessings, Asklepios is still with us.

We can study the Asklepian tradition. We can adapt it to our contemporary medical needs. We can integrate it into our philosophy of living. We can practice it in personal, professional, and communal ways. We can find in it inspiration to help restore purpose and direction to our lives and repair our relationship with divinity. We can find in it an ancient but still potent path to wholeness for ourselves, our community, even our cosmos.

It may be the Fates who send us our trials. He sends us their remedies through which we may unfold our destinies. We do not know what to call him. We may as well call him Asklepios.

These are his blessings, and for them we are deeply grateful.

# NOTES

## FOREWORD

1. Maud Oakes and Joseph Campbell, *Where the Two Came to Their Father: A Navajo War Ceremonial*, Bollingen Series I (New York: Pantheon Books, 1943).

2. C. A. Meier, *Ancient Incubation and Modern Psychotherapy*, reprint, 1949 (Evanston, Ill.: Northwestern University Press, 1967).

3. Carl Kerényi, *Asklepios: Archetypal Image of the Physician's Existence*, trans. Ralph Manheim, Bollingen Series LXV: *Studies of Archetypal Images in Greek Religion* (New York: Pantheon Books, Inc., 1959).

4. Kerényi's work, like many of its sister publications in the Bollingen Series, including those of Jung and Campbell, serves to bring the dimension of myth and symbol to the modern world.

5. Jean Houston, *A Mythic Life: Learning to Live Our Greater Story* (San Francisco: HarperSanFrancisco, 1996); Sam and Anne Valley-Fox Keen, *Your Mythic Journey: Finding Meaning in Your Life Through Writing and Storytelling* (Los Angeles: Jeremy P. Tarcher, Inc., 1973); David Feinstein and Stanley Krippner, *Personal Mythology: The Psychology of Your Evolving Self; Using Ritual, Dreams, and Imagination to Discover Your Inner Story* (Los Angeles: Jeremy P. Tarcher, Inc., 1988); Stephen Larsen, *The Mythic Imagination: Your Quest for Meaning Through Personal Mythology* (New York: Bantam Books, 1990).

6. James Hillman, *The Soul's Code: In Search of Character and Calling* (New York: Random House, 1996).

7. Kerényi, *Asklepios*, xxv.

8. Kerényi quotes Walter F. Otto in *The Muses and the Divine Origin of Singing and Speech*, xxii.

9. Kerényi, *Asklepios*, 26.

## CHAPTER 1: THE WOMEN OF TROY

1. Henry Miller, *The Colossus of Maroussi* (New York: New Directions, 1954), 79.

2. Editor's Notes in Louise Mahdi, Steven Foster, and Meredith Little, eds., *Betwixt and Between: Patterns of Masculine and Feminine Initiation* (La Salle, Ill.: Open Court, 1988), 415.

3. C. A. Meier, *Ancient Dream Incubation and Modern Psychotherapy*, trans. Monica Curtis (Evanston, Ill.: Northwestern University Press, 1967), 56.

4. Stathis Papalexandros, a scholar and teacher of ancient Greek in the Paransos mountain village of Arachova, personal communication.

5. Liddell and Scott, *Greek-English Lexicon* (Oxford: Oxford University Press, 1995), 1-2. The word *abaton* was transliterated into the Bible as *abaddon* and finally demonized by Christianity as a synonym for Hell.

6. Meier, 5, 58, 115-116. Erwin Rohde points out that in the ancient world, incubation deities such as Asklepios (there were others) could not appear anywhere, but were bound to places that were believed to be their dwelling places. Further, in incubation, the god always appeared in person or in one of his totem forms. Dream healing only occurred under these conditions: through personal action on the part of the god at his particular sacred residence. Erwin Rohde, *Psyche: The Cult of Souls and Belief in Immortality Among the Ancient Greeks*, trans. W. B. Hills (Chicago: Ares Publishers, 1987), 106-107.

7. Emma J. Edelstein and Ludwig Edelstein, *Asclepius: Collection and Interpretation of the Testimonies* (Baltimore and London: Johns Hopkins University Press, 1998). For locations of Asklepeia in Bulgaria and their ruin sites today, I am grateful to Prof. Francine Frank, University at Albany, personal communication.

8. Savas Kasas, "Some Medical Treatments in Ancient Korinth," trans. Anne Kasas, in *Important Medical Centers in Antiquity* (Athens: Editions Kasas, 1990), 8.

9. Mary Renault, *The Last of the Wine* (New York: Vintage, 1975), 254-257.

10. Guiseppe Roccatagliata, *A History of Ancient Psychiatry* (New York: Greenwood, 1986), 12.

11. Roccatagliata, 8.

12. Will Durant, *The Life of Greece* (New York: Simon and Schuster, 1939), 96.

13. To understand the extensive damage this refusal did to developing male psyches, see Robert Bly, "The Erosion of Male Confidence," in Mahdi, *Betwixt and Between*, 189-200.

14. Ανάθεμα is both an ancient and modern Greek word and carries much greater weight than our English word *anathema*. In ancient Greek, anathema was a thing devoted to evil, an accursed thing. In modern Greek, the phrase ανάθεμα σου, *anathema sou*, is used only with utmost seriousness to call a curse down upon someone. It is among the most pained verbal expressions in modern Greek and is never used casually, as we might use "damn you!" Hekabe was both cursing the Greek conquerors of Troy, calling evil down upon them, and crying out in anguish that damnation and evil had befallen her people and city.

15. To understand moral inversion as a central component of combat veterans' post-traumatic stress disorder, and its recognition and correction as central to their healing, see Edward Tick, "Satori in the Hut," *Pilgrimage* 19, no. 3 (May-Aug. 1993):21-27; and Edward Tick, "The Vietnam War and the American Shadow," *Spring: A Journal of Archetype and Culture*, no. 62 (Fall/Winter 1997): 71-87.

16. Friedrich Nietzsche, *The Birth of Tragedy* (New York: Modern Library, 1954), 20-21, 33-43.

17. Joseph Campbell, *The Masks of God: Primitive Mythology* (New York: Viking, 1959), 50.

18. Meier, 417.

## CHAPTER 2: THE MYTH OF ASKLEPIOS

1. Robert Graves, *The Greek Myths* (New York: Penguin, 1990), Vol. II, 332.

2. Pindar, "Pythian Ode," in Edelstein, *Asclepius*, Vol. I, Testimony 54, 33.

3. Papalexandros, personal communication.

4. Liddell and Scott, 124; Georg Autenrieth, *A Homeric Dictionary* (Norman: University of Oklahoma Press, 1958), 49.

5. All descriptive quotes in retelling the myth in this chapter are taken from Pindar's "Third Pythian Ode," in Roy Arthur Swanson, trans., *Pindar's Odes* (Indianapolis: Bobbs-Merrill, 1974), 74-79.

6. Kerényi, *Asklepios*, 48.

7. Homer, *Iliad*, I:268, trans. Robert Fitzgerald (Garden City, N. J.: Doubleday, 1974).

8. Nikos Kazantzakis, *Report to Greco*, trans. Peter Bien (New York: Simon and Schuster, 1965), 292.

9. Kazantzakis, 292.

10. Vusamazulu Credo Mutwa, *Song of the Stars*, ed. Stephen Larsen (Barrytown, N.Y.: Station Hill, 1996).

11. Joseph Campbell with Bill Moyers, *The Power of Myth*. Edited by Betty Sue Flowers (New York: Doubleday, 1988), 47-8.

12. Reinhard Struckmann, "Asklepios in Epidauros: Sources of Health," in Kasas, 22.

13. Joseph Campbell, *The Masks of God: Occidental Mythology* (New York: Viking, 1971), 25. It is curious that in such a complete survey of world mythology as Campbell has achieved with *The Masks of God*, this is his only reference to Asklepios. We will examine this later in a consideration of the inhibition and suppression of this archetype in Western culture.

14. Edward F. Edinger, *The Eternal Drama: The Inner Meaning of Greek Mythology* (Boston: Shambhala, 1994), 135.

15. Apollodorus, quoted by Meier, 5.

16. Struckmann, 21; Joseph L. Henderson, "Ancient Myths and Modern Man," C. G. Jung, ed., *Man and His Symbols* (New York: Dell, 1973), 153.

17. Struckmann, 22.

18. Campbell, *Masks of God*, 25-26.

19. Meier, 26.

20. Yannis N. Stavrakakis, "Subway to the Past," *Archaeology Today* 53, no. 2 (March/April 2000): 39.

21. Homer, *Iliad*, XXXIII: 168-169.

22. Kasas, 10.

23. Marilyn Rouvelas, *A Guide to Greek Traditions and Customs in America* (Bethesda, Md.: Attica Press, 1994), 120-121.

24. I. A. Richards, *Why So, Sokrates?: A Dramatic Version of Plato's Dialogues* (London: Cambridge University Press, 1964), 39. It must be noted that Richards' dramatic versions of the *Dialogues* are edited and include relevant passages from additional dialogues. In other strict translations of the *Phaedo*, Plato's absence due to illness is mentioned but not his attendance at the Asklepian temple.

## CHAPTER 3: DREAM, MYTH, AND RITUAL

1. James Hillman, *The Dream and the Underworld* (New York: Harper and Row, 1979), 201.

2. For a full exploration of the meaning of *kairos* and its differentiation from ordinary time, and for an explication of other key mythic aspects of growth and healing, see Edward Tick, "The Mythic Dimensions of Healing," *Voices: The Art and Science of Psychotherapy* 32, no.4 (Winter 1996): 15-20.

3. Thomas Patrick Lavin, personal communication.

4. Edinger, 3.

5. Homer, *Odyssey*, trans. Robert Fitgerald (Garden City, N.J.: Doubleday, 1961), XII: 143-207.

6. Campbell, *The Power of Myth*, 74.

7. Norma Lorre Goodrich, *Priestesses* (New York: Harper Perennial, 1989), 9.

## CHAPTER 4: CONSCIOUS MYTHMAKING

1. Stephen Larsen, *The Mythic Imagination* (New York: Bantam, 1980), 25.

## CHAPTER 5: BIRTHPLACE AND HOMELAND

1. W. K. C. Guthrie, *The Greeks and Their Gods* (Boston: Beacon Press, 1954), 217. For a full discussion of this debate over Asklepios's divine or human nature, see "God or Hero? Asklepios," in Guthrie, 242-259, as well as the Edelsteins' extensive analysis.

2. There is a second myth of Asklepios's origins that places him at Epidauros in his infancy. We hear that story when we revisit Epidauros later.

3. Quoted by Guthrie, 245.

4. Guthrie, 245.

5. *Iliad* II, 729 ff.

6. *Iliad* IV, 200-234.

7. Ancient and modern scholars alike have been hard put to date the Trojan War accurately. Estimates range from 1334 to 1135 BCE. Here we use the date estimated by the 1932-38 Cincinnati Expedition, the major excavators of Troy after Schliemann's initial discovery. See the report of the Cincinnati Expedition published as C. W. Blegen, *Troy and the Trojans* (New

York: Barnes and Noble, 1995), 162-163.

8. Pindar, "Third Pythian Ode," in Swanson, 74.

9. Mary Renault, *The Bull From the Sea* (New York: Pantheon, 1962), 76.

10. Guthrie, 245.

11. *Inscriptiones Graecae*, in Edelstein, *Asclepius*, Vol. I, Testimony 516, 292-293. Note the correspondence to Christian belief regarding the relationship of the father and son aspects of deity. The father must be honored and receive sacrifice in order for us to approach the more accessible and compassionate son to receive a direct intervention in our healing. This archetypal pattern clearly predates and finds repetition, depth, and preservation in the Christian tradition.

## CHAPTER 6: HEALING SANCTUARY

1. Some scholars believe that the spread of the Asklepian cult was slow and steady, as generations of healers learned their crafts from their fathers or mentors and carried it through the Mediterranean world. Others believe that Asklepios remained a hero for centuries. They argue that during particular times of crisis and emergency, especially the plague in Athens around 430 BCE (examined in chapter 9), Asklepios transformed within just a few generations from a relatively minor hero into a god of great power, importance, and following. For the later interpretation see, for example, E. R. Dodds, *The Greeks and the Irrational* (Berkeley and Los Angeles: University of California Press, 1971), 193.

2. Apollodorus, *The Library of Greek Mythology*, trans. Robin Hard (Oxford: Oxford University Press, 1997), 58.

3. Clementine writings, Edelstein, *Asclepius*, Vol. I, Testimony 119 and 120, 57-58.

4. Nicholas Gage, *Hellas: A Portrait of Greece* (New York: Villard, 1987); Charles Seltman, *The Twelve Olympians* (New York: Thomas Crowell Company, 1960), 179 ff. Notice that this lesser-known version of the myth also gives Asklepios a rescue from near death and thus a symbolic rebirth or resurrection during infancy. Seltman's interpretation is that the Thessalian and the Argive Asklepios were originally two distinct heroes with separate myths that eventually merged into one healing god.

5. Kerényi, 50.

6. Seltman, 179ff.

7. Hygieia is the root of the English word *hygiene. Panaceia* itself is an English word. And Iaso is the root of the Greek word *iatros,* meaning "doctor."

8. Barbara Walker, *The Woman's Encyclopedia of Myths and Secrets* (New York: Harper and Row, 1983), 420, 766-767.

## Chapter 7: Earth-Walking Savior

1. I Corinthians 20.

2. Kasas, 7.

3. Kasas, 15.

4. Kasas, 11ff. There is some evidence and belief that different Asklepia specialized in treating different conditions.

## Chapter 8: Raising the Dead

1. Euripedes, *Hippolytus,* trans. David Grene, in *Euripedes I: Four Tragedies,* ed. David Grene and Richard Lattimore (Chicago: University of Chicago Press, 1955), 219-220.

2. Renault, *The Bull from the Sea,* 310.

3. *Oxford Classical Dictionary,* ed. M. Cary et al. (London: Oxford University Press, 1961), 431.

4. Ovid, *The Metamorphosis,* trans. Horace Gregory (New York: Mentor, 1958), 430.

5. *Inscriptiones Graecae,* Edelstein, *Asclepius,* Vol. I, Testimony 423, 234.

6. Cary et al., 526.

## Chapter 9: Beautiful and Besieged

1. Thukydides, *History of the Peloponnesian Wars,* II, 47 in M. I. Finley, ed., *The Greek Historians* (New York: Viking, 1959), 273-274.

2. Thukydides, II, 52 and 53, in Finley, 277.

3. V. K. Lambrinoudakis, *Argolida: Archaeological Sites and Museums of the Argolid* (Editions Apollo, n.d.), 135.

4. Quoted by Guthrie, 247.

5. Plutarch, "Perikles," *Selected Lives and Essays,* trans. Louise Ropes Loomis (Roslyn, N.Y.: Classics Club, 1951), I, 143.

6. Quoted by Guthrie, 247.

7. *Sophokles*, Edelstein, *Asclepius*, Vol. I, Testimony 587, 326.

8. *Etymologicum Magnum,* Edelstein, *Asclepius*, Vol. I, Testimony 591, 327.

9. Personal communication.

10. *Inscriptiones Graecae*, Edelstein, *Asclepius*, Vol. I, Testimony 423, 253.

## Chapter 10: The Father of Medicine

1. Richards, 12-13.

2. Durant, 344.

3. Steven B. Katz, Professor of English at North Carolina State University, personal communication.

4. Durant, 343.

5. Riccotagliata, 163 ff.

6. Pliny, *Natural History*, in James Longrigg, *Greek Medicine: From the Heroic to the Hellenistic Age* (New York: Routledge, 1998), 42. Longrigg warns that this story may be legendary, since the temple may not have been built until after Hippokrates' time. The chronology of the large Asklepian sanctuary of Kos will be presented later, as well as its probable scope during Hippokrates' childhood. If this story is legendary, it is certainly illustrative, for it is established that Asklepian healing was practiced on Kos before Hippokrates' time and that his father and grandfather were Asklepiads.

7. Kerényi, 48.

8. Ibid., 47-52.

9. Ibid., 51.

10. Longrigg, 133-134.

11. Despite extensive archeological exploration, medical tools have not been found at all Asklepian sites. At some sites, for example Korinth, numerous votives given in thanksgiving for healing have been unearthed, but none of the medical instruments that we would expect were necessary to bring about such healings. This has led to the conclusion that some sites exclusively practiced dream healing, with significant success.

12. Ludwig Edelstein, *Ancient Medicine*, trans. C. Lillian Temkin (Baltimore: Johns Hopkins University Press, 1987), 239-246.

13. Πανος Δ. Ατιοστολιδης, *Επμηνευτικο Λεξικο Πασων Των Λεξεων Του Ιπποκρατουε* (Athens: Εκδοσεις Γαβριηλιδης, 1997). My search in this modern lexicon of classical Greek Hippokratic terminology did not yield a single instance of the word *abaton* or other words in the Hippokratic canon related to the practice of dream healing. Further, Longrigg stresses that the entire body of Hippokratic writing is almost completely absent of references to magic or superstition. It seems that Hippokrates left dream healing strictly to the priests and more traditional or religiously oriented Asklepiads. He further argues, along with some other recent scholarship, that the Asklepiads were not priest-physicians at all, but rather members of a physicians' guild descended from a clan of hereditary physicians. See Longrigg, 48-49.

14. Riccotagliata, 163 ff.

15. Kerényi, 56 ff.

16. Ibid., 61.

17. Katz, personal communication.

18. Longrigg, 42-43.

## CHAPTER 11: TO THE IMPERIAL CITY

1. Edelstein, *Asclepius*, Vol. II, 252.

2. *Facta et Dicta Memorabilia*, Edelstein, *Asclepius*, Vol. I, Testimony 848, 433.

3. Ovid, *Metamorphosis*, XV, 433. Unless otherwise noted, all verse quotes of Asklepios's arrival in Rome throughout the rest of this section are taken from the Horace Gregory translation of Ovid cited above.

4. Kerényi, 15-17.

5. Ibid., 17.

6. *Fasti*, Edelstein, *Asclepius*, Vol. I, Testimony 855, 450.

7. Kerényi, 14.

8. *Inscriptiones Graecae*, Edelstein, *Asclepius*, Vol. I, Testimony 438, 251.

9. *Claudius*, Edelstein, *Asclepius*, Vol. I, Testimony 858, 451.

10. Estimates of the number of Asklepian sanctuaries in the early Roman Empire range from 186 to 410. See Edelstein, *Asclepius*, Vol. II, 251.

11. Edelstein, *Asclepius*, Vol. II, 253.

12. Marcus Aurelius, *Meditations*, I:17, in *Marcus Aurelius and His Times,* trans. George Long (Roslyn, N.Y.: Classics Club, Walter J. Black, Inc., 1945), 19.

13. Patricia Cox Miller, *Dreams in Late Antiquity* (Princeton, N.J.: Princeton University Press, 1994), 114.

## CHAPTER 12: HARMONIZING SCIENCE AND SPIRIT

1. Acts 19:27.

2. Quoted in case display in Archaeological Museum in Selcuk, Turkey.

3. Edelstein, *Ancient Medicine*, 250 and elsewhere.

4. Oribasius, *Collectiones Medicae*, Edelstein, *Asclepius*, Vol. I, Testimony 425, 239.

5. Edelstein, *Ancient Medicine*, 245n.

## CHAPTER 13: THE ANCIENT PSYCHIATRIST

1. Edelstein, *Ancient Medicine*, 275-277.

2. *Aristides*, Edelstein, *Asclepius*, Vol. I, Testimony 317, 159-160.

3. *In Platonis Rem Publicam,* Edelstein, *Asclepius,* Vol. I, Testimony 309, 153.

4. Edelstein, *Asclepius,* Vol. I, Testimony 302, 150.

5. Edelstein states that it was a principle of ancient medicine that it is part of the physician's art to know who can and cannot be cured and that physicians were discouraged from treating the incurable. He further holds that this view is humanized and made comprehensible when we understand that those who suffered either chronic diseases or conditions beyond the scope of human knowledge went to the temples seeking cure. See *Ancient Medicine*, 244-245.

6. Roccatagliata, 26.

7. Miller, 190.

8. *Inscriptiones Graeciae*, Edelstein, *Asclepius*, Vol. I, Testimony 287, 140. It is noteworthy that Telesphoros is not even mentioned in Apollodorus's ancient mythology, in Robert Graves's exhaustive or Edith Hamilton's popular collections of the Greek myths.

9. *Dubitationes et Solutiones*, Edelstein, *Asclepius*, Vol. I, Testimony 313, 154.

10. C. G. Jung, *Memories, Dreams and Reflections* (London: Routledge and Kegan Paul, 1963), 215.

11. Kerényi, 88.

12. Stephen Larsen, personal communication.

13. Kerényi, 58.

14. Ibid., 57.

15. Meier, "Ancient Incubation and Modern Psychotherapy," in Mahdi, 419.

16. I adapt these names from the translation of τελεσφορος, *telesforos,* originating from τελος, *telos,* completion or consummation, and φερω, *fero,* to bear, carry, endure, suffer, bring, etc. See Liddell and Scott, 798. Kerényi believes that the completion might indicate death, but the ancient connotations of the word could equally indicate the completion of the death-rebirth cycle in the disease and healing process, or the fulfillment of dream visions.

17. Anne Macguire, "Jung's First Dream," in Mahdi, 64; Meier, 38 ff.

18. Meier, 38.

19. Edelstein, *Asclepius,* Vol. I, Testimony 409, 207.

20. Roccatagliata, 193.

21. Edelstein, *Asclepius,* Vol. II, 147.

22. Edelstein, *Asclepius,* Vol. II, 147. See also Meier, 58.

23. *Subfiguratio Empirica,* Edelstein, *Asclepius,* Vol. I, Testimony 436, 250.

24. Miller, 46.

25. Quoted in Miller, 46.

26. *De Libris Propriis,* Edelstein, *Asclepius,* Vol. I, Testimony 459, 263.

27. Galen, *Opera Omnia,* cited in Meier, 3.

28. *De Antidotis,* Edelstein, *Asclepius,* Vol. I, Testimony 595, 331.

29. *De Sanitate Tuenda,* Edelstein, *Asclepius,* Vol. I, Testimony 413, 208-209.

30. *Commentarius in Hippocratis Epidemias,* Edelstein, *Asclepius,* Vol. I, Testimony 402, 202.

31. This is not the common interpretation of Galen. For example, one contemporary physician/philosopher presents the more prevalent view that

"Galen ... was said to be arrogant and claimed miraculous cures. He had a ready explanation for every problem and a reason for every phenomenon, all based on 'scientific' theories. . . Although Galen wrote [extensively] . . . he rarely, if ever, mentioned soul." Mike Denney, "Mickey Mantle Meets Prometheus," *Spring: A Journal of Archetype and Culture*, no. 65 (Spring/ Summer 1999): 135-136. My contention here is that Galen's "miraculous cures" and testimony of familiarity with the god were perfectly aligned with the practice of temple medicine and that his own sophisticated scientific humoral medicine elucidated the embedding of the ways of the soul in the matter and energy patterns of the body.

32. For a complete summary of Aristides' life and work and the various scholarly interpretations of it, see Miller, 184-204, from which some of this presentation is drawn. Miller draws extensively from Aristides' autobiographical work, *Sacred Tales*. References to Aristides' records of his dreams and his writings that witness Asklepian practices and the interpretation of its principles are taken from this and the approximately fifty testimonies attributed to Aristides included in Edelstein. Miller presents scholarly critiques of Aristides' psychological and cultural matrix, demonstrating how his psychosomatic illness and Asklepian response are emblematic of his times. My interpretation is more universalistic and archetypal, stressing the dimensions of Aristides' illness and healing that are emblematic of the timeless unfolding of a destiny. I return to this theme and its expression today in Parts IV and V.

33. Edelstein, *Asclepius*, Vol. I, Testimony 418, 211.

34. *Sacred Tales,* quoted by Miller, 185.

35. Edelstein, *Asclepius*, Vol. I, Testimony 408, 206.

36. Edelstein, *Asclepius*, Vol. I, Testimony 323, 165.


## CHAPTER 14: ASKLEPIOS AND CHRIST

1. *De Vita Constantini*, Edelstein, *Asclepius*, Vol. I, Testimony 818, 419-420.

2. Edelstein, *Asclepius*, Vol. II, 256.

3. *Historia Ecclesiastica,* Edelstein, *Asclepius*, Vol. I, Testimony 819, 420.

4. Quoted by Roccatagliata, 76, 74.

5. I Corinthians 23.

6. Roccatagliata, 75.

7. Ibid., 76.

8. *Oxford Classical Dictionary,* 548; Seltman, 181.

9. Robert Wickiewicz, M.D., personal communication. The taking of the Hippokratic Oath faded during the third century until it disappeared entirely, not to return until the Renaissance with its reawakened interest in the classical world.

10. Quoted in Roccatagliata, 73.

11. Richard Geldard, *The Traveler's Key to Ancient Greece* (Wheaton, Ill.: Quest Books, 2000), 253; Roccatagliata, 74.

12. Roccatagliata, 74.

13. Miller, 117. Thecla, too, derives from the matriarchal tradition. Her name originally meant "Famous One" and was one of the titles of Artemis at Ephesus. See Walker, 990.

14. Dorothy Mills, *The Book of the Ancient Romans* (New York: G. P. Putnam's Sons, 1927), 297.

15. Edelstein, *Ancient Medicine,* 244n.

16. Edelstein, *Asclepius,* Vol. II, 256.

17. Meier, in Mahdi, 418.

18. Julian, *Contra Christ*, Meier, 66.

19. Marinus, *Vita Procli*, Edelstein, *Asclepius,* Vol. I, Testimony 582, 322.

20. Meier, 24-25.


## CHAPTER 15: A SAINT IN THE MOUNTAINS

1. These stories, along with others, will also be reported in Louise Mahdi, ed., *In the Spirit of St. Nicholas* (Wheaton, Ill.: Quest Books, 2002). I am grateful for Louise's inspiring companionship in traveling to Greece with me in search of healing stories from archaic and modern spiritual traditions.

2. Meier, xii–xiii.


## CHAPTER 16: MODERN DREAM HEALING

1. John Astin, "Why Patients Use Alternative Medicine: Results of a National Survey," *JAMA* 279, no. 19 (May 1998): 1548.

2. Astin, 1550-1551.

3. Robert Wickiewicz, "A Modern Physician in Search of his Soul," *Pilgrimage: Reflections on the Human Journey* 26 (2000/01): 54-55.

4. Astin, 1552.

5. While it appears that new developments in theoretical science are propelling us toward a new paradigm that will be characterized by chaos, dynamism, and interrelatedness, it will take generations for our applied sciences to transform their philosophies and practices to align with the shift. The theory and practice of medicine and health are from the philosophical point of view still firmly rooted in the paradigm characterized by Newtonian and Cartesian principles and from the cultural point of view shaped by the dominant values of mechanization, technological address, utilization, and cost effectiveness that characterize our society.

6. "Joseph Campbell and the Power of Myth with Bill Moyers," Public Broadcasting System Interviews (New York: Mystic Fire Video and *Parabola* Magazine, 1988).

7. See Astin for statistical validation of this claim.

8. Gene Wolfe, *Soldier of the Mist* (New York: Tor Books, 1987), 176.

9. *In Platonis Rem Publicam*, Edelstein, *Asclepius*, Vol. I, Testimony 309, 153.

10. Personification and active imagination are the essence of Hillman's and other archetypal psychologists' strategies. These dimensions are found in many key psychospiritual writings since Jung. For a cogent and holistic general explication of the importance of these dimensions in making psychology work, see especially James Hillman, *Re-Visioning Psychology* (New York: Harper Perennial, 1992). Herein I apply these principles to the study of Asklepios. We should recognize that these principles can be applied with great value to the study of any god image as representing particular aspects of divinity and giving us ways to practice its unfolding in our individual lives.

11. Hillman, *Re-Visioning*, 34.

12. Larsen, 25.

13. Hillman, *Re-Visioning*, 33.

14. Ibid., 34.

15. Ibid., 97.

16. *Inscriptio Pergamena*, Edelstein, *Asclepius*, Vol. I, Testimony 513, 291.

17. Edward C. L. Smith, *The Body in Psychotherapy* (Jefferson, N.C.: McFarland, 1985), 139, 140, 143, 145.

18. Meier, xiii-xiv.

19. Meier, xiv.

20. Sigmund Freud, *The Interpretation of Dreams*, trans. James Strachey (New York: Avon, 1969), 67n.

21. Kerényi, (subtitle of his book *Asklepios*)

22. Kerényi, xxv.

23. Meier, 3-4.

24. Jean Houston, *A Mythic Life* (New York: HarperCollins, 1996), 128-129.

25. Larsen, 222.

26. Many theorists from Jung and Joseph Campbell through humanistic psychologists such as Rollo May and Ira Progoff have noted that the essential distinctions between myth and dream are 1) between the personal and the transpersonal, and 2) between the individual and collective. Both are symbolic experiences that differ in how and to whom they manifest.

## Chapter 17: The Ship of Death and Life

1. The island of Poros, though tiny and simple, provides many riches for the spirit. I refer interested travelers or readers to my articles on this island and its cultural and spiritual offerings: "Counsel from the Dead: George Seferis and Poros," *Key West Review* 1, no. 2 (Fall 1988): 82-92; "The Gift of Turtle," *Pilgrimage: Psychotherapy and Personal Exploration* 17, no. 4 (Sept./Oct. 1991): 2-10; "On an Island, Barely, in Greece," *The New York Times*, Sept. 22, 1996, 20, 24.

2. C. G. Jung, *Psychology and Religion: East and West,* Vol. 11 of *Collected Works*, trans. R. F. C. Hull (New York: Bollingen Foundation, 1958), 508.

3. Plutarch, "Letter of Consolation to His Wife," *Selected Lives and Essays*, Vol. II, 325.

4. Mircea Eliade, *Rites and Symbols of Initiation: The Mysteries of Birth and Rebirth* (Woodstock, Conn.: Spring Publications, 1994), x.

5. Meier, 116.

6. C. G. Jung, *Psychology and Alchemy,* Vol. 12 of *Collected Works*, trans. R. F. C. Hull (Princeton, N.J.: Bollingen Foundation, 1993), 317.

7. D. H. Lawrence, "The Ship of Death," *The Complete Poems of D. H. Lawrence* (New York: Viking, 1971), 716-718.

## CHAPTER 18: "WHAT DREAM THE GOD HAS SENT"

1. See Book XI of Homer's *Odyssey*. I often use this story of Odysseus's descent to Hades as a road map for people whose souls are wandering, saturated with the pain of loss and death. Homer's tale provides us with the map for our necessary encounter with the dead in order for us to achieve the same mission as Odysseus—getting instructions for finding the route to our true homes.

2. This quotation comes from the movie version of *Zorba the Greek*. In the novel, the dialogue is somewhat different, but it expresses the same sense of the human spirit in rebellion against unjust loss and death. See Nikos Kazantzakis, *Zorba the Greek*, trans. Carl Wildman (New York: Simon and Schuster, 1952), 247 ff.

3. Euripedes, *Hecuba*, in *Euripedes III: Four Tragedies*, trans. William Arrowsmith (Chicago: University of Chicago Press, 1958), 14-15.

4. Euripedes, *Hecuba*, 37, 40.

5. Hillman, *The Dream and the Underworld*, 146.

6. Edelstein, *Asclepius*, Vol II, 148n.

## CHAPTER 19: SOKRATES ON KRETE

1. Edelstein, *Asclepius*, Vol. II, 249-250n.

2. Evidence gathered from displays in the Archaeological Museum in Iraklion, Krete's capital.

3. Philostratus, *Vita Apollonii*, Edelstein, *Asclepius*, Vol. I, Testimony 792, 400.

4. *Inscriptions Creticae*, Edelstein, *Asclepius*, Vol. I, Testimony 791, 400.

5. *Inscriptions Creticae*, Edelstein, *Asclepius*, Vol. I, Testimony 426, 239-240.

6. Plato, *Phaedo*, in Richards, 40.

7. Plato, *Apology*, in Richards, 23, 27, 28.

8. Plato, *Krito*, in Richards, 36.

9. Ibid., 48.

## CHAPTER 20: THE SNAKE RETURNS

1. Numbers 21:4-9. Various translations say that the serpent was "brazen" or "brass." "Copper" is the more accurate translation. Similar serpents have

been uncovered in archaeological excavations, and the biblical incident occurred near an important ancient copper mine. See W. Gunther Plaut, ed., *The Torah:A Modern Commentary* (New York: Union of American Hebrew Congregations, 1981), 1161.

2. J. H. Hertz, ed., *The Pentateuch and Haftorahs* (London: Soncino Press, 1981), 660.

3. *Encyclopedia Judaica*, Vol. 5 (Jerusalem and New York: Macmillan & Co., 1971), 957-959.

4. Artemidorus, *Onirocritica*, II, 13, in Edelstein, *Asclepius*, Vol. I, Testimony 703, 367.

5. Macrobius, *Saturnalia*, I, 20, in Edelstein, *Asclepius*, Vol. I, Testimony 301, 148-150.

6. Thomas Patrick Lavin, "Carl Alfred Meier e le radici della terapia," *Psicologia Analitica Contemporanea*, a cura di Carlo Trombetta (Milano, Italy: Studi Bompiani, 1989), 41.

7. Henderson, 153.

8. Hillman, *The Soul's Code*, 59.

9. Thomas Lavin, personal communication.

## CHAPTER 21: ASKLEPIOS MAKES HOUSE CALLS

1. Marinus, *Vita Procli*, in Edelstein, *Asclepius*, Vol. I, Testimony 446, 257.

2. N. Michael Murphy, *The Wisdom of Dying: Practices for Living* (Boston: Element Books, 1999), 181-197. As a hospice specialist, Murphy leads "Death and Dying" workshops in the United States and Europe and practices his own modern versions of Asklepian retreats based on these principles. His workshops actually combine two Greek mystery traditions. He guides his questers toward the Asklepian goal of healing for intractable conditions as well as the goal of the Eleusinian Mysteries, practice in and comfort with the experience of dying.

3. Thomas Lavin, personal communication.

## CHAPTER 22: THE FUTURE OF ASKLEPIAN MEDICINE

1. Plutarch, "Pericles," Vol. I, 134.

2. Joseph Campbell, *The Masks of God: Creative Mythology* (New York: Viking, 1975), 4.

3. Houston, 161-162.

4. See, for example, Denney for a thorough review of the literature and analysis of the soul complications of liver transplant surgery. Denney cites numerous liver transplant studies documenting significant post-operative complications due to patient experiences of a foreign soul, spirit, or personality being transferred from the donor to the recipient.

5. Steven B. Katz, "Out of Hospital," *Archives of Family Medicine* 8, no. 1 (Jan./Feb. 1999). The physicians' response to his poem derives from a personal communication.

6. Steven B. Katz, "Preface," in Elizabeth S. Spragins, *Metaphoric Analysis of the Debate on Physician Assisted Suicide* (Lewiston, Maine: Edwin Mellen Press, 1999), iv. Katz credits Kenneth Burke for the scene, act, and agent analysis of medical interventions.

7. Plato, 311.

8. Plutarch, "The Passing of the Oracles," Vol. II 394-415.

9. Elizabeth Cominos, Jungian translator and scholar in Athens, personal communication.

10. Houston, 312.

11. Lavin, especially 21-22.

12. Rade Nicholas Pejic, "The Symbol of Medicine: Aesculapius or Caduceus?" *JAMA* 275, no. 18 (April 24, 1996): 1232.

13. Murphy, 182.

14. James Hillman in *The Soul's Code* demonstrates the operations of this philosophy, explicating the ways that trouble, challenge, the accidental, the unexpected, and the traumatic contribute toward unraveling hidden destinies in a great many creative lives.

15. Marcus Aurelius, V:8, 76-77.

## Chapter 23: The Blessing of Asklepios

1. Rouvelas, 57.

2. Revelation 2:10.

# INDEX

Quest Books
encourages open-minded inquiry into
world religions, philosophy, science, and the arts
in order to understand the wisdom of the ages,
respect the unity of all life, and help people explore
individual spiritual self-transformation.

Its publications are generously supported by
The Kern Foundation,
a trust committed to Theosophical education.

Quest Books is the imprint of
the Theosophical Publishing House,
a division of the Theosophical Society in America.
For information about programs, literature,
on-line study, membership benefits, and international centers,
see www.theosophical.org
or call 800-669-1571 or (outside the US) 630-668-1571.

To order books or a complete Quest catalog,
call 800-669-9425 or (outside the US) 630-665-0130.

Theosophy teach the
purpose of life is
spiritual emanipation
and claim that the human
soul undergoes reincarnation
upon bodies death

"the accomplished"
"bringer of into"
"bearers of fruit"

Telesphorus
"This is telesphorus
who summons the
dead vapors
of this cosmos
and glows
like a star
out of the
depths;
He points
the way...
to the gates of the
sun and to the
land of dreams"
Carl Jung

telos
/
completion
fulfillment/goal

phino
/
bring/bear
carry